# Crazy Wisdom

*Wes "Scoop" Nisker*

**1Ѳ** TEN SPEED PRESS
BERKELEY, CALIFORNIA

1⦿

Ten Speed Press
Box 7123
Berkeley, CA 94707

Cover design by Fifth Street Design
Book design by Sarah Levin
Typeset by Wilsted & Taylor

Library of Congress Cataloging-in-Publication Data

Nisker, Wes.
  Crazy wisdom / Wes Nisker.
    p.
  ISBN 0-89815-350-6 (paper)  0-89815-352-2 (cloth)
  1. New Age movement.   2. Philosophy—History.   3. Wisdom—History.
  4. Paradox—History.   I. Title
  BP605.N48N57  1990
  149—dc20   89-38111CIP

Printed in the United States of America

1   2   3   4   5 — 94   93   92   91   90

Excerpt from *The Branching Moments* translated by Coleman Barks and John Moyne, copyright © 1988. Reprinted by permission of Copper Beach Press, Providence, RI.

Excerpt from *Open Secret* translated by Coleman Barks and John Moyne, copyright © 1984 by Threshold Books. Reprinted by permission of Threshold Books, Putney, VT.

Excerpt from *Unseen Rain* translated by Coleman Barks and John Moyne, copyright © 1986 by Threshold Books. Reprinted by permission of Threshold Books, Putney, VT.

Excerpt from *This Longing* translated by Coleman Barks and John Moyne, copyright © 1988 by Threshold Books. Reprinted by permission of Threshold Books, Putney, VT.

Haiku from *Haiku: Volume One, Eastern Culture* translated by R. H. Blyth, copyright © 1981 by R. H. Blyth. Reprinted by permission of The Hokuseido Press, Tokyo.

Haiku from *Haiku: Volume Two, Spring* translated by R. H. Blyth, copyright © 1981 by R. H. Blyth. Reprinted by permission of The Hokuseido Press, Tokyo.

Haiku from *Haiku: Volume Three, Summer-Autumn* translated by R. H. Blyth, copyright © 1982 by R. H. Blyth. Reprinted by permission of The Hokuseido Press, Tokyo.

Haiku from *Haiku: Volume Four, Autumn-Winter* translated by R. H. Blyth, copyright © 1982 by R. H. Blyth. Reprinted by permission of The Hokuseido Press, Tokyo.

Excerpts from *Silence* by John Cage, copyright © 1961 by John Cage. Reprinted by permission of University Press of New England, Hanover, NH.

Excerpt from *Timescale* by Nigel Calder, copyright © 1963 by Nigel Calder. Reprinted by permission of Viking Penguin, a division of Penguin Books USA, Inc., New York.

Excerpts from *The Myth of Sisyphus and Other Essays* by Albert Camus, translated by Justin O'Brien, copyright © 1955 by Alfred A. Knopf, Inc. Reprinted by permission of the publisher.

Excerpts from *The Experts Speak* by Christopher Cerf and Victor S. Navarsky, copyright © 1984 by Christopher Cerf and Victor S. Navarsky. Reprinted by permission of Pantheon Books, a division of Random House, New York.

*To my parents, Jack and Esther Nisker,*
*whose wisdom allowed me my own craziness,*
*and whose love I will cherish always.*

# Table of Contents

# Introduction

*Crazy Wisdom* is autobiographical. Not that I am especially wise, or necessarily crazy, but ever since I can remember I have looked somewhat askance at the world. My personal heroes have always seemed to possess a quality that might well be described as *crazy* wisdom. Chuang Tzu, Gautama the Buddha, the Baal Shem Tov, Albert Camus, Mark Twain, Rumi, Jack Kerouac—these and other controversial voices have attracted and nourished me. Often they have been there to reassure me that my own moments of mystical vision or absurdist clarity were valid and wondrous. In a sense, I am paying homage to my teachers and heroes by introducing them to each other in the pages of this book, bringing them together under the rubric of "crazy wisdom."

I have always felt as though I had only one foot on the ground, the other searching for a toehold in some other realm where I might gain a wider or more critical perspective. This tendency to be both a participant in and an observer of life may have begun during my childhood in a small Nebraska town. I was the only Jewish kid in school, and I recall the persistent sense that I was an outsider, watching from a distance and wondering about my place. This detachment—alternating between bemusement and alienation—has continued throughout my life, leading me to look for other outsiders; those who also view the world from a nonordinary perspective. The research for *Crazy Wisdom* started with my earliest attempts to find the companionship of like-minded individuals.

As I grew up, I was increasingly amused and horrified by life, especially as I saw it being lived in mid-century, Midwestern, middle-class America. It seemed to me that the human condition was essentially absurd, and that the justifications offered by church, state, and school were meaningless, if not laughable.

In my late teens, I began reading the existentialist philosophers and Beat poets, and found that their attitudes fit my own. I heard my own outrage and sorrows in Nietzsche's diatribes and Camus's laments, while Allen Ginsberg's poetry and Jack Kerouac's novels showed me a kindred desire for an all-embracing state of grace, or at least the release of the wild spirit. These writers confirmed my sense that there was another way to look at things, a different way of living.

I was equally drawn to the era's satirists and jesters. Lenny Bruce and Mort Sahl spoke for me, mocking the ways of the world, and Alfred E. Neuman's silly smile seemed an appropriate response to life. "What, me worry?" sounded like as good a philosophy as any.

My urge to be a critic and a jester led me, in 1968, to take a job as newscaster and commentator at KSAN-FM in San Francisco, America's first full-blown "counterculture" radio station. Since KSAN was the voice of the psychedelic and anti-war movements, I was allowed to be as politically radical and stylistically outrageous as I wished. I began presenting the news by putting together collages of sound—splicing the voices of politicians together with bits of poetry, rock and roll lyrics, interviews with people in the streets, and sound effects. I cut up one of Richard Nixon's speeches and moved his devious euphemisms around until he ended up telling the truth as I saw it, and then played the altered version over the Beatles singing "Everybody's got something to hide, 'cept for me and my monkey," followed by people in the streets talking about the bombing of Cambodia.

I also interjected my own version of the "larger perspective" into my daily news features, drawing on historical themes and cosmological overviews. America became another Roman empire, the earth a planet hurtling blindly through space—or perhaps a hunk of matter-energy in a universe governed by entropy. My broadcasts thus conveyed my fundamental skepticism about the veracity as well as the ultimate significance of what passes for the daily news. The phrase I coined to end each feature referred to both the content and the style of my reports: "If you don't like the news, go out and make some of your own."

My continuing interest in the work of the Beat writers and people like Alan Watts and Ram Dass, as well as my own experiments with mind expansion of various sorts, led to a growing curiosity about Eastern spiritual traditions. In 1970 I decided to take a break from the turmoil of counterculture radio and travel to Asia, where I hoped to find a teacher, or at least experience something of Hinduism and Buddhism firsthand. After a few months, I ended up in Bodhgaya, India, practicing Buddhist meditation just a few hundred yards from the tree where the Buddha supposedly attained his enlightenment. In meditation I found myself firmly in the role of both participant and observer. I was also still applying the standard journalist's questions—Who? What? Where? When? Why? How?—but now the subject under investigation was myself.

It was shocking to discover how confused and conditioned my mind was. Just sitting still, I found that I was not in control of my own thoughts or emotions—my mind had a mind of its own. It became clear to me that the untrained mind is a source of great delusion and suffering, both for myself and for others. I began to experience Buddhist meditation as an antidote to this condition, a comprehensive discipline that offers a different understanding of life, as well as another way of being in the world.

I first encountered the phrase "crazy wisdom" in my study of Buddhism and Taoism, where it is sometimes used to describe the realizations and teaching methods of the more radical Eastern sages. I also began to discover many similarities between the beliefs of my Western cultural heroes and the ways of the Eastern spiritual traditions. I realized that twentieth-century existentialism, the Beat movement, and some expressions of Western psychology corresponded closely with the ideas and practices of the Eastern crazy wisdom masters. Meanwhile, books such as *The Tao of Physics* and *The Dancing Wu Li Masters*, with their depictions of a theoretical universe that seemed to contain its own crazy wisdom, gave me a new interest in the physical sciences. I began to read about the latest findings in such fields as evolutionary biology, genetics, and astrophysics. All of these ideas wove themselves together into a pattern in my mind, which has become the fabric of *Crazy Wisdom*.

The material for this book developed directly out of two ongoing projects. In 1984, I began leading crazy wisdom workshops and seminars with my friend Paul Krassner, the stand-up satirist and editor of the *Realist* magazine. Paul is the consummate jester: an incisive iconoclast and one of the most spontaneously playful people on the planet. Some of the material in this book grew out of the research and preparation for our workshops.

In 1984, I also became coeditor, with Barbara Gates, of the *Inquiring Mind*, a journal of the Buddhist vipassana (insight) meditation community in the West. I began to explore the themes of this book in my regular *Inquiring Mind* column, "The Dharma and the Drama," and in many ways my work on the journal led directly to the writing of *Crazy Wisdom*.

So, that's where this book comes from. Before we begin in earnest, here's a caveat or two. While some people may object to their personal heroes and idols being labeled as "crazy," they should understand that my use of this word carries with it the deepest admiration. Also, I am well aware of the paucity of women's voices in *Crazy Wisdom*. This is more the fault of history than of my own research and experience. It is not that women have had nothing to say, but rather that few historians have recorded their words and deeds. Perhaps a revised edition in the next century will find this imbalance corrected, especially since much of today's crazy wisdom contains a feminine perspective that may well prove to be a major component of the next accepted version of truth.

Lastly, although this book moves through the realms of art, science, philosophy, and religion, I am not a scholar in any of these fields. My expertise in a particular discipline is only as thorough as my own interests have dictated. I see myself as a generalist, and *Crazy Wisdom* as a speculative romp, an attempt to find a common pattern—a philosophy if you will—in the synthesis of my intellectual and spiritual interests.

# Acknowledgments

I gratefully acknowledge the many people who in so many ways contributed to the writing of this book. My deepest love and gratitude go to my daughter Rose, who keeps me on my toes and is such a joy in my life; to my soul mate Terry Vandiver, whose love and friendship are a constant inspiration; and to Mudita, a dear companion on many paths.

I offer special thanks and great respects to my first meditation teacher, S. N. Goenka, and to my close friends and spiritual mentors Joseph Goldstein, Jack Kornfield, and Sharon Salzberg, who are continuing sources of wisdom and love.

In the most direct way, this book would be much different and less than what it is without the excellent advice and guidance of my dear friend and editor Shoshana Tembeck Alexander. I am deeply grateful for her vision. For both practical and emotional support I also extend love and thanks to Jan Buffum for keeping the family together; to Catherine Ingram, whose sympathetic ear and heart were never more than a phone call away; to Perry Garfinkel for being a brother in so many ways and to Ariana Garfinkel for being Rose's friend; to Barbara Gates and the entire staff of *Inquiring Mind* for their love and encouragement; to Robert Fraser for scientific consultations about nothing and *for* nothing; to Djuna Odegard for her enthusiasms; to Jeff Greenwald for his irrepressible wit and tough-love critiques; and to Dan Clurman for keeping my computer humming through it all, with a little language philosophy thrown in for good measure.

I offer heartfelt appreciation to Phil Wood at Ten Speed Press for believing in me and letting me write the book I wanted to write. Also, I extend very special thanks to Mariah Bear, whose editorial advice was extremely valuable to me throughout this endeavor. Her good humor and patience eased the work considerably. Also, thanks to Sal Glynn and the entire Ten Speed staff for their amiable assistance, and to George Young, whose sagacity guided the manuscript into book form.

# PART I

## *The Crazy Wisdom Story*

CHAPTER ONE

# The Beginning
# Is the Middle

Where can I find a man who has forgotten words?
I would like to have a word with him.

CHUANG TZU

A special kind of wisdom is loose in the world. This wisdom is difficult to codify or categorize and it refuses to be institutionalized. It is called *crazy* wisdom. And so it is, both crazy, and wisdom.

Crazy wisdom is the wisdom of the saint, the Zen master, the poet, the mad scientist, and the fool. Crazy wisdom sees that we live in a world of many illusions, that the Emperor has no clothes, and that much of human belief and behavior is ritualized nonsense. Crazy wisdom understands antimatter and old Sufi poetry; loves paradox and puns and pie fights and laughing at politicians. Crazy wisdom flips the world upside down and backward until everything becomes perfectly clear.

You will find crazy wisdom flowing through all of human history, bubbling up here and there, now and then, pointing out different ways of looking at things, reminding people to take it easy, and providing a necessary counterpoint to self-righteousness. From the Taoists to the Dadaists; from the Book of Ecclesiastes to Mark Twain's *Letters to the Earth*; in the parables of Chuang Tzu and the Baal Shem Tov; out of the cyclonic whirl of Rumi's dervish poetry and the profound nonsense of Samuel Beckett's confused characters; lurking beneath the unruly hair of Albert Einstein and between the bushy

To see truth, contemplate all phenomena as a lie.

THAGANAPA

Everything you know is wrong.

THE FIRESIGN THEATER

eyebrows of Groucho Marx; inside the howly voice of Allen Ginsberg and from behind the rags of Lily Tomlin's bag lady: Whatever tone it speaks in and whatever disguise it wears, crazy wisdom arises again and again to expose us to ourselves and to remind us of the strange impossible nature of our enterprise here on earth: life.

Crazy wisdom is the skeptical voice inside us that doubts our importance in the world and questions our belief in a higher purpose. It is the nagging suspicion that both our reasons and our reasoning are mistaken.

Crazy wisdom laughs at our ridiculous ways and shows compassion for the suffering that results from them. It presents us with the bigger picture, as well as ways to step lightly through it.

Crazy wisdom is the humbling knowledge of the immensity of the cosmos and the inevitable change and transformation that will ultimately wear away all our achievements. It is the grinning face of death, and the hollow sound of our question "Why?" echoing back at us from the void.

If you understand, things are just as they are. If you do not understand, things are just as they are.
ZEN BUDDHIST SAYING

# A Very Brief History

Although we have no records to prove it, a little crazy wisdom must have been around even in prehistoric times. No doubt some contrary ancient sage was present to tell the cave people that capturing fire would create as many problems as it would solve. Crazy wisdom must be at least as old as conventional wisdom. Every god has both believers and disbelievers. True and false are constant companions.

Although clear precedents can be found in early writings from the Indian subcontinent, a crazy wisdom approach to life did not truly come of age until the sixth to fifth centuries B.C., in China. There, out of the nameless, inexpressible source of all things, the Tao, crazy wisdom emerged—full bodied, fully enlightened, and full of mischief.

4

For of the wise man as of the fool there is no enduring remembrance, seeing that in the days to come all will have been long forgotten. How the wise man dies just like the fool! For all is vanity and a striving after wind.
*Ecclesiastes*

If you think that you know much, you know little.
KENA–UPANISHAD

> To remain whole, be twisted.
> To become straight, let yourself be bent.
> To become full, be hollow.
> *Tao Te Ching*

Standing at the very center of these paradoxes, the old Taoists shrugged and let out a sigh of relief, accepting that they could not resolve them. From that great breath, crazy wisdom has spread across the planet with little heed to chronology or causal connections, taking on many different names and shapes through the ages. It remains a wild, elusive creature.

> The greatest music cannot be heard.
> The greatest form has no shape.
> *Tao Te Ching*

The ideas and attitudes that we are calling "crazy wisdom" come from many sources. The most complete expressions of a crazy wisdom point of view can be found in Taoism, Zen and Tibetan Buddhism, and Sufism. The legacy of these traditions is carried on primarily by independent teachers, sometimes called "crazy wisdom masters," each with their own version of truth as well as a variety of methods for imparting their madness. They do not require their followers to hold particular beliefs, but instead give them techniques to develop their own individual perception of the truth.

> Who is it that is dragging this corpse around?
> ZEN KOAN, A SPIRITUAL EXERCISE

Crazy wisdom also finds expression in the work of certain artists, writers, and philosophers, both Eastern and Western, each with an individual twist on the crazy wisdom themes. The artistic side of crazy wisdom, like its spiritual counterpart, consists primarily of personal visions connected by a common spirit. Crazy wisdom also makes an appearance in folklore and mythology, where archetypal figures such as the clown, the trickster, the jester, and the fool act out the human comedy of errors. These popular characters are great teachers of crazy wisdom, revealing human nature in all its extremes of wisdom and foolishness.

Lately, crazy wisdom has found a strange bedfellow in modern

5

Nothing is more real than nothing.
SAMUEL BECKETT

Molecular psychology represents the most fundamental heresy ever committed by science, and we will have to embrace it. We will have to look into the mirror, surrender illusion, and make peace with the fact that we're staring at a machine.

JON FRANKLIN
*Molecules of the Mind*

science, where recent discoveries have overturned many previous certainties. The latest scientific theories and findings reveal the inconceivable vastness of the universe, as well as underlying unity and interdependence. Many of our most sacred beliefs about ourselves are also being called into question.

Crazy wisdom does not exist in any history books and has never been traced as a distinct tradition. Here, we give name and shape to this unconventional understanding of life, which in some cases implies a manner of living as well. We will fashion "crazy wisdom" from both secular and spiritual sources, both ancient and modern, and from both Eastern and Western cultures, showing it to be the gritty core of many esoteric teachings and an essential part of the human story.

## The Principles of Crazy Wisdom

The principles of crazy wisdom are not Ten Commandments or Four Noble Truths or Eternal Forms. We offer the following principles simply as touchstones to help you keep your bearings as we explore some difficult mental terrain in our search for crazy wisdom. Some of these principles might seem contradictory—pointing back to the way you came or in two directions at once—but you must keep in mind that forward is not always the way to crazy wisdom and sometimes you don't need to move at all.

While many crazy wisdom followers may accept some of these "principles," others will refuse all attempts to classify their wordless understanding. If you wish to follow along, it is advisable to leave preconceptions and conceits, as well as the all-too-rational mind and the all-too-civilized self, behind. Let it all go . . . and let's go.

> Being a Sufi is to put away what is in your head—
> imagined truth, preconceptions, conditioning—
> and to face what may happen to you.
> ABU SAID

6

Mythology breaks the whole of life into a vast, horrendous Divine Comedy.

JOSEPH CAMPBELL

## The Challenger

One essential principle of crazy wisdom can be found in its name: It is *crazy* wisdom, not conventional wisdom. Many people included in our crazy wisdom lineage would tell you that crazy wisdom is the *only* wisdom, and that conventional wisdom is just the commonly agreed upon lies of any given era.

Conventional wisdom is the habitual, the unexamined life, absorbed into the culture and the fashion of the time, lost in the mad rush of accumulation, lulled to sleep by the easy lies of political hacks and newspaper scribblers, or by priests who wouldn't know a god if they met one. Crazy wisdom is the challenge to all that; it dismantles assumptions accepted as truth, unmasking ourselves and our societies.

Crazy wisdom is intrinsically contrary, often opposing even the loyal opposition, sometimes standing completely off the scales of ordinary human judgment. Consequently, crazy wisdom usually is perceived as a threat to the powers of church and state—those institutions that claim to own the truth and then sell it to people through persuasion or force. Often, followers of crazy wisdom challenge the established order through protest, personal sacrifice, art, or guerilla theater. At other times, they walk away into the mountains to live a simple life away from the insanity of institutions and the madness of mobs.

> Happy is it to practice the yoga of renouncing one's own country.
>
> MILAREPA, TIBETAN YOGI

## What Do You Know, Anyway?

Cocks crow
Dogs bark
This all men know.
Even the wisest
Cannot tell
Whence these voices come
Or explain
Why dogs bark and cocks crow
When they do.

CHUANG TZU

7

I don't make jokes. I just watch the government and report the facts.

WILL ROGERS

8

If crazy wisdom knows anything, it is that we don't know. We don't know who we are, why we are, where we are, or what this life and universe are about. Even with the brave new knowledge and expanded worldview of the twentieth century, we still do not know the answer to these perennial questions, and perhaps we never will.

We may be able to describe the world as we see it, give names to things, and even tentatively understand how some processes work, but we don't have a clue as to *why* things are the way they are. Or why they are at all.

> What's fire? You can tell me about oxidation, but that doesn't tell me a thing.
>
> JOSEPH CAMPBELL

We can explain how the respiratory system functions, but who can speak of the mystery of breath? Even if we think we understand the evolution of the human species, we still don't know where it's going next or why it developed in the first place. Although many spiritual schools claim to lead to self-knowledge, we cannot know ourselves completely. It is impossible to see the exact nature of a box when you are inside of it.

We may admit that we cannot know the *ultimate* meaning of life, yet we still assume that we can and will understand the laws of nature and how the universe works. However, looking back through history at our knowledge of the world, we find that basic "facts" change with every century and every civilization. By now it should be evident that what we know, or think we know, is perceived through a dense series of veils—culture, language, historical moment, and biological development. We and the world around us are always hidden from ourselves by ourselves. In his book *The Decline of the West*, Oswald Spengler investigates the ways that each civilization sets limits to its own understanding. He explains our particular bias this way:

> What the West has said and thought, hitherto, on the problems of space, time, motion, number, will, marriage, property, tragedy, science, has remained narrow and dubious, because men were always looking for *the* solution of *the* question. It was never seen that many questioners

implies many answers, that any philosophical question is really a veiled desire to get an explicit affirmation of what is implicit in the question itself . . .

Crazy wisdom also understands that the many conflicting answers to the unanswerable questions are what get humanity into its deepest troubles. Whether over God, Government, or Gross National Product, all wars are holy wars, fought by people who think they alone know the truth.

## We Think Too Much

> Many complain of their looks, but none complain of their brains.
> YIDDISH PROVERB

Another principle of crazy wisdom is that humans don't know how to think. Or maybe we just think too much. In either case, what passes for reason often turns out to be unreasonable in the end. Our so-called rational mind is deeply conditioned, psychologically and culturally, and what is labeled reasoning is often just the mind making excuses for emotional needs and reactive behavior. Reason has become our ideology, but we may not yet be able to tell it apart from wishful thinking. It may also be that the intellect is overvalued and even overdeveloped. It may be that we think so much we can't think, and know so much we don't know anything.

> The evolution of the brain not only overshot the needs of prehistoric man, it is the only example of evolution providing a species with an organ which it does not know how to use.
> ARTHUR KOESTLER

Reason may be humanity's greatest boon but it is also our bitterest curse, perhaps even our fatal flaw. What reason has gained for us by giving us some degree of mastery over our world, it has taken away by separating us from that world. If the separation increases much more, it may become a permanent split.

The act of thinking can be tiresome and is often painful. Some-

> A man's worst enemies can't wish on him what he can think up himself.
> YIDDISH PROVERB

times it feels like we are locked into the prison of our mind and given a life sentence. Our punishment is to suffer under a life of sentences; the train of thought runs over our lives.

> Man's great misfortune is that he has no organ, no
> kind of eyelid or brake, to mask or block a thought,
> or all thoughts, when he wants to.
>
> PAUL-TOUSSAINT-JULES VALÉRY

Reason and the intellect are important tools for survival, as well as natural wonders that give us the capacity to create great flying machines and figures of speech. However, it appears that reason and the intellect only prepare the ground for crazy wisdom, which—like the universe itself—often seems to blossom out of nothingness. Even the greatest scientists say that it is not the rational mind that comes up with the most significant discoveries; something else is taking place. When the apple hit Isaac Newton on the head, it must have knocked all the knowledge out so gravity could finally get in. That gravity, however, did not bring Newton *or* the Western world back down to earth.

> If you are depressed, you are too high up in your
> mind.
>
> CARL JUNG

## *We Think Too Much of Ourselves*

Crazy wisdom does not believe that humans, as individuals or as a species, are necessarily the ultimate purpose for the universe—the reason for the existence of billions of galaxies full of suns and planets and eons and eons of time. By force of habit, unyielding vanity, or perhaps a genetically encoded belief, we still think and behave as though the whole show was created for our sake and that our own history is somehow the major concern of the cosmos. Such a belief might be reasonable if we also still believed the sun goes around the earth. We should know better by now. As science pushes back the boundaries of space and time, it also puts us in our place, shrinking our significance relative to the uncountable solar systems and the light-years of time.

The most radical crazy wisdom does not view our personal human history (or even the evolution of the species) as movement

Man, here's your greatness:
your meat is useless,
your bones don't make
    ornaments,
your skin can't be played on
    an instrument.

KABIR

toward a higher state. What makes us believe that things are advancing? Who is to say that we are better off now than we ever were? For that matter, who is to say that we are better off now than before we were at all?

> Belief in progress is a doctrine of idlers and
> Belgians.
>
> CHARLES BAUDELAIRE

Looking at the human species circa the twentieth century, we can only guess that evolution is not yet finished. If we *are* the end product, then we must assume that the cosmic design is, at best, somewhat flawed. Furthermore, if we don't mutate our way into some sleek new species, we will probably be going the way of the dinosaurs. Yet in spite of, or perhaps even because of, our impermanent condition, crazy wisdom often finds great love and compassion for all humanity. If it doesn't appear that way at first glance, it's just because some of the heavy melodrama and sentimentality have been removed from the story.

> For the present, the comedy of existence has not
> yet "become conscious" of itself. For the present,
> we still live in the age of tragedy, the age of morali-
> ties and religions.
>
> FRIEDRICH NIETZSCHE

## A Different Way of Knowing

> The knowledge beyond knowledge is my
> knowledge.
>
> KABIR

Crazy wisdom is about another way of knowing. Some call it intuition or vision. Artists might say they are touched by the Muses, while some spiritual masters refer to "direct seeing," "revelation," or "the wisdom that surpasseth understanding." Some modern seekers say crazy wisdom comes to us through a different part of the brain, perhaps the mysterious right hemisphere, or else through the heart. Maybe it happens through an as yet undiscovered organ.

Whatever the pathway or process might be, in order to hear

crazy wisdom we need to somehow shut off or turn down the grinding noise of the rational, analytic gears. Crazy wisdom requires that we get at least a little bit out of our minds. This can be done through prayer, meditation, nature, art, poetry, stories, and song.

I would like to learn, or remember, how to live. I come to Hollins Pond not so much to learn how to live as, frankly, to forget about it. That is, I don't think I can learn from a wild animal how to live in particular—shall I suck warm blood, hold my tail high, walk with my footprints precisely over the prints of my hands?—but I might learn something of mindlessness, something of the purity of living in the physical senses and the dignity of living without bias or motive. The weasel lives in necessity and we live in choice, hating necessity and dying at the last ignobly in its talons. I would like to live as I should, as the weasel lives as he should. And I suspect that for me the way is like the weasel's: open to time and death painlessly, noticing everything, remembering nothing, choosing the given with a fierce and pointed will.

ANNIE DILLARD
*Teaching a Stone to Talk*

Some pathways to crazy wisdom are more direct than others. The spiritual masters, especially those in the Orient, have invented many techniques to move people out of their rational minds and into another mode of understanding. Unsolvable puzzles, repetitious chanting, elaborate visualizations, and even shouts, frights, and well-timed physical blows are used to drive people "crazy wise."

Another way crazy wisdom gets wise and crazy is by gaining many perspectives: by changing points of view, getting into another place or a distant space and looking at things from there; by finding an odd angle, climbing high for an overview, seeing what is behind it all or underneath it all, stepping outside or going inside. With all due respect to Albert Einstein, crazy wisdom has known for a long time that a lot depends on where you're standing and how fast you're going. There are many ways of looking at things.

Behead yourself!
RUMI

Sometimes I go about pitying myself,
and all the time
I am being carried on great winds across the sky.
OJIBWAY SAYING

## Nothing is Real

13

Illusion is the only reality.
GUSTAVE FLAUBERT

The inherent baselessness of physical and mental
objects is called reality.
AVATAMSAKA SUTRA

Crazy wisdom has always suspected that the world is not what it appears to be; what we ordinarily perceive as reality is not reality at all. For ages the saints and sages have been trying to tell us this through the languages of mysticism and poetry. Now contemporary scientists are saying much the same thing in the terms of physics, biology, and astronomy. According to the scientists, "reality" is even stranger than anyone imagined.

The latest scientific theory proposes that the world may not even exist if someone is not here to perceive it. Modern science has destroyed matter. Unraveled reality. Literally pulled the rug out from under us. The world we have always believed to be solid and predictable turns out to be just a play of shadow and light. The theory of quantum mechanics has turned the physical world into a lying, deceiving scoundrel and made our own five senses and central nervous systems into coconspirators in an elaborate "reality sting," a fraud carried on successfully since time immemorial. And the sting goes deeper. It turns out that space and time, as well as matter and energy, have been married for at least fifteen billion years, and all along we have been led to believe that they were single. *We are constantly being deceived!*

Recent discoveries in science reveal worlds so enormous and so tiny and so strange that they must be the great cosmic joke of some Creator who doubles over with laughter every time a scientist discovers another bizarre twist to the reality puzzle. From superclusters of galaxies that measure hundreds of millions of light-years across to particles so small that they have no mass; from the Principle of In-

We now know that the moon is demonstrably not there when nobody looks.
N. DAVID MERMIN

Reality is a wave function traveling both backward and forward in time.
JOHN L. CASTRI

determinacy to a universe containing multiple realities, everything appears to be something other than what it appears to be. If scientists can be believed, the fact of the matter is that matter is not a fact. Nobody seems to have a clue as to what is going on.

14

> The unconscious is the true psychic reality; in its inner nature it is just as much unknown to us as the reality of the external world, and it is just as imperfectly communicated to us by the data of consciousness as is the external world by the reports of our sense-organs.
>
> SIGMUND FREUD

To study Buddhism is to study ourselves. To study ourselves is to forget ourselves.

ZEN MASTER DOGEN

It is not only the external world that deceives us, but our internal world as well. For centuries, some mystics and poets have told us that we are not ourselves; furthermore, we have no separate "self." Few have taken them seriously, thinking they were only being poetical and mystical. Now psychologists and biologists tell us the same thing; the self we think we are is not the real self, or we have many selves. What's more, these so-called "selves" are determined almost completely by genes, chemicals, and early conditioning. The conclusion scientists are approaching but do not yet have the audacity to state is that, in fact, there exists no independent "self" at all. We simply don't own one. The "self"—that is to say, what we think of as the individual—is as much of an illusion as the world of matter.

Of course, there is always another side to the story. Crazy wisdom admits that the current scientific picture of reality may be as far off base as the previous scientific picture. Not only that, but mystics may be deceived as grandly by the universe as physicists and psychologists. Nonetheless, the continual reevaluations of reality and the endless new revelations about the strange and impossible nature of things should at least lead us to the following conclusion: We may never understand what is going on, and we may be sorry if we ever do.

Do what you will, this
Life's a Fiction
And is made up of
Contradiction.

WILLIAM BLAKE

> When you eventually see
> through the veils to how things really are,
> you will keep saying again
> and again,

"This is certainly not like
we thought it was!"
RUMI

## The Truths Will Set Us Free

What we are calling "crazy wisdom" is an enterprise of exposing the many sides of truth until there is no truth, and that's the truth. Crazy wisdom shows us the part of ourselves that Christians disapprovingly call our "animal nature"—the Coyote in us all—or the part of us that the Zen master might call our "original face." Crazy wisdom looks at things from the sky above and the mud below, through a telescope and a microscope, from the head and the heart and the loins, all in the hope that we will gain varied perspectives and play our roles in this bittersweet melodrama of life with a little more ease and grace. But wait! This doesn't mean crazy wisdom will necessarily solve our problems or save the planet.

Everything is going to become unimaginably
worse, and never get better again. If I lied to you
about that, you would sense that I'd lied to you,
and that would be another cause for gloom.
KURT VONNEGUT, JR.

This process of revelation may, indeed, turn out to be somewhat uncomfortable. Crazy wisdom removes our many layers of masks and costumes, takes away our clocks and compasses, our automobiles and house keys, and calls into question our most cherished beliefs in God, Country, Family, and Future. All visions, including nightmares, must be addressed. Crazy wisdom even finds it important to remind us that we will die.

We die, and we do not die.
SHUNRYU SUZUKI

While some of crazy wisdom's revelations sound harsh, others are joyous and full of wonder. In fact, there may be an equal amount of each type, or at least two different ways of looking at everything. Crazy wisdom's insights inspire a wide range of responses, from pessimism and gloom to great ecstasy. But even in a critical mood,

Only the shallow know themselves.
OSCAR WILDE

those who possess crazy wisdom most often soften up a hard-edged insight with a song, a poem, some humor, or a little sleight of hand.

In the process of exploring crazy wisdom, we may stumble across some truth. Even if we do, we might not recognize it. Or if we did, we would pick it up, and before you could say "quark" or "synapse," it would disappear right out of our hands. Just like these "principles" of crazy wisdom will now vanish into the rest of this book.

> Since everything is but an apparition, perfect in
> being what it is, having nothing to do with good or
> bad, acceptance or rejection, one may well burst
> out in laughter.
>
> LONG CHEN PA
> TIBETAN MEDITATION MASTER

## Crazy Wisdom: The Book

In this book we will weave the various threads of these crazy wisdom principles together into a crazy quilt, perhaps an insecurity blanket; one that won't necessarily keep us warm at night but can make us more alive during the day. Through many cultures and characters, we will search for the common motifs to pattern our cloth, a patchwork we hope will hold together. At the very least, this crazy wisdom quilt may serve as a cover for some of our more wild ideas and unconventional impulses. Some people might even end up wearing it as a robe.

We will meet many disparate characters who embody crazy wisdom. They will include sweet, gentle beings such as St. Francis of Assisi, who would go to great trouble to spare the life of a single earthworm. There will also be sharp-edged curmudgeons, the likes of Friedrich Nietzsche or H. L. Mencken, who will pull the tail of all our sacred cows. Crazy wisdom is the fulcrum on which good and bad balance perfectly, the carousel on which both saint and sinner ride. As we meet these characters, it will be up to you, the reader, to decide—if you care to make any such distinctions—who is sinner and who is saint. After all, one person's Harpo Marx may be another's Meyer Baba (both were silent). Deciding who sits on the higher throne, Jesus of Nazareth or Mark Twain, is up to each individual.

Even the physicists have "proved" that reality depends on the observer. Revelation, like everything else, is in the eyes of the beholder.

In part one, we will become acquainted with crazy wisdom through a few of the archetypal characters who live it and define it. We will trace crazy wisdom's historical roots through both Eastern and Western cultures, ending the section in the lofts of twentieth-century artists and poets. Then, in part two, we will explore the ways in which people arrive at crazy wisdom. We will even conduct an exercise in crazy wisdom perspectives, as we embark on a journey across the landscape of the mind and the universe, asking fundamental questions about the human condition and the laws of nature. We end the book with a grand tour of the twentieth century, which we will examine as a transition period, an apocalyptic and, some would say, unfortunate testament to the truths of crazy wisdom. It is our world, and welcome to it.

> Let us settle ourselves, and work and wedge our feet downward through the mud and slush of opinion, and prejudice, and tradition, and delusion and appearance, that alluvion which covers the globe, through Paris and London, through New York and Boston and Concord, through church and state, through poetry and philosophy and religion till we come to a hard bottom and rocks in place, which we can call reality, and say, This is, and no mistake; and then begin, having a *point d'appui*, below freshet and frost and fire, a place where you might found a wall or a state, or set a lamppost safely, or perhaps a gauge, not a Nilometer, but a Realometer, that future ages might know how deep a freshet of shams and appearances had gathered from time to time.
>
> **HENRY DAVID THOREAU**

# CHAPTER TWO

# The Cast

You may never get to touch the Master, but you
can tickle his creatures.

THOMAS PYNCHON

## Archetypes

Crazy wisdom makes its appearance through archetypal characters who arise in every culture to challenge convention. Getting to know these archetypes will give us a feel for the mythic quality and common heritage of crazy wisdom, as well as provide a way to recognize the crazy wisdom in some of the historical figures we will meet throughout this book.

The clown, the jester, the trickster, and the fool are the four crazy wisdom archetypes. Although they have been known to trade costumes and steal each other's riffs and magic tricks, each challenges us in their own special way—with questions, stories, or laughter, or by offering their own radically different version of reality. Because these archetypes have devised some brilliant disguises, it may appear at times that they have nothing at all to do with wisdom. Some of them put on masks to unmask us. Others remove all their masks. Some mimic and mime to show us who we are.

The common message conveyed by the four archetypal characters is the crazy wisdom of doubt. They spread doubt about our beliefs, our abilities, our motives, our institutions, our sanity, our loves, our laws, our leaders, even our alliteration. Clowns and jesters have grave doubts about our attitude. "Is this seriousness really appropriate?" Others, such as the spiritual crazy wisdom masters—the holy fools—call into question our entire understanding of ourselves and the world.

The four archetypes share an uncanny ability to escape the trouble they inevitably get themselves into: The clown gets bopped, the trickster is dismembered and blown apart, the jester may have his head cut off by the king or be hit by rotten fruit thrown from the audience, and the great fool is about to fall off a cliff or be martyred by an angry mob. But just when it seems that all is lost, they rise again, recovered and whole, even from death. (The dismembered Coyote reassembles; Jesus Christ rises into everlasting life.) Because of their humor or their innocence, or because their revelations are so important, these crazy wisdom characters are immortal.

Although these four are at times banished from the institutions of church and state, they can often be found hanging out with the common folk. Over time, they have made their way into the stories, legends, and songs of the people.

## The Clown

> The comic spirit masquerades in all things we say
> and do. We are each a clown and do not need to put
> on a white face.
>
> JAMES HILLMAN

The most human of the crazy wisdom archetypes is the clown. The clown's too-big mouth is grotesquely grinning or super-sad, mocking our mortal moods. We laugh because the clown is one of us, pathetic and lovable, trying hard, but always flailing and failing. (Shy about being introduced, the clown leans over to tie his shoe and . . . oh no, the inevitable tangled-up tango begins! Accompanied by silly circus music.)

The clown shows us our awkward human condition and encourages us to laugh at ourselves. We all are clowns, always getting fouled up, mixed up, thwarted by circumstance. We climb the ladder only to find it is leaning against the wrong wall. We search for hats that are already on our heads. We plan our days only to find that the days have other plans.

The clown points out our vulnerability. Although he is eager and hopeful, we know he will not succeed. His great triumph is the sheepish grin or silly shrug he displays after his failures. "Oh well, that's the way it goes." The clown quickly forgets the past and moves on to the next disaster.

The clown's world, in which all of us live, is not a practical joke—it is an *impractical joke*. It is the world of Laurel and Hardy moving a piano, or of Elmer Fudd trying to get wid of the wabbit. In this clown's world, appliances don't work right. We try to clean things up but in the process make them even dirtier. Just having a body sometimes seems an absurd condition. We run in circles wearing shoes that don't fit, so we get nowhere and get blisters on the way. ("Aye, there's the rub.") The clown is living proof of the second law of thermodynamics; in this world, all things tend toward chaos and dissolution.

Some say the clown's white face is the mask of death, grinning out from within us at our feeble attempts to create order and meaning out of life's three-ring circus. In the end, says the white face, we are always the butt of the joke.

The clown is also the everyman figure, personified by Charlie Chaplin caught in the machinery of modern times, or lured to the gold rush with the rest of the crowd. He is the unfortunate immigrant, the ordinary sadsack guy buffeted by forces of history and his own foolishness yet surviving somehow, sometimes managing a foolish grin, and occasionally even jumping up and clicking his worn-out heels as he walks into the sunset. The clown falls over for us, and stands up for us, too.

The clown is the lighter side of dark forces, chaos made benign, the subconscious as silly. This makes the clown the most acceptable and lovable of all the crazy wisdom archetypes.

## The Jester

No matter how much restriction civilization imposes on the individual, he nevertheless finds some way to circumvent it. Wit is the best safety valve modern man has evolved;

20

In the end, everything is a gag.

CHARLIE CHAPLIN

The clown is the primitive comedian.

GEORGE SANTAYANA

the more civilization, the more repression, the more need there is for wit.

SIGMUND FREUD

Jesters are the wits and critics. They expose the establishment's lies and make light of the contemporary social scene. While the clown reveals the timeless foibles of humanity, the jester takes on the social and political behavior specific to the current age.

The jester has appeared in many guises: as playwright and pamphleteer, roaming minstrel and balladeer, actor in the commedia dell'arte, master of ceremonies at a cabaret or vaudeville show; as cartoonist, satirist, parody writer; and as the contemporary stand-up comedian.

People should be taught what is, not what should be. All my humor is based on destruction and despair. If the whole world were tranquil, without disease and violence, I'd be standing in the breadline—right in back of J. Edgar Hoover, Director of the F.B.I.

LENNY BRUCE

Unlike the all-too-human clown, sometimes the jester is barely human—a character whose teeth and tongue are equally sharp. ("Doesn't that slay you.") He gets away with dangerous revelations by making them funny.

The jester works with words: While the clown mimes, the jester mimics. As has been said, the pen is mightier than the sword. The jester slices the *s* off *sword* and thrusts with the word. The jester jests and jousts with his sharp tongue, hurling barbs, needles, jabs, sticking it to them, laying them low, killing them.

The jester takes the wind out of politicians' sails, deflates inflated rhetoric, punctures hypocrisy and hype-ocracy, bureaucracy and bore-ocracy, until they are shown to be nothing but hot air, the laughable breeze made by the human species fawning over itself and flapping its jaws.

The court jester is the king's own fool and often his best advisor. While others are afraid to tell the king the truth, the court jester, "playing the fool," points out both the king's weaknesses and political realities. He had better be funny because his head is at stake.

21

No matter how cynical you get, it is impossible to keep up.

JANE WAGNER

America has the best politicians money can buy.

WILL ROGERS

Seriousness is the only refuge of the shallow.

OSCAR WILDE

The aim of a joke is not to degrade the human being but to remind him that he is already degraded.

GEORGE ORWELL

FOOL: The sweet and bitter fool
      Will presently appear;
      The one in motley here,
      The other found out there.
LEAR: Dost thou call me fool, boy?
FOOL: All thy other titles thou hast given away:
      That thou wast born with.

SHAKESPEARE

*The Tragedy of King Lear*

One of the jester's most famous tracts came from the pen of Jonathan Swift during the Irish famine in the early 1700s. In the following excerpt from "A Modest Proposal," Swift's biting sarcasm lays bare society's indifference to the bitter suffering of the poor.

> I have been assured by a very knowing American of my acquaintance in London, that a young healthy child well nursed is at a year old a most delicious, nourishing and wholesome food, whether stewed, roasted, baked, or boiled, and I make no doubt that it will equally serve in a fricassee, or a ragout.
>
> I do therefore humbly offer it to public consideration, that of the hundred and twenty thousand children already computed, twenty thousand may be reserved for breed, whereof only one fourth part to be males, which is more than we allow to sheep, black-cattle, or swine. . . . That the remaining hundred thousand may at a year old be offered in sale to the persons of quality and fortune, through the kingdom, always advising the mother to let them suck plentifully in the last month, so as to render them plump, and fat for a good table.

The jester also challenges religious beliefs, perhaps never more thoroughly than in the artistry of Mark Twain. His most irreverent writing, collected in *Letters from the Earth*, was not published until the 1940s, nearly thirty years after Twain's death. If sections of this book has been released in his lifetime, Twain might well have been lynched. In it he dares to take on none other than Jehovah Himself.

He says, naively, outspokenly, and without suggestion of embarrassment: "I the Lord thy God am a jealous God." You see, it is only another way of saying, "I the Lord thy God am a small God; a small God, and fretful about small things." He was giving a warning: he could not bear the thought of any other God getting some of the Sunday compliments of this comical little human race. . . .

Twain portrays God as not only vain, but also malicious. He questions why people would love a God who doles out such atrocities.

The Christian begins with this straight proposition . . . God is all-knowing, and all powerful. Then, having thus made the Creator responsible for all pains and diseases and miseries . . . which He could have prevented, the gifted Christian blandly calls him Our Father!

Twain, like the best of jesters, is not being humorous just for humor's sake. Through cutting wit, he presents a crazy wisdom point of view, his dark assessment of both Creator and creation.

Man is a Religious Animal. Man is the only Religious Animal. He is the only animal that has the True Religion—several of them. He is the only animal that loves his neighbor as himself and cuts his throat if his theology isn't straight.

What do you call Love, Hate, Charity, Revenge, Humanity, Magnanimity, Forgiveness? Different results of the one Master Impulse: the necessity of securing one's self approval.

There are times when one would like to hang the whole human race, and finish the farce.

The jester works with words, sometimes making words themselves the target. The joker or punster creates confusion and laughter by showing us that words often have two meanings—the double entendre or the Freudian slip. Sometimes the truth is in the mistake, and in the misspoken word we hear the true meaning behind the intended meaning. At other times there is no meaning there at all.

24

> One morning I shot an elephant in my pajamas. How he got in my pajamas I don't know. Then we tried to remove the tusks, but they were embedded so firmly we couldn't budge them. Of course, in Alabama the Tuskaloosa. We took some pictures of the native girls, but they were not developed. But we're going back again.
>
> GROUCHO MARX

Nonsense either reveals the inherent meaninglessness of words or creates new meanings for them. The pun can be the lowest form of humor or the highest. In other words, some types of nonsense make more sense than others.

> Hearasay in paradox lust.
> JAMES JOYCE
> *Finnegans Wake*

In *Finnegans Wake*, James Joyce created his own language, based on English but thickened with multilingual puns, onomatopoeia, and word associations that present the reader with a maze of meanings. With his sustained wordplay and rhythms, Joyce makes the description of a sexual encounter resonate beyond ordinary language.

> Pharoah with fairy, two lie, let them! Yet they wend it back, qual his leif, himmertality, bullseaboob and rivishy divil, light in hand, helm on high, to peekaboo durk the thicket of slumbwhere, till their hour with their scene be struck for ever and the book of the dates he close, he clasp and she and she seegn her tour d'adieu, Pervinca calling, Soloscar hears. (O Sheem! O Shaam!), and gentle Isad Ysut gag, flispering in the nightleaves flattery, dinsiduously, to Finnegan, to sin again and to make grim grandma grunt and grin again while the first grey streaks steal silvering by for to mock their quarrels in dollymount tumbling.

The greatest of word jesters can deconstruct a language and speak in strange tongues that we all understand. Words are only commonly agreed-on sounds, when spoken, or symbols, when written. When the game is revealed as the game it is, we are exposed, grunting and humming to one another in the elaborate music of language.

Instead of relying heavily on the pun or even the pen, some jesters venture into the streets or go to the seat of power to make their point, displaying crazy wisdom through their idiosyncratic behavior or through defiant acts of political theater.

Diogenes the Cynic, an infamous figure in ancient Greece, walked the streets of Athens with a lantern at night, telling people he was looking for an honest man. Diogenes, who despised worldly possessions and lived in a bathtub, still gained much respect as a philosopher. When visiting Diogenes, Alexander the Great asked if he could do him a favor. Diogenes replied, "Yes. Remove your shadow." Legend has it that Diogenes once masturbated on the Parthenon steps, requesting those who masturbated in the privacy of their homes to join him in a public display of honesty.

The twentieth century has demanded outrageous acts of defiance from its jesters, and they have responded. In the late 1960s, the American counterculture staged many acts of protest through guerilla theater events. "Yippies" (members of the Youth International Party) threw money from the balcony of the New York Stock Exchange onto the trading floor below. To protest the Vietnam War, the same group gathered thousands of people to surround the Pentagon, and after sticking flowers into the rifles of the soldiers who guarded the building, the protesters chanted "om" in unison, in an attempt to levitate the massive building. They claimed success.

Because jesters are "nay-sayers," they often speak the truth, saying no to obvious lies, absurdities, and injustices. In the worldly realm of relative truths, jesters are the champions of crazy wisdom.

All "isms" should be "wasms."

ABBIE HOFFMAN

## The Trickster

> Since everybody laughs at me, I will laugh at them.
> IKTOMI, OGLALA TRICKSTER

The tricksters are the rascals of myth and folklore. Sometimes they appear as bumbling creators of the world, the source of all our troubles; at other times they are nothing more than ribald sex fiends.

Whichever role they play, the tricksters do not abide by ordinary codes of behavior. They emerge from a time before good and evil, and their crazy wisdom is to act out our uncivilized, primal nature. In *The Trickster*, Paul Radin explores the trickster's universality.

26

> No generation understands him fully, but no generation can do without him. Each had to include him in all its theologies, in all its cosmologies, despite the fact that it realized that he did not fit properly into any of them, for he represents not only the undifferentiated and distant past, but likewise the undifferentiated present within each individual.

The mythical tricksters are a combination of god and beast, and are among the oldest human images of the divine. Native American tricksters like Coyote may have been creator deities of hunter-gatherer tribes—creators who were later kicked out of heaven by tamer and more orderly agricultural gods. Although many people now believe in a more noble creator, some still think that the trickster is to blame for the way things are.

Radin recounts a Blackfoot Indian myth which tells how, when Old Man (the trickster) was creating things, he would have made a worse mess if it hadn't been for Old Woman. She insisted on helping Old Man decide how people should be fashioned. He agreed to listen only if *he* could have the final say; luckily, it didn't quite work out that way.

*In the beginning of the world, Coyote was more foolish than he is now.*

YAQUI LEGEND

> "Well," said Old Man, "let the people have eyes and mouths in their faces; but they shall be straight up and down."
>
> "No," said Old Woman, "We will not have them that way. We will have the eyes and mouths in the faces, as you say; but they shall all be set crosswise."
>
> "Well," said Old Man, "the people shall have ten fingers on each hand."
>
> "Oh no!" said Old Woman, "that will be too many. They will be in the way. There shall be four fingers and one thumb on each hand."
>
> "Well," said Old Man, "we shall beget children. The genitals shall be at our navels."

"No," said Old Woman, "that will make child-bearing too easy and the people will not care for their children. The genitals should be at the pubes."

When the trickster Coyote is given the role of creator, he always makes a mess of things. In the beginning, it is told, Coyote had a sack full of stars that he was supposed to place in the sky. He was doing a good job at first, putting the stars in neat rows, but he got bored and restless, and finally flung the remaining stars where they are now. This kind of thing happened with many of Coyote's jobs as creator. How might the world have looked if Coyote had taken more care?

After carelessly creating the universe, the trickster becomes wild nature made flesh, arriving in the village to sniff around for some action. When the trickster Coyote visits the Indian tribes of North and Central America, he has absolutely no manners. It is said that he even laughs through his anus. By most accounts, he is also a shameless sex fiend, called "cunt-craving coyote" by the Hopi, and in one story even having sex with his own daughter. In the following Maidu story, adapted from Malcolm Margolin's *The Way We Lived*, Coyote reveals his lovable, loathable, lascivious self.

> The trickster is a collective shadow figure, an epitome of all the inferior traits of character in individuals.
>
> CARL JUNG

## MAIDU COYOTE STORY

As Coyote went about everywhere he met Cottontail Rabbit and came to the place where he made his camp.

"Well," said Coyote, "Are we going together to the dance?"

"Yes! We will dance when it grows dark," said Cottontail.

Then it was night and they heard singing and dancing all about. So they went toward the music until Coyote said to Cottontail, "Stop a minute! You had better stay here. Women are very careful and suspicious of me," he said. "If I have this penis on, they are afraid of me. So you keep it for me here. When the women think I am all right, I will whistle. When you hear the whistle, bring my penis along." So Cottontail agreed and stayed there.

Meanwhile Coyote went off and arrived at the dance. He started dancing and two very pretty women fell in love with him. They followed him off to the place near where Cottontail was waiting.

Then Coyote whistled, but there was no reply. He whistled again.

"What are you doing?" said the girls.

"Oh, just whistling," Coyote said. Then the girls laughed, and put their legs over him. "Why don't you wait, you two!" he said.

Now, after Coyote had walked down to the dance and left Cottontail behind, two Star-Women came along and Cottontail followed them. After a while Cottontail made love to the oldest woman, making her moan and sigh. The younger woman said to the older woman, "How can such a little man make you moan like that? Such a tiny fellow can't make me do that!" said the youngest. Then Cottontail made love to the youngest woman and also made her moan and sigh.

Meanwhile Coyote stayed with the two women he was with until it was light. Then in the morning he went to the house where Cottontail was staying. Rushing in, Coyote looked angry. "Why didn't you come with my penis when I whistled? I have a good mind to kill you," he said.

"Two women came along and I followed them," said Cottontail.

"Then what did you do?" said Coyote.

"I entered them with your penis," he said.

"Oh!" said Coyote.

"I made the two girls moan and sigh," said Cottontail.

"Oh yes!" said Coyote, "My penis will make women moan and sigh." Coyote felt as if he had been making love all night, and his anger disappeared.

When Cottontail handed it over, Coyote washed and cleaned it with water and put it away. He went off again the next morning.

Given the chance, would we be as ribald as the scroungy dog-cat, Coyote? To find out, you might try to locate Coyote sometime. He seems to have survived the modern world better than some other tricksters, and he can still be seen around campfires and powwows, sneaking into zendos, or hanging around coffeehouses and red-light districts. In a recent book, *Coyote's Journal*, a group of contemporary writers tell of Coyote's ways. Some have even learned things about Coyote's past that were not known before.

## WHY DOGS SMELL EACH OTHER'S BUTTS
### *by Lowell Jaeger*

When he asked, the dogs refused him.
You are unclean, they told Coyote,
you are not a dog.
So the dogs undressed for their sweatbath
and entered the sweatlodge without him.

Coyote envied the glossy fur coats
the dogs had hung outside the lodge.
He thought of stealing them,
but he decided not to.

29

Instead he threw the long coats
in a great pile,
and wiped his muddy feet across them.
Then he set fire to the sweatlodge roof
and said in a loud voice:
Oh what will the dogs do now,
Coyote has taken their fur!

From behind a rock, Coyote sat laughing
as the naked dogs rushed
into the cold out-of-doors,
grabbing for a coat,
afraid there might be too few
to cover everyone.

Years later, as the story goes,
with every dog zipped in someone else's fur,
dogs smell each other's butts,
looking for their own.

Meanwhile Coyote is still grinning,
off in the hills somewhere,
rolling in red dirt,
thinking how crude
to be a dog,

how much more clean,
how much more fun
to be Coyote.

Coyote is most often seen with his head back, muzzle facing upward, howling at the moon. The secret of his crazy wisdom can be
understood by listening closely to his cry. In it one can hear a bittersweet mixture of all experience. In Coyote's howl we hear both longing and laughter, mocking and moaning.

Even though he loves to steal the stage, Coyote is just one of the animal forms that the trickster takes. In North and Central American Indian tribes he also appears as Raven, Crow, or Hare; in Europe as Reynard the Fox; in Africa as the spider Ananse; and in the American South as B'rer Rabbit.

Aspects of the trickster appear in the deities and mythical characters of many cultures. The Hindu's Lord Krishna is part trickster and loves to play jokes on mortals (if you were a god, wouldn't you?), especially the young girls, the milkmaids, whom he dazzles with his divine radiance and magic powers.

One of Lord Krishna's roles is to steal people's certainty, to rob them of their pride. That is also one of the functions of the Greek god Hermes, Zeus's messenger, who often delivers messages that people would rather not receive. A West African trickster god named Edshu also loves to create uncertainty and chaos among humans. Once Edshu went for a walk, wearing a hat that was red on one side and white on the other. He walked down the path between two farmers' fields, waving at both of them and making sure they each saw his hat. Later, when the farmers talked to each other, they got into an argument over the hat's color, one having seen the red side and the other the white. Just as they were ready to kill each other over this disagreement, Edshu revealed himself and his hat trick.

The fact that Coyote and other tricksters are making a comeback is evidence that the crazy wisdom of these mythological rascals refuses to be paved over. Where the brush begins to thicken, just outside the boundaries of our civilized encampment, the trickster howls at night to remind us of the chaos that lives all around.

## The Fool

Lord, what fools these mortals be.
SHAKESPEARE

If the fool would persist in his folly, he would become wise.
WILLIAM BLAKE

The fool is the most potent of the archetypes and also the most capable teacher of crazy wisdom. There are actually two types of fool: the foolish fool and the great fool. The foolish fool is inept and silly, a clown of the mind. The great fool is wise beyond ordinary understanding. The foolish fool is the one we see every day when we look into the mirror or walk down the street. The great fool is the rarest of beings.

Innocence is the trademark of both fools. The innocence of the foolish fool makes him clumsy and unsophisticated because he tries to live according to convention. The great fool, however, does not try to fit in; in his innocence, he lives by his own rules. The foolish fool and his money are soon parted, but the great fool gives his money away. The foolish fool always gets lost, while the great fool is at home everywhere. The great fool has different values from the rest of us and therefore is crazy wisdom's master of ceremonies.

> Einstein was a man who could ask immensely
> simple questions.
>
> JACOB BRONOWSKI
> *The Ascent of Man*

The great fool, like Einstein, wonders about the obvious and stands in awe of the ordinary, which makes him capable of revolutionary discoveries about space and time. The great fool lives outside the blinding circle of routine, remaining open to the surprise of each moment. We are the foolish ones, complacent in our understanding. We take for granted the miraculous dance of creation, but the great fool continuously sees it as if for the first time. The revelations of the great fool often show us where we are going, or—more often— where we are.

## THE FOOL IS A CARD

The great fool shows his true face as the Fool, the first card in the tarot deck. He is the master of ceremonies, smiling and welcoming us to the show, the Grand Illusion, the parade of archetypal characters to follow. The Fool announces that what we are about to see is only a melodrama, and that we should not take these masks or matters too seriously. Our personalities are just put-ons, personae, roles we are given to play. We just read the lines and flesh out scenes; there's really not much we can do about the plot. Our destiny is, after all, written in the cards.

In the tarot the Fool is portrayed wandering in the sunshine with his knapsack and little dog, seemingly without a care in the world

3 I

Start a huge, foolish project,
like Noah.
It makes absolutely no
    difference,
what people think of you.
RUMI

If others had not been
foolish, we should be so.
WILLIAM BLAKE

and with no particular place to go. And he is about to step off the edge of a cliff! Perhaps the Fool knows he will go over the cliff but continues to smile because he also knows he will never hit bottom. The Fool understands that he, the cliff, and the bottom are all illusions.

The Fool is the only unnumbered card in the tarot deck; he represents the nothingness from which the universe emerged. As the zero, the Fool himself has no value; he is outside the boundaries of number or sequence, outside all categories, beyond good and evil. With the Fool, anything can happen, and all things, even death, are equally worthy of his perpetual smile.

Since the Fool has no number, he can also be seen as the last card. Or we might envision him as leading us from the nothingness at the beginning into the nothingness at the end—out of the void, through the valley, and finally over the cliff and back to the void. And all of us will be there, right behind the Fool, each of us in the costumes and roles of other tarot characters, all together on our way to the inevitable conclusion.

Finally, as a testament to his power, the Fool is one of the few characters from the tarot deck to make it into our modern playing cards. He becomes the Joker—always wild, and almost always welcome. Like the Fool, the Joker is without number or trump, and therefore above all numbers and trumps. He has no specific value and so is of the greatest value. The Joker is mightier than the Kings and higher than the Aces.

### FOOL AROUND

The fool can be found playing the central role in folk stories from around the world. All of the crazy wisdom principles can be seen in these stories, with the fool acting out the extremes of either wisdom or folly. One of the most famous of fools is Mulla Nasrudin, who is especially popular in the Arabic world. The Muslim mystics use stories about Nasrudin as spiritual lessons, giving him the role of either village idiot or eccentric sage. In the following story Nasrudin plays the great fool, teaching crazy wisdom to the people.

When Nasrudin was asked to speak to the congregation at the mosque, he went up to the front and asked, "Oh people, do you know what I have come to tell you?" The crowd answered, "No." Nasrudin then said, "If you don't know what I have come to tell you, then you are too ignorant to understand what I was going to say." And he left the mosque. But the people knew he had great wisdom, so they invited him back the next week. This time when Nasrudin asked the congregation if they knew what he was going to tell them, the crowd answered, "Yes." "Fine," said Nasrudin, "then I don't need to waste your time." And once again he left the mosque. But once again the people invited him back, thinking the next time they could convince him to talk. When he arrived on the following week, Nasrudin again asked the congregation if they knew what he was going to tell them. This time, half of the people answered back "Yes," and half of them answered back "No." "Fine," said Nasrudin, "then those who know should tell those who don't know, and I will be on my way."

A Hasidic story reveals a rabbi's wise and crazy teaching methods. One day this great fool was visited by a very poor man. The man complained that he had to live in a tiny one-room house with his wife, six children, and mother-in-law. It was so crowded he couldn't stand it any longer; he was losing his mind.

"Do you have any animals?" the rabbi asked.

"Yes, chickens and a goat," the man replied.

"Good," said the rabbi. "Bring the goat into the house to live with you."

The poor man objected, but finally agreed to follow the rabbi's suggestion. A week later the man came back to the rabbi, even more exasperated, saying, "I brought the goat into my house and now it is worse than before. I can't stand it! What should I do now?"

The rabbi said, "Go home and also bring the chickens into the house to live with you." The man objected again, but finally did as he was told. A week later he came back to the rabbi, dazed and crazed, crying, "It is impossible now in my house, rabbi! Help me! Help me!"

The rabbi said, "Go home and take out the goat and the chickens." The man did as he was told and a few days later came back to the rabbi, smiling and grateful, saying, "Rabbi, my house is now so spacious and peaceful! You are certainly the wisest man who ever lived."

There is a Chinese story about a wise farmer who knew about the impossibility of knowing and the arbitrary nature of human judgments. In the story, the farmer's horse runs away and his neighbor comes to offer sympathy, saying, "Too bad about your horse." The farmer simply replies, "Maybe." The next day the farmer's horse comes back leading two wild horses into the stable. This time the neighbor congratulates the farmer, saying, "What a lucky break!"

Again the farmer replies, "Maybe." The next day the farmer's son breaks his leg trying to tame one of the wild horses, and again the neighbor comes over to offer sympathy. "Too bad," says the neighbor. Once again the farmer simply replies, "Maybe." The next day the recruitment officer from the king's army comes through the region taking all the young men of fighting age, but since the farmer's son has a broken leg he is left behind. The story can go on and on.

In each of these stories, the wise fool knows the answer; ordinary mortals turn out to be the foolish ones. Sometimes, however, the foolish fools get the stories all to themselves, with no one to help extract them from their ridiculous and sometimes pitiful ways.

One day Nasrudin was sitting in the marketplace in front of a basket full of hot peppers, eating one after the other. His eyes were watering, his face was red and contorted, and he was obviously suffering greatly, but still he continued to eat the hot peppers. When someone finally asked him why he was doing this, Nasrudin replied, "I'm looking for a sweet one."

There is a Christian story of unknown origin, which concerns a foolish fool who is also very religious. The most modern version of the story tells of this pious man living in a small town in Europe when a big flood occurs. As the water rises in the town and begins to fill the houses, a rescue boat comes to take the pious man to safety. However, the man waves the boat away, saying, "Don't worry about me. I believe in God and He will save me." Later, as the water rises higher, the man is forced to climb up onto the roof of his house, and once again the boat comes by. Once again the pious man waves the boat away, crying, "Don't worry, I believe in God and He will save me!" Finally, just as the waters reach the chimney and the man has to stand on tiptoe to breathe, a helicopter flies over and throws a rope down to him. However, the pious man refuses to grab the rope, and a few minutes later is swept away and drowns. When the pious man reaches heaven he gets an audience with God, and after bowing, he says with consternation, "My Lord, I was your faithful servant, who worshiped you daily, loving you and trusting in you, but when the flood came, you would not save me. Why, Lord, why?" God looks at the man with a puzzled expression and says, "That's odd. I was sure that I had sent you two boats and a helicopter."

Animals are often given the starring roles in folk stories about wise and foolish fools, as in Aesop's fables or the Buddhist Jataka tales. In one Jataka tale, a monkey reaches into a trap to grab a banana, but the size of the banana prevents him from removing his hand from the trap. The foolish monkey simply has to let go of the banana and he will be free, but his greed keeps him trapped until the hunter arrives.

While we are on the subject of foolish fools, they say that during the days of the second Hasidic movement in the 1700s, there was a town in Poland named Chelm—some claim it was a mythical place while others insist it was real—which was governed by a counsel of fools who believed themselves to be very wise. They even called themselves "the wise men of Chelm." In Jewish folklore, these wise men of Chelm have become the object of derision and laughter to all but themselves.

It has been told that the wise men of Chelm once found themselves in a heated dispute over which was more important to humanity, the sun or the moon. After much bickering and debate, the head rabbi finally decided to settle the issue once and for all. With impeccable logic he proclaimed, "The moon comes out at night when it is completely dark, allowing us to see at least a little. But the sun shines only in the daytime when it is light and we don't need it. Therefore, I say that the moon is more important than the sun."

A group of rabbis was once laughing at the foolishness of the wise men of Chelm, when the oldest and wisest rabbi among them said, "Anyone who thinks that he is not a fool shows his ignorance. As the Talmud itself claims, 'The world was delivered unto fools.'"

In these folk stories we learn much about the ways of fools and their extremes of wisdom and folly. However, the great fool is most vital to our saga of crazy wisdom, making it important to meet this archetype in a historical context also. We will be surprised to discover that many of us pray to some form of the great fool almost daily. Our worship is directed toward those fools who have become figureheads of the world's religions.

## THE HOLY FOOLS

> None attains to the Degree of Truth until a thousand honest people have testified that he is a heretic.
>
> JUNAID OF BAGHDAD, SUFI

36

Some think, perhaps, that it is peace which I have come to cast upon the world. They do not know that it is dissension which I have come to cast upon the world.

JESUS OF NAZARETH

The holy fools arise from the spiritual subcultures, the esoteric and mystical underground of the world's great religious traditions. They know a different reality than the rest of us and live every moment in accordance with their understanding, no matter what the cost. They are divine madmen. Among the better known are Lao Tzu, Buddha, and Christ—all challengers of conventional truth, all masters.

Although today it may seem inappropriate to label these holy men "fools," they probably were called that in their own time. Certainly more people thought them foolish than wise. Lao Tzu, if he existed at all, was a crazy visionary poet who reputedly turned down good jobs with the king in order to live secluded in the mountains. In the important circles of court and city life they probably laughed when Lao Tzu's name or ideas were mentioned.

Gautama, the Buddha, was no doubt viewed as just one of the more popular cult leaders of his time. He set up communal dwellings in the forest where he taught his followers to reject ordinary worldly pursuits and to replace them with an odd-sounding doctrine called "the middle path." If the Buddha were alive and teaching today, many parents would certainly arrange to have their children kidnapped from his community and deprogrammed.

In his own time, Jesus was considered a kook. He became a hero among the poor because he ministered to them and dared to challenge the authority of church and state, but respectable people probably saw him as a scruffy, wandering street person. Not only was Jesus labeled a fool, he sometimes accepted the role, and deliberately "played the fool" as part of his radical protests.

> Like the jester, Christ defies custom and scorns crowned heads. Like a wandering troubador, he has no place to lay his head. Like the clown in the circus parade, he satirizes existing authority by riding into town replete with regal pageantry when he has no earthly power.
>
> HARVEY COX
> *The Feast of Fools*

Many Eastern sages called themselves fools; their acceptance of that label is a key to their crazy wisdom. Chuang Tzu says that the one who knows he is a fool "is not the biggest fool." Lao Tzu boasts "others are sharp and clever, but I alone am dull and stupid."

The holy fools are found in two distinct streams of crazy wisdom. In one, Taoists and Zen masters learn to ride the currents and surrender to the flow. They become friends with insecurity, making doubt their guide and each moment their god. In the other stream, visionaries like Christ or the Sufi poet Rumi pass through doubt into the certainty of their own uncommon visions and lose themselves in love of God or the oceanic Oneness, living thereafter in an altered state.

> An image crosses the heart: "Return to your origin." The heart flutters all around and away from the world of colours and perfumes, clamoring: "Wherefore the Origin?" while tearing apart its adornments, because of its love.
>
> RUMI

Holy fools see through the veils of illusion to the unity of all existence. When Jesus proclaims he is the son of God, he is saying that we are all children of God, all emanating from the same divine source. So too, the Taoist or Zen master understands that all things are one, and our separate "selves" are just a painful illusion. To the most radical sages, even the simple act of naming is a habit that falsely separates us from the rest of creation.

Holy fools agree that false identification with the "self" fosters fear, hatred, and greed, which in turn result in violence and war. Consequently, holy fools usually live simply or in voluntary poverty. They believe that wealth builds up the self and too many possessions block the path to unity.

Identification with the poor almost inevitably forces the holy fool into the role of rebel, leading populist movements that shake up the existing political and spiritual orders. State and church tend to scratch each other's backs, and when you challenge one you threaten the other. The greatest of holy fools have been out of favor with the priesthood and often in trouble with the law.

Gautama, the Buddha, broke away from Hinduism to demonstrate that truth was not the exclusive realm of Brahman priests and that salvation had nothing to do with caste, rituals, or offerings. The Buddha taught that anyone could practice liberation and achieve it.

37

A rabbi whose congregation does not want to drive him out of town isn't a rabbi.

TALMUDIC SAYING

The Great Way is not difficult for those who have no preferences.

THIRD ZEN PATRIARCH

It is easier for a camel to go through the eye of a needle, than for a rich man to enter into the kingdom of God.

JESUS OF NAZARETH

I do not call a man a Brahman because of his birth or of his
mother. He is supercilious in his mode of address and he
is wealthy: but the poor man who is free from attachments,
him I call indeed a Brahman.

BUDDHA
*The Dhammapada*

Lao Tzu and the Taoists yanked on Confucius's beard and said,
"The Way is the other way." The Taoists rejected the followers of
Confucius and their stuffy moralism, with its formal codes of duty to
family and society. The Taoists understood that virtue does not come
from obeying rules but from an inner understanding. They refused
to be false to themselves and to the Tao, the nature of things.

Confucius will deck things out in feathers and paint, and
conduct his affairs with flowery phrases, mistaking side
issues for the crux. He is willing to distort his inborn nature
in order to make himself a model for the people, not even
realizing that he is acting in bad faith.

CHUANG TZU

Jesus, a Jew, denounced the corruption of the Jewish establishment of Judea, the Roman collaborators. He chased the money
changers out of the synagogue, gave up all his possessions, and
preached to the lowest classes. There is little doubt why the authorities called him mad and put him to death.

For as the lightning flashes and lights up the sky
from one side to the other, so will the Son of man
be in his day. But first he must suffer many things
and be rejected by this generation.

*Luke 17:24*

The Chan and Zen Buddhists overturned the priestly piety of the
earliest Indian Buddhist schools. Influenced by the Chinese Taoists,
the Zen masters rebelled against formalized teaching methods and
adherence to scripture, creating their own practices and interpretations of the path as they went along. While the Indian Buddhists
taught rejection of the world for the sake of enlightenment, most

Zen masters refused to make any distinction between this world and another. Zen attempted to break down all dualities.

> No suffering, no origination, no stopping, no
> path, no cognition, also no attainment.
> HEART SUTRA, ZEN MAHAYANA TRADITION

39

Whirling out of Islam came the Sufi masters, mad with dancing and chanting the names of God. They offered the faithful a simple and joyous means of knowing and loving Allah. Similarly, the Hasidic rabbis arose out of Judaism in the diaspora. In the midst of constant danger and uncertainty, they led the people in song and dance in praise of the Lord. The Baal Shem Tov declared that the peasant who sat at the back of the synagogue and could only whistle the prayers was as delightful to God as the learned scholar who could recite the Talmud. A similar message comes through the black Southern Baptist gospel tradition and the hypnotic, ecstatic singing of Krishna devotees: "If I can't dance, I don't want to be in your religion."

I would believe only in a god who could dance.
FRIEDRICH NIETZCHE

Holy fools are often religious revolutionaries. Some even write their own scriptures, or their lives become scripture. After their deaths come the charlatans, and then the churches. Chances are, if the great crazy wisdom masters who gave their names to the world's major religions came back today, they would, without exception, refuse to join their own churches.

In singing and dancing is the voice of the Law.
ZEN MASTER HAKUIN

## A FOOL FOR NOW

Mohandas Gandhi, a holy fool, was recently among us. With only a spinning wheel and a copy of the Hindu "Song of God," Gandhi, the Mahatma or "great soul," challenged the British Empire and the whole of Western civilization. According to Gandhi, religion and politics are inseparable, and both should be lived according to the primary principle of nonviolence.

God has no religion.
MAHATMA GANDHI

> When the practice of nonviolence becomes universal, God will reign on earth as He does in heaven.

Gandhi's nonviolence means refusing to harm or kill any living being, and is a complete way of life. This principle led Gandhi to employ tactics of nonviolent resistance against the British in India, and also formed the cornerstone for his ideal of village socialism.

> Centralization as a system is inconsistent with a
> nonviolent structure of society. By the nonviolent
> method, we seek not to destroy the capitalist, we
> seek to destroy capitalism.

Gandhi understood there would be violence as long as there were extremes of rich and poor in the world. When he was in Europe he saw how Western capitalism and urban life fostered greed and disharmony. Therefore, while most of the developing world rushed toward Western-style industrialization, Gandhi urged India to develop small cottage industries and foster cooperative village life. He believed that village society could save India from the evils of the twentieth century, and would set an example the rest of the world could follow. In Gandhi's vision, only by living simply in small-scale communities could people find social harmony, individual happiness, or spiritual fulfillment.

> There is no limit to the measure of sacrifice that one may
> make in order to realize *oneness with all life*, but certainly that
> ideal will set a limit to your wants. That is the antithesis of
> the position of modern civilization which says, "Increase
> your wants."

Like so many of the holy fools before him, Gandhi dedicated his life to helping the poor, and he lived as one of them. When he died, his only possessions were his spinning wheel, a figurine of the See No Evil, Hear No Evil, Speak No Evil monkeys, his spectacles and walking staff, and a few pieces of homespun clothing.

> There comes a time when an individual becomes
> irresistible and his action becomes all-pervasive in
> its effects. This comes when he reduces himself
> to zero.

Once, Gandhi visited England's King George wearing only a loincloth, shawl, and sandals. Later, when questioned about the propriety of his attire, Gandhi replied, "The King was wearing enough for both of us." On another occasion, when Gandhi was asked what he thought of Western civilization, he answered, "I think it would be a good idea."

Gandhi was an exemplary modern holy fool, challenging the

dominant behavior of the twentieth century—the pursuit of wealth and practice of warfare. He came to his own definition of God, declaring that "Truth is God," and not the other way around as commonly stated. Above all, he practiced his profound message to the modern world that nonviolence must be the guiding principle of religion and politics, of all human activity.

> If I seem to take part in politics, it is only because politics encircle us today like the coil of a snake from which one cannot get out, no matter how much one tries. I wish therefore to wrestle with the snake.

Gandhi has been compared to both Jesus and Buddha; although he became a powerful influence throughout the world, his methods were often ridiculed and his message ultimately ignored. India opened itself to Western industry, driving millions into overcrowded cities; every nation continued to amass weapons. Like the holy fools before him, Gandhi tried to move the world in another direction, and although by our standards it appears that he failed, his legacy is yet to be determined.

*Everything we do is futile, but we must do it anyway.*
MAHATMA GANDHI

> Satisfaction lies in the effort, not in the attainment.
> Full effort is full victory.

The holy fools have had varying degrees of success with their truths. Some of them found the right symbols and metaphors for their time and—creating new myths out of their own lives—were posthumously accorded the status of deity. They gave humanity a miraculous rebirth, a new beginning to the eternal cycle. Through their rebellious visions and deeds these holy fools become founders of new spiritual orders, new symbolic representations of the meaning of it all.

With the holy fools, our exploration of the crazy wisdom archetypes is completed. Through the clown, jester, trickster, and fool, we have discovered different ways in which crazy wisdom is manifested. Despite all our pretensions, some character inevitably comes around to lift the veils of illusion and respectability—and to pull down our pants. Someone with crazy wisdom always ends up looking us in the eye, and elsewhere, and laughing like Coyote, scowling like Mark Twain, or smiling compassionately like the Buddha. The

*And what rough beast, its hour come round at last, Slouches toward Bethlehem to be born?*
WILLIAM BUTLER YEATS

four archetypes will continue to appear in these pages under various assumed names. Their distinctive characteristics should become clearer as we proceed to look at crazy wisdom throughout history and follow its emergence in both Eastern and Western cultures. We will begin in the Orient, since that is where crazy wisdom made its first recorded appearances and gave some of its most brilliant performances.

# CHAPTER THREE

# Crazy Eastern Wisdom

The most complete expressions of a crazy wisdom point of view are contained in Taoism and Zen Buddhism. Neither is exactly a philosophy or religion: the early masters of Taoism and Zen Buddhism did not promote a god or even much of a metaphysical system. These Eastern holy fools saw life not as a puzzle to be solved, but as a mystery to be lived. Instead of the typical Western concerns with intellectual certainty or individual salvation, Taoist and Zen Buddhist masters saw their state of grace as one of just "being"—living without ideology, analysis, or a higher meaning. In learning this state, they made nature their teacher and medium. The Taoists and Zen Buddhists sought to embed themselves from moment to moment in the web of life.

In their meditations, Eastern sages reached a level of understanding that would not develop in the West until nearly two thousand years later. They recognized that the mind is undisciplined and thoroughly conditioned, and that each individual is an unstable flow of thoughts, emotions, and changing identities. They saw that the idea of a free agent called the "self" is largely a fiction. Furthermore, long before the Western world got a glimpse of just how big the universe is, Eastern sages seem to have grasped intuitively its enormous reaches of space and time. They believed that the vastness of the universe is beyond human comprehension, and that within this context

This very earth is the Lotus Land of purity,
And this very body is the Body of Buddha.
ZEN MASTER HAKUIN

the individual does not have much freedom or significance. Since each person is subject to the overriding forces of biological and cosmic evolution, no one is able to control or even understand their destiny. For all these reasons, in the Taoist and Zen Buddhist scheme of things little emphasis is placed on worldly knowledge or accomplishments. The life of any one person living in a particular time and place is simply not afforded the same weight as it is in the Western Judeo-Christian tradition.

The crazy wisdom of Taoists and Zen masters may sound especially crazy to Westerners, and often not so wise. It does not justify existence; it is not about reason or faith. You don't pray to anything or even *do* much of anything. Sometimes you hardly move. Both truth and salvation are a matter of acceptance, of just being. From that simple, earthbound premise grows the Taoist and Zen Buddhist expressions of crazy wisdom.

# How Now, Great Tao?

Someday there will be a great awakening when we know that this is all a great dream. Yet the stupid believe they are awake, busily and brightly assuming they understand things, calling this man ruler, that one herdsman—how dense! Confucius and you are both dreaming! And when I say you are dreaming, I am dreaming, too. Words like these will be labeled the Supreme Swindle. Yet after ten thousand generations, a great sage may appear who will know their meaning.

CHUANG TZU

Therefore the sage keeps to the deed that consists in taking no action and practices the teaching that uses no words.

LAO TZU

Lao Tzu and Chuang Tzu are the quintessential crazy wisdom masters and the founding fathers of Taoism, most easily described as a radical Eastern existential philosophy that emerged in the sixth to the fifth century B.C. in China. Lao Tzu is the reputed author of the Tao Te Ching, the fundamental Taoist text. He is the more serious of the two: the philosopher of paradox and vast perspectives, a poet who knows the Tao and can almost talk about it. Chuang Tzu is much lighter, a storyteller who uses parable and humor to mock ordinary human understanding. Chuang Tzu turns everything upside down to show us the Way, saying:

> Who can look on non-being as his head, on life as
> his back, and on death as his rump? Who knows
> that life and death, existence and annihilation, are
> all a single body? I will be his friend.

Taoism's basic principle is that all things are one. Many spiritual traditions discuss fundamental unity, but Master Lao and Master Chuang draw the most extreme conclusions from this concept. For them, the unity of all things means that no distinction can be made between life and death, right and wrong, holy and profane, or any other "this and that." Opposites depend on each other for existence and have no independent meaning. The Taoist holy fools stand right in the middle of the paradox, where all dualities converge. Here, in the middle, is where Chuang Tzu finds the logic of crazy wisdom.

> Right is not right; so is not so. If right were really right, it
> would differ so clearly from not right that there would
> be no need for argument. If so were really so, it would
> differ so clearly from not so that there would be no need for
> argument. Forget the years; forget distinctions. Leap into
> the boundless and make it your home!

Master Chuang and Master Lao call their unifying principle the Tao, which means "the Way." The Tao is "the way" things are, in the laws of nature, the course of events, the flux of matter and energy. In spite of its all-encompassing presence, Master Chuang and Master Lao do not make the Tao into a deity. The Tao is more about physics than metaphysics. If we do not speak Jehovah's name, it is because we are told not to. We *cannot* speak of the Tao because we can't begin to describe it.

Master Tung-kuo once asked Chuang Tzu, "This thing called the Tao—where does it exist?" Chuang Tzu answered, "It is in the piss and dung." The unity of the Tao encompasses everything, including the piss and dung and the Taoists themselves. Master Chuang and Master Lao understand that most of our problems are caused by our creating a separate identity and special importance for ourselves. In-evitably, once we set ourselves apart from the rest of creation, we are in conflict with it. Making distinctions and choices develops a tense, sometimes adversarial relationship with what is bigger than us and with what essentially *is* us. The illusion that we are separate and spe-cial is the root of our suffering.

> Hope and fear are both phantoms
> that arise from thinking of the self.
> When we don't see the self as self,
> what do we have to fear?
>
> LAO TZU

Since the "self" sticks to us like skin, removing it requires total commitment. The Taoist master may spend many years in difficult study and training to achieve the elusive state called "non-being." Any accumulation of knowledge, wealth, or fame is a hindrance to this spiritual goal; their pursuit builds up pride in the self, blocking the path to unity.

Chuang Tzu refused to let pride sway him. Once when he was fishing in the P'u River, two messengers arrived from the Prince of Ch'u and asked Chuang Tzu to become prime minister of the realm. Chuang Tzu kept fishing and, without turning his head, said, "I have heard that there is a sacred tortoise in Ch'u that has been dead for three thousand years. The king keeps it wrapped in cloth and boxed, and stores it in the ancestral temple. Now would this tortoise rather be dead and have its bones left behind and honored? Or would it rather be alive and dragging its tail in the mud?"

"It would rather be alive and dragging its tail in the mud," said the two officials.

Chuang Tzu said, "Go away! I'll drag my tail in the mud!"

Both Lao Tzu and Chuang Tzu disagreed with the popular ideas of the philosopher Confucius. They saw Confucius as a self-righteous crusader who went around admonishing people to prac-tice virtue, be dutiful to their elders, and obey the authorities. The Taoist holy fools just didn't believe things work that way. Listen to Chuang Tzu:

> All this talk of goodness and duty, these perpetual pin-pricks, unnerve and irritate the hearer; nothing, indeed, could be more destructive of his inner tranquility. If you

indeed want the men of the world not to lose the qualities
that are natural to them, you had best study how it is that
Heaven and Earth maintain their eternal course . . . thus
you too shall learn to follow the course that the Way of
Nature sets; and soon you will reach a goal where you will
no longer need to go round laboriously advertising goodness and duty, like the town-crier with his drum, seeking
for news of a lost child. No, Sir! What you are doing is
to disjoint men's natures!"

Chuang Tzu and Lao Tzu believe that harmony can be achieved
only by letting things develop organically. The Taoists' fundamental
psychological and political premise is that neither morality nor truth
can be imposed artificially. Furthermore, human attempts to figure
out and arrange things are precisely what lead to difficulty and
disharmony.

The Taoist holy fools doubt our plans and ambitions, and their
contrary conclusions often sound shocking. For example, Lao Tzu
baldly states, "Exterminate learning and there will no longer be wor-
ries." How would philosophers and scholars in the West react to this
idea? Go ahead, try to impart this message to the Secretary of
Education.

> When a foolish man hears of the Tao,
> he laughs out loud.
> If he didn't laugh
> it wouldn't be the Tao.
>
> LAO TZU

Lao Tzu knows that his crazy wisdom sounds like nonsense to
most people. After all, he recommends that we give up our reasonable approach to life and our desire to understand, give up any idea
we might have of *purposeful* existence, give up our pursuit of wealth
or fame or happiness. He and Chuang Tzu suggest that we are going
about this business of living the wrong way. Chuang Tzu has a
suggestion:

> I cannot tell if what the world considers "happiness" is
> happiness or not. All I know is that when I consider the way
> they go about attaining it, I see them carried away head-
> long, grim and obsessed, in the general onrush of the

47

Give up sainthood,
  renounce wisdom,
And it will be a hundred
  times better for everyone.
Give up kindness, renounce
  morality,
And men will rediscover
  filial piety and love.
  *Tao Te Ching*

Do you think you can take
  over the universe and
  improve it?
I do not believe it can be
  done.
  *Tao Te Ching*

human herd, unable to stop themselves or to change their direction. All the while they claim to be just on the point of attaining happiness. My opinion is that you never find happiness until you stop looking for it.

Chuang Tzu is proposing nothing less than total freedom, which can be achieved only by "non-doing." It sounds contradictory, especially to rational Western humanists, that we might gain control by giving up control, but Chuang Tzu claims there is no alternative. We continually forget that we are dwarfed by the landscape of galaxies, swept by immense natural forces; that we are nothing but dust in the great winds of chance and change. To Taoists, freedom is understanding we are not in control and never will be. The only struggle is to stop struggling.

There was a man who was so displeased by the sight of his own shadow and so displeased with his own footsteps that he determined to get rid of both. The method he hit upon was to run away from them. So he got up and ran. But every time he put his foot down there was another step, while his shadow kept up with him without the slightest difficulty. He attributed his failure to the fact that he was not running fast enough. So he ran faster and faster, without stopping, until he finally dropped dead. He failed to realize that if he merely stepped into the shade, his shadow would vanish, and if he sat down and stayed still, there would be no more footsteps.

Master Chuang and Master Lao follow only one law: the law of the Tao. This principle is simple to state but very difficult to practice. In order to follow the Tao, one must first get to know the Tao; those who wish to know the Tao may spend many years in meditation, training the mind, taming desires, learning how to let go of everything. Once empty and quiet, however, one can hear what the Tao says and see what direction it takes. Master Chuang invites us to step out of our confusing schemes and distinctions and desires and into the Tao's cool, meandering stream. This is the Way.

> Do not be an embodier of fame; do not be a storehouse of schemes; do not be an undertaker of projects; do not be a proprietor of wisdom. Embody to the fullest what has no end and wander where there is no trail. Hold on to all that you have received from Heaven but do not think you have gotten anything. Be empty, that is all. The Perfect Man uses his mind like a mirror—going after nothing, welcoming nothing, responding but not storing. Therefore he can win out over things and not hurt himself.

# Zen What?

> Shut your mouth, close your lips, and say something!
>
> ZEN MASTER PAICHANG

The name "crazy wisdom" may have been coined originally to describe the antics and achievements of Zen Buddhists. Zen masters invented many techniques to awaken and develop crazy wisdom, including shouts, blows to the head, riddles, belly laughs, and blasphemy. In Zen crazy wisdom reaches the limits of both craziness and wisdom. A great Zen sage cuts off his eyelids so he can meditate longer without falling asleep; a student cuts off his arm to demonstrate to the master that he is ready for the teachings; one master shouts so loudly that his disciple, although "enlightened" by the shout, becomes deaf; another kills a cat when his students fail to save it by saying the correct words; and stories abound of masters and disciples hitting each other with their staffs.

Kwatz! (Ho!)
ZEN MASTER LIN-CHI
Kwan! (Ho!)
ZEN MASTER UMMON

> When you say "yes," you get thirty blows of my staff; when you say "no," you get thirty blows of my staff just the same.
>
> TOKUSAN

When you have a staff, I will give you one; when
you have none, I will take it away from you.

HUI-CH'ING

Zen, the hybrid of Taoism and Buddhism, was born in China in
600 A.D., and later spread to Japan, where it came into full bloom.
However, many Zen followers trace their lineage to India, to about
500 B.C., when the Buddha presented his teachings to a group of
more than one thousand disciples at the Mount of the Holy Vulture.
When it was time to speak, the Buddha paused, then simply held up
a flower. Only one person in the entire assemblage understood the
gesture. A monk named Kasyapa saw, beyond words and concepts,
exactly what the Buddha meant and was immediately enlightened.
According to some, Kasyapa's sudden, direct insight into the perfection of things as they are was the beginning of the path of Zen. This
path is summed up for many by what are known as the Four Great
Statements of Zen:

> A direct transmission outside the scriptures;
> No dependence on words and letters;
> Direct pointing to reality;
> Seeing into one's own nature and attaining Buddhahood.

Everyone says that very little can be said about Zen, yet a
great many people have said a great deal about Zen. There seems to
be an overwhelming, often futile, desire to try to describe the
indescribable.

> Logically considered, Zen may be full of contra-
> dictions and repetitions. But as it stands above
> all things, it goes serenely on its own way.
>
> D. T. SUZUKI

> Zen passes through all our definitions and remains
> Zen as before.
>
> R. H. BLYTH

Because it is not about knowing anything, the Zen master's crazy
wisdom is beyond logic and language. Zen is about a way of *being*.
But if we can't talk about Zen, then how can we talk about Zen?

Zen is not letting yourself
be horsewhipped into
words about it, so as you
read these words just
unfocus your eyes and stare
at the blurry page.

JACK KEROUAC

A monk asked Zen Master Tosu, "Am I correct when I understand the Buddha as asserting that all talk, however trivial or derogatory, belongs to ultimate truth?" Master Tosu said, "Yes, you are right." The monk went on, "May I then call you a donkey?" The master hit the monk with a stick.

Zen holy fools are out of their minds and want to drive you out of yours. The message in their madness is that their madness is the message.

The crazy wisdom of the Zen master transforms ordinary experience back into ordinary experience. Most experience is *extra*ordinary, overlaid with our preconceptions and judgments and filtered through our pragmatic desire to find a "use" for everything. Practicing Zen is to move beyond desire, emotion, ideas, or words and to experience each moment without qualification. Now we have more words about what is beyond words.

When asked perfectly serious questions about the meaning of Zen or about the nature of mind or enlightenment, Zen masters often answer with statements such as: "The cypress tree is in the courtyard," "The cat is climbing the pole," "The moon is clearly visible," or "Have you had your breakfast?"

> Zen is the unsymbolization of the world and all the things in it.
>
> R. H. BLYTH

A disciple asked Zen Master Bokuju, "We have to dress and eat every day. How can we escape from all that?" The master replied, "We dress; we eat." The disciple remained puzzled and said, "I do not understand." Bokuju replied, "If you do not understand, put on your clothes and eat your food."

Zen holy fools have clear, direct experience of the world from moment to moment, making them capable of continuous spontaneity and playfulness. Zen is perfectly crazy wisdom.

Master Shih-kung asked the disciple if he could take hold of empty space. The disciple made a grasping movement in the air with his hand but Shih-kung exclaimed, "You got nothing!" The disciple then asked, "What, then, is your way?" Whereupon Shih-kung took hold of the dis-

51

Zen is the madman yelling: "If you wanta tell me that the stars are not words, then stop calling them stars!"
JACK KEROUAC

If you want to see it, see into it directly; but when you stop to think about it, it is altogether missed.
TAO-WU

We have two eyes to see two sides of things, but there must be a third eye which will see everything at the same time and yet not see anything. That is to understand Zen.
D. T. SUZUKI

Everything you do is Zen.
BODHIDHARMA

ciple's nose, gave it a sharp twist and called out, "That is the
way to take hold of empty space!"

ALAN WATTS
*The Spirit of Zen*

Form is emptiness and emptiness is form.
PRAJNA PARAMITA SUTRA

## Blasphemy for Buddha

The Buddha is a bull-headed jail-keeper, and the
Patriarchs are horse-faced old maids!
ZEN MASTER FENG

A disciple once asked Zen Master Ummon, "What
is the Buddha?" Ummon answered, "A dried
dung-stick!"

Yun-men once related the legend to his monks, according
to which the Buddha at his birth pointed toward heaven
with one hand and the earth with the other, and taking
seven steps forward looked toward the four quarters of the
earth, exclaiming: "Above and beneath heaven, I alone
am the honored one." Yun-men then declared, "If I had
seen him at the time, I would have cut him down with my
staff, and given his flesh to dogs to eat, so that peace could
prevail over all the world.

M. CONRAD HYERS
*Zen and the Comic Spirit*

Zen Buddhist crazy wisdom has no heroes, not even the Buddha
himself. The Buddha and the idea of Buddhahood are bondage for
the mind. Attachment to even the image of the Buddha—that sweet,
compassionate, half-smiling face—is an obstacle to one's own freedom. Ironically, setting enlightenment as our goal ensures that we
won't get there. Having an objective implies that we are headed
someplace, that we are not here in this moment in which, if we could
give up our spiritual ambition, we would already be enlightened.

Whatever you encounter, slay it at once: on meeting a
buddha slay the buddha; on meeting a patriarch slay the
patriarch; on meeting your parents slay your parents; on
meeting your kinsman slay your kinsman; and you attain
emancipation.

RINZAI

Zen holy fools consider only one thing to be holy: their moment-
to-moment Zen. Being requires constant homage to the eternal
now.

Ganto said, "If you want to know the last word, I'll
tell you, simply—This! This!"

Blue Cliff Record, Case 51

# The Eastern Crazy Wisdom
# Poets' Society

We may not be aware of it, but at one time or another, each of us
has probably paid homage to a famous Asian holy fool, the half-
mythical, half-flesh-and-blood character named Hotai, better
known as the Laughing Buddha. He is the potbellied figure whose
statue appears in Chinese souvenir shops and restaurants, who
brings good luck if his stomach is rubbed. His hands are sometimes
extended upward as if he holds up the sky with his crazy dance, and
a big silly grin crosses his broad face. Supposedly, the Laughing Buddha was modeled after an actual wandering Chinese Zen monk
named Keishi, who some people believe was Maitreya, another in-
carnation of Buddha, who arrived unexpectedly in this jolly, rotund
form. By contrast, Gautama, the Buddha from India who is wor-
shipped worldwide, is depicted traditionally as trim, handsome, and
extremely dignified, with perfectly symmetrical features and just the
slightest of smiles, as faint as the Mona Lisa's. This sublime smile is
one of the many emblems of the Buddha's spiritual state. A passage
in orthodox Indian Buddhist literature claims that spiritually advanced people display less pronounced laugh responses, and that the
most enlightened beings will not even show their teeth when they
smile. Flying in the face of this stuffy monastic ideal, the folk hero

Hotai came along to proclaim that you can be enlightened and still have a belly laugh. You can have great realizations of suffering and emptiness and yet emerge a playful, joyous fat man who drinks a little wine now and then and would rather play hide and seek with children all day than chant sutras with a bunch of old monks in a stifling hot temple. The great enlightened crazy wisdom of the formal Buddhist path is just not crazy enough for some. In *Zen and the Comic Spirit*, Conrad Hyers writes:

> According to legend Ho-tai (the laughing Buddha) refused the designation of Zen master, as well as monastic restriction, and instead walked the streets with his sack over his shoulder, giving gifts to children.

The Laughing Buddha symbolizes an entire subculture of crazy wisdom artists, the wandering poet-seekers of China and Japan, many of whom were also Taoist or Zen Buddhist monks. This spiritual-poetic subculture spans centuries and includes some of the finest Asian writers and artists. They were usually great lovers of nature and wild places, and many of them became wanderers, living from moment to moment and often from hand to mouth. They shunned official religious institutions, as well as the business of ordinary people, and chose to live free, practicing only their art and the art of liberation.

> Abandon this fleeting world, abandon yourself,
> Then the moon and flowers will guide you along the Way.
> RYŌKAN

## Vagabond Verse

Poetry is the special medium of spiritual crazy wisdom, the form of expression that comes closest to creating a bridge between words and what is wordless. We will now turn to a few Asian holy fools who were also poets, and let them come as close as possible to capturing the essence of Eastern crazy wisdom in words. We begin with the Taoist and Zen Buddhist poets.

Crazy wisdom themes are eloquently and simply stated in the work of these poet-seekers. They placed no value on scholastic learning or knowledge of scripture and renounced wealth and fame. We can imagine them shrugging with either disdain or detachment when talking about the human condition or, for that matter, their own fate. In poetry, they describe clearly what they see from the perspectives of their enlightenment and vagabond travels.

> My life may appear melancholy,
> But traveling through this world
> I have entrusted myself to Heaven.
> In my sack, three sho of rice;
> By the hearth, a bundle of firewood.
> If someone asks what is the mark of enlightenment or
>     illusion,
> I cannot say—wealth and honor are nothing but dust.
> As the evening rain falls I sit in my hermitage
> And stretch out both feet in answer.

Ryōkan, who lived in the late eighteenth and early nineteenth centuries, is one of the best-known and most-beloved figures in all of Japanese history. He was a wandering crazy wisdom Zen poet who called himself the Great Fool. Although his enlightenment was certified and he could have become head priest at a temple or monastery, Ryōkan refused any official position and lived in a mountain hermitage. From there he often took long walks through villages where he played with the children and drink sake with the farmers. He preferred the common people over priests, and according to stories about him, Ryōkan recited his poetry to the villagers whenever asked.

> Shaggy hair past the ears,
> A worn-out robe resembling white clouds and dark smoke.
> Half drunk, half sober, I return home,
> Children all around, guiding me along the Way.

In one of his most celebrated poems, Ryōkan evokes the elusive Zen state of grace, the perfect harmony of simply being.

> With no-mind, blossoms invite the butterfly;
> With no-mind, the butterfly visits the blossoms.
> When the flower blooms, the butterfly comes.

When the butterfly comes, the flower blooms.
I do not "know" others.
Others do not "know" me.
Not-knowing each other we naturally follow the Way.

Cold Mountain and Stonehouse are the assumed names of two Chinese crazy wisdom poets. Imagine two figures barely visible stepping through a Chinese landscape painting, shrouded in mists and dwarfed by sky and cliffs, their robes tattered, their faces cragged like the mountains they inhabit. In the painting they are almost invisible; that is the way they want to be because that is the way it is. They seek no fame or fortune and shun the pursuits of everyday life. Instead, they beg for their food, write poetry, and meditate. Sometimes witty, sometimes wistful, they live close to the clouds where they tune in to the natural rhythms and seasonal cycles, learning to be in harmony with the Tao or their own Buddhist understanding. They get cold and lonely on the mountain and sometimes they go hungry, but they would not change places with anyone.

> I settled at Cold Mountain long ago,
> Already it seems like years and years.
> Freely drifting, I prowl the woods and streams
> And linger watching things themselves.
> Men don't get this far into the mountains,
> White clouds gather and billow.
> Thin grass does for a mattress,
> The blue sky makes a good quilt.
> Happy with a stone underhead
> Let heaven and earth go about their changes.
> COLD MOUNTAIN

Cold Mountain (Han-shan), who named himself after his favorite cliff dwelling, lived in the late seventh century during the T'ang dynasty and was reputed to have great wisdom. He and his sidekick Pick Up (Shih-te) are now considered "Immortals" in Chinese folklore. Cold Mountain and Pick Up worked for a while in the kitchen of a large monastery, and many famous paintings portray these legendary madmen leaning on brooms and laughing uproariously. According to stories about them, they were always singing and clowning around, often making fun of the priests and monks from the region.

Like his Japanese counterpart, Ryōkan, Cold Mountain refused to take any lofty position in a temple or monastery. When a famous priest came to visit him in the kitchen where he worked, Cold Mountain ran away into the mountains and never was seen again. Thereafter, he led a hermit's life of poverty and freedom, writing poems on cliffs and stones and pieces of wood.

> wise ones you ignore me
> I ignore you fools
> neither wise nor foolish
> don't hear of me henceforth
> at night I'll sing to the moon
> at dawn I'll dance with the clouds
> how can I stop my mouth and hands
> and sit up straight with all this hair

Stonehouse was a fourth-century Chinese mountain poet who may have helped smooth down the forest paths that Cold Mountain wandered three centuries later. Although little is known about Stonehouse's life, the poetry attributed to him has survived and has recently been translated and published in the West. Stonehouse states with elegant simplicity the Taoist poets' philosophy of freedom.

> this body's existence is like a bubble's
> may as well accept what happens
> events and hopes seldom agree
> but who can step back doesn't worry
> we blossom and fade like flowers
> gather and part like clouds
> worldly thoughts I forgot long ago
> relaxing all day on a peak

## The Moment of Haiku

Japanese haiku poets are like Zen clowns, giving poignant and sometimes humorous glimpses into their bittersweet experience of life.

Developed primarily by Japanese Buddhist monks and meditators, haiku marries poetry and Zen by expressing a moment's awareness simply and directly. Just as the great Western spiritual poets Dante and Milton focused their mythopoetic verse through a Christian lens, the poets writing haiku attempt to transcribe their Zen experience. As the scholar of Eastern culture R. H. Blyth writes, "Haiku is a kind of satori, or enlightenment, in which we see into the life of things."

Haiku is an articulation of the Zen ideal in that it finds the spiritual in the ordinary, saying to us, "Just this." The poet rarely interprets or explains the image or scene being presented, and abstraction or metaphoric flight is almost always absent. The aim is to convey one moment's experience, and if the moment contains difficult thoughts or sentiments, the poet simply places these in the context of the haiku, where they become a matter of fact. The personal story is just another aspect of the fleeting scene.

> I leave.
> You stay.
> Two autumns.
> BUSON

A poet writing haiku focuses on a single experience, but often notices two elements: what is perceived in the world and what is perceived in the mind. The poet plays these two perceptions off each other to create poetic tension. Bashō, the father of contemporary haiku, calls this interplay "surprising comparison" and describes its effect by saying, ". . . the mind goes, and then it comes back again."

The haiku form limits the poet to three lines that total seventeen syllables (in Japanese), requiring great precision of expression. Like the sparse brush strokes of a Japanese or Chinese ink drawing, the haiku paints a picture and evokes a mood with the fewest of words.

> —the world of dew is only a world of dew
> and yet—
> and yet—
> ISSA

---

58

In these latter day
degenerate times,
cherry blossoms
everywhere!

ISSA

Where there are humans
you'll find flies,
and Buddhas.

ISSA

Issa is one of the best-loved Japanese haiku poets; like Saint Francis of Assisi, he had great affection for all forms of life. In his poetry, Issa often addresses himself to the birds, animals, and insects.

For you fleas too,
the night must be long,
it must be lonely.

Even among the insects
some can sing,
some can't.

Don't kill the fly!
Look—it's begging you,
wringing its hands and feet!

O snail
climb Mt. Fuji,
but slowly, slowly!

Issa and other haiku masters, like many Asian poet-seekers, had great love for the natural world, considering nature a teacher, studying the cycles of birth and death and the ways of other creatures. This led to a long-standing convention, followed in many haiku, that somewhere in each poem there be a reference to the season. These closing haiku are a year's cycle, with one extra for good measure.

Clouds come from time to
    time—
and bring a chance to rest
from looking at the moon.
        BASHŌ

People coming, people going
Over the spring moor—
For what, I wonder?
        SHIKI

I put the brazier
By my skirt, but my heart
Was far from it.
        ISSA

Ears of my old age;
the summer rains
falling down the rainpipe
        BUSON

The old calendar
Fills me with gratitude,
Like a sutra
        BUSON

Deep autumn;
My neighbor—
How does he live?
        BASHŌ

## From the Roof of the World

I see this life as a conjuration and a dream.
Great compassion rises in my heart
For those without a knowledge of this truth.
        MILAREPA

The Tibetan Buddhist tradition has also produced great poet-seekers, such as the ascetic Milarepa who taught transcendental wisdom through his improvisational songs. Milarepa chose to live in extreme poverty in the austere cold of the Himalaya Mountains, mastering himself and the elements at the same time. When a king over several provinces sent a messenger to invite Milarepa to the royal palace for an audience, Milarepa refused, saying, "I am likewise a mighty king, of the Wheel that Revolveth; and a king who aboundeth in riches is in no wise happier or mightier than I."

Milarepa dedicated himself to gaining control over his mind and achieving full enlightenment. He knew this task had nothing to do with wealth or comfort. It also had nothing to do with religion or holy scriptures. As he stated,

> Accustomed long to meditating on the Whispered Chosen
> Truths,
> I have forgot all that is said in written and printed books.
> Accustomed long to know the meaning of the Wordless,
> I have forgot the way to trace the roots of verbs.
> I have forgot all creeds and dogmas.

Another holy fool of the Himalayas was the rascal Tibetan saint Drukpa Kunley. Through his outrageous behavior, Kunley taught people how to let go of religious formality and be open to all of life. Once, it is told, Kunley came to a village where the people were being very devout, bowing to this virtue or that deity. Kunley chimed in with his own litany, which included:

> I bow to fornicators discontented with their wives;
> I bow to crooked speech and lying talk;
> I bow to ungrateful children;
> I bow to wearers of the cloth who break their vows;
> I bow to professors attached to their words;
> I bow to tramps who reject a home;
> I bow to the bums of insatiate whores.

Like many crazy wisdom masters, Kunley made sure that "sinners" and the poor were included in the realm of the holy, as deserving of praise as gods or the clergy. In *The Divine Madman*, Keith Dowman translates this song in which Kunley sings of his own qualities.

Dancer in the indestructible stream of magical illusion,
Unifier of the welter of inconsistencies and absurdities,
Power-holder turning the Wheel of Bliss and Emptiness,
Hero perceiving all things as deception,
Nauseous Recalcitrant disgusted with temporal
    attachment,
Little Yogin piercing others' illusory projections,
Vagabond selling Samsara short,
Light-traveller making his lodging his home,
Fortunate Wayfarer perceiving his Mind as the Lama,
Champion understanding all appearance as the mind,
Diviner of Relativity knowing unity as multiplicity,
Naljorpa tasting the one flavour of all things—
These are some of the masks I wear!

In the words of Kunley and other Asian poet-seekers, we have found the many expressions of Eastern crazy wisdom—humorous, ironic, enthusiastic, detached, compassionate, contradictory. If the poets failed to capture Eastern crazy wisdom for us, a blow from a Zen master's staff might be the only recourse left. However, we should not feel discouraged; experiencing a little confusion is sometimes necessary in Eastern crazy wisdom. Furthermore, the mad ways of the Eastern holy fools may make more sense after we search for crazy wisdom in the West. In the Western traditions our rational minds should feel somewhat more at home—at least for a while. Now, Westward ho! (Kwatz!)

# CHAPTER FOUR

# Crazy Western Wisdom

In much wisdom is much grief; and he that increaseth knowledge increaseth sorrow.

*Ecclesiastes*

The Western expressions of crazy wisdom are more scattered and obscure than those of the East and, therefore, more difficult to trace. Outside of a few small groups of Western religious mystics, including those of native American origin, little development of spiritual crazy wisdom has occurred in the West. Until existentialism appeared in the late nineteenth century, no movement in Western philosophy dealt with the ideas that are so integral to Eastern cultures. Wayward Western philosophers or artists may have arrived at their own understanding, but crazy wisdom has not taken root in the Western psyche or, until recently, been given wide consideration. The reasons for this are deep-rooted.

As we noticed, understanding Eastern crazy wisdom requires a stretch, if not a complete snap, of the Western mind. A Zen poet once remarked, "It is like trying to discuss the color of milk with a blind man." The major difficulty results from disparate attitudes toward reason in the East and the West. Over the centuries Eastern and Western seekers of wisdom have been involved in two somewhat different games of consciousness. Consider the following statements:

> Reason is the true self of every man, since it is the supreme and better part.
>
> **ARISTOTLE**

Stop thinking, and end your problems.
LAO TZU

A kind of East-West split exists in the world psyche. Using terms from modern physiology and psychology to examine this separation of mental powers, we find that the planet is divided in much the same way as is the brain: into two hemispheres, each with its own methods for understanding. Broadly speaking, Eastern and Western seekers of wisdom have taken two fundamentally different approaches.

Virtue is knowledge.
PLATO

If you try to know it, you have already departed from it.

CHUANG TZU

Early on in their experiments with consciousness, Eastern sages, seeking inner peace, attempted to gain control over their thoughts and emotions. As they gazed inward they discovered the intellect to be an unreliable and often treacherous tool. The rational mind, though often motivated by greed or fear, nonetheless tricks itself into believing in its own logic and stability. Eastern holy fools also saw the intellect as an agent of separation, geared toward manipulating the external world for self-preservation. They began to understand that our rational mind, although necessary to survival, leads to painful alienation from ourselves and the rest of creation.

On another side of the planet, the Western seekers of wisdom, beginning with the Greeks, became infatuated with the rational mind. They came to honor reason and the intellect as all but divine powers. This belief in the mind's supremacy placed humans above the rest of creation and fostered an intense identification with the individual "self" or "soul" in the Western psyche. The Western enterprise came to center on developing the intellect and strengthening the self as a way of knowing and controlling the world.

A fair amount of crazy wisdom is nevertheless concealed within this dominant Western world view. Finding it requires that we follow two separate trails. One is the circuitous trail of philosophy, the other is that of the Western holy fools. We will first follow the latter

63

Oriental man remains intuitive, not rational. The lifting of reason out of the primeval waters of the unconscious is a Greek achievement.

WILLIAM BARRETT

The world is ruled by letting things take their course.

LAO TZU

route as it leads around the fringes of the intense, stormy worlds of Jehovah and Jesus Christ. The spiritual trail of Western crazy wisdom looks similar to the Eastern path except that, instead of bamboo, cactuses line the roadside.

> One of the elders said: Either fly as far as you can
> from men, or else, laughing at the world and
> the men who are in it, make yourself a fool in many
> things.
>
> THOMAS MERTON
> *Wisdom of the Desert*

A few holy fools have infiltrated the mainstream Judeo-Christian-Islamic tradition, living barely within the boundaries of the established order. (Sometimes, after their deaths, they are allowed to enter the sanctuary as saints and heroes.) Like their Taoist and Zen counterparts, the Western holy fools attempt to lose themselves in union with all of creation, but they differ by usually having an agent, an intervening presence called God or Christ or Mohammed. And whereas many Eastern masters emphasize unity with the *ordinary* nature of things, the Jewish, Christian, and Muslim mystics instead seek something extraordinary. They yearn for *ecstatic* union, full of flames and visions and all manner of special effects.

Like all crazy wisdom masters, holy fools of the West made up their own spiritual practices. They usually left the churches and temples behind, heading off alone to the desert, or to the slums and shtetls to live with the poor. They knew that true wisdom was rarely found in institutions or in proximity to the wealthy and worldly-wise.

Praise him according to his
excellent greatness.
Praise him with the sound
of the trumpet:
Praise him with the psaltery
and harp.
Praise him with the timbrel
and dance:
Praise him with stringed
instruments and organs.

*Psalm 150*

Sell whatever thou hath,
and give to the poor, and
thou shalt have treasure in
heaven; and come, take
up the cross, and follow me.

JESUS OF NAZARETH

# Fools for Christ

In the fourth century A.D. the first Christian hermits left their churches for the desert sands, the sparse landscape where Jesus and Moses had found truth, and where Western holy fools have often had visions. These fervent individuals, who came to be known as the "desert fathers," were willing to pay a lonely, burning price for their own experience of the Divine.

> Blessed Macarius said: This is the truth, if a monk
> regards contempt as praise, poverty as riches,
> and hunger as a feast, he will never die.
>
> THOMAS MERTON
> *Wisdom of the Desert*

The desert fathers attempted to diminish themselves through austerity until they became one with the divine. In the stillness and solitude of the desert they sought unity with all creation. This path is reminiscent of that chosen by many Taoist and Buddhist masters—a simple but difficult life. Like the Eastern sages, the desert fathers also believed that language, and in particular scripture, is inadequate for either promoting or explaining spiritual experience.

> When Abbot Pambo was asked to say a few words
> to the very important Bishop of Alexandria, who
> was visiting some of the Desert Fathers, the elder
> replied: "If he is not edified by my silence, there
> is no hope that he will be edified by my words."
>
> THOMAS MERTON
> *Wisdom of the Desert*

During the Middle Ages, the Eastern Orthodox Church recognized a few divine madmen in its ranks, individuals who came to be called, after Saint Paul, "fools for Christ's sake." Some of these fools were street dwellers who hung around red-light districts and reputedly drank more than just sacramental wine. Symeon of Emesa walked around naked and was punished once for throwing nuts at people praying in church. Eventually some of these madmen were canonized as saints. Although they did not exactly fit the saintly ideal, they were so loved and revered by those who knew them (usually the poor) that the church concluded they must have had God in their hearts.

St. Francis of Assisi was an early thirteenth-century mystic who lived crazy wisdom completely. After his sudden enlightenment he stripped naked and renounced his inheritance, declaring himself forever after "married to Lady Poverty."

In 1209 Francis founded his order of "Little Brothers" who sought union with God through abstinence and poverty. The extreme behavior and appearance of his early followers apparently embarrassed the church, and finally a local bishop asked Francis to take them off the streets and find decent clothes and housing for them. Francis refused, explaining, "If we had possessions we would need weapons for their defense."

Francis is remembered for his gentle nature and his love for all creatures. According to legend, after a rainstorm he would pick up the earthworms, removing them from the streets so they would not be stepped on. The Order of Little Brothers was widely known for their joyous and playful ways, and Francis referred to himself and his followers as "jesters of the Lord."

# Righteous Ones

Alas! the world is full of enormous lights and mysteries, and man shuts them from himself with one small hand!

BAAL SHEM TOV
in *Tales of the Hasidim* by Martin Buber

Many Hasidic rabbis fit into the crazy wisdom canon, most notably the founder of Hasidism, the Baal Shem Tov—the "possessor of the good name." Like so many holy fools, the Baal Shem Tov was a hero of the poor and oppressed. His flock consisted of Eastern European Jewish peasants who lived in the early eighteenth century during the pogrom years. The Baal Shem Tov and his later Hasidic disciples rejected elitism and the intellectual squabbles of rabbinical schools, teaching that the simplest people and prayers were God's favorites. The Baal Shem Tov claimed that:

The lowest of the low you can think of, is dearer to me than your only son is to you.

The Baal Shem Tov had little regard for wealth or material comforts. He prophesied:

Before the coming of the Messiah there will be great abundance in the world. The Jews will get rich. They will become accustomed to running their houses in the grand style and moderation will be cast to the winds. Then the lean years will come; want and a meagre livelihood, and the world will be full of poverty. The Jews will not be able to satisfy their needs, grown beyond rhyme or reason. And then the labor which will bring forth the Messiah will begin.

While most of Judaism merely waited for the Messiah's return for deliverance from woes and oppression, the Baal Shem Tov taught people to live in the moment, with great energy and joy. "If I love God," he asked, "what need have I of a coming world?" He showed his followers the "sparks of God in all things," and like St. Francis, he talked to animals and trees. However, in *Tales of the Hasidim*, Martin Buber tells of one tree that the Baal Shem Tov avoided.

> It is said that once, when all souls were gathered
> together in Adam's soul, at the very moment
> in which he stood poised beside the Tree of Knowl-
> edge, the soul of the Baal Shem got up and left,
> and did not eat of the fruit of the tree.

The Baal Shem Tov was one of the zaddikim, a line of rabbis known as the "righteous ones." These rabbis were a forceful influence, much like the Eastern Zen masters who, after having an experience of god or enlightenment, helped others arrive at their own. Like their Asian counterparts, the zaddikim rarely preached and instead transmitted wisdom through parables and riddles or singing and dancing. Often they were living examples of crazy wisdom— they taught by "being." One Hasidic student tells how he came to know the holy book: "I learned the Torah from all the limbs of my teacher."

# Whirling Words:
# The Poetry of Rumi

Give up owning things and being somebody. Quit existing.

RUMI

Out of the thirteenth-century Islamic world dances Mavlana ("The Awakened One") Djalal-od-Din Rumi, one of the world's greatest spiritual poets. Although Rumi's wisdom has much in common with that of Asian holy fools, his passionate love for the divine places him firmly in the Judeo-Christian-Islamic tradition of the West. Rumi is revered by millions, especially throughout the Muslim nations where devotees are often heard chanting his poetry, which is considered by some to be second in importance only to the Koran. Rumi founded one of the most influential Sufi brotherhoods, an order that emphasized music and whirling dancing as the path to awakening. The members of Rumi's order came to be known as "whirling dervishes."

> Today, like every other day, we wake up empty
> and frightened. Don't open the door to the study
> and begin reading. Take down the dulcimer.
> Let the beauty we love be what we do.
> There are hundreds of ways to kneel and kiss the ground.

Rumi knew, three centuries before Copernicus, that the earth revolves around the sun, and that nine planets make up the solar system—a fact not discovered in the West until 1930. He wrote that we would find a miniature solar system inside an atom if it were possible to cut into one.

> All the atoms in the air and in the desert,
> Let it be known, are like madmen.
> Each atom, happy or miserable,
> Is in love with the Sun of which we can say nothing.

Much of Rumi's verse was created in an improvisational manner, the spontaneous combustion of a spirit on fire, and transcribed by followers as they listened to him speak in pure song. Rumi's legacy includes the *Divan*, a volume with 42,000 lines of poetry, and the *Mathnawi*, his masterwork, a six-volume collection of stories, aphorisms, jokes, and over 51,000 verses. Some of this verse is currently being retranslated into English, further spreading the influence of this mystical poet and crazy wisdom master.

> Out beyond ideas of wrongdoing and rightdoing,
> there is a field. I'll meet you there.

> When the soul lies down in that grass,
> the world is too full to talk about.

Ideas, language, even the phrase 'each other'
doesn't make any sense.

Although he was a master of words, Rumi always looked beyond them; neither language nor knowledge was important to his
love of the divine. Like his Asian counterparts, Rumi refused official
recognition as a wise man.

The people here want to put me in charge. They want me
to be Judge, Magistrate, and Interpreter of all the texts. The
Knowing I have doesn't want that. It wants to enjoy itself.
I am a plantation of sugarcane, and at the same time I'm
eating the sweetness.
    Knowledge that is acquired is not like this. Those who
have it worry if audiences like it or not. It's a bait for popu-
larity. Disputational knowing wants customers. It has no
soul. Robust and energetic before a responsive crowd, it
slumps when no one is there.
    The only real customer is God. Chew quietly your
sweet sugarcane God-Love, and stay playfully childish.
Your face will turn rosy with illumination like the rosebud
flowers.

Rumi sees all phenomena, including the self, as transitory
expressions of a divine intelligence. With that understanding, he
finds great love and acceptance for the way things are: the one cosmic
dance.

Think of how PHENOMENA come trooping
out of the Desert of Non-existence
into this materiality.
    Morning and night,
they arrive in a long line and take over
from each other, "It's my turn now. Get out!"

A son comes of age, and the father packs up.
This place of phenomena is a wide exchange
of highways, with everything going all sorts
of different ways.
    We seem to be sitting still,
but we're actually moving, and the Fantasies
of Phenomena are sliding through us

like ideas through curtains.
　　They go to the well
of deep love inside each of us.
They fill their jars there, and they leave.

There is a source they come from,
and a fountain inside here.
　　Be generous.
Be grateful. Confess when you're not.

We can't know
what the Divine Intelligence
has in mind!
Who *am* I,
standing in the midst of this
thought-traffic?

Rumi and the Baal Shem Tov typify the holy fool of the West: a lover of all life, especially those in need; empty of knowledge and self, but full of God. The Western holy fools' belief in a supernatural deity distinguishes them from the Taoist or Zen masters, with their nontheistic grounding in the natural world. The Eastern holy fools find unity with all things through a cool, detached acceptance, while the Western approach was one of passionate love for creation as the manifestation of God.

The holy fools of both East and West come to their own realizations, but they do not ask us to believe them. Instead, they respond to our questions with further questions or with riddles and parables. Often these holy fools teach crazy wisdom just by being themselves. If we watch closely, we might learn from them how to live, with simple acceptance of, and even great love for, life.

# The Sacred Clowns

Another brand of Western crazy wisdom comes through the guise of the trickster rather than that of the holy fool. In Native American religions these tricksters are called "sacred clowns." While the tricksters of myth usually take on animal forms, sacred clowns appear as costumed humans, usually with sex on their minds and outsized phalli between their legs. They disrupt the solemn proceedings at religious ceremonies or sometimes lead special bawdy rituals of their own.

In the Zuni pueblo, sacred clowns are called Koyemshis, or "mud-heads"—a name derived from the pink clay they wear on their heads, which some say are made up to resemble phalli. When these tricksters appear to announce an approaching religious festival, their liturgical part sounds obscene. In *Pueblo: Gods and Myths*, Hamilton A. Tyler quotes from this ritualized scatology:

> After so many days, eight days, on the ninth day
> you will copulate with rams.

An example of the way in which sacred clowns perform religious duties in native cultures is presented in Jerome Rothenberg's *The Technicians of the Sacred*. He describes a Cherokee ritual called the "Booger Event." Sacred clowns—called boogers—enter the sacred circle and begin breaking wind and making foul noises. Each booger has an obscene name such as Big Balls, Asshole, Rusty Asshole, Burster, Swollen Pussy, Sweet Prick, Piercer, and so on. Once inside the circle, the boogers act like madmen, falling on the ground and pushing at the male spectators as if to get at their wives and daughters. After a while, the boogers begin a dance. Each booger's name is taken in turn as the first word of a song that is sung while that booger dances a solo, using awkward, grotesque steps. The audience applauds each mention of his name, while the other dancers thrust out their buttocks and occasionally display the large phalli concealed under their clothing. These phalli may contain water, which is sprayed on the spectators. Finally, female dancers enter the circle to be the boogers' partners. As soon as they do, the boogers increase their sexual exhibitions, closing in on the women from behind and gyrating in simulated intercourse.

72

Christian missionaries must have been shocked to witness such events, especially as part of a religious ceremony, and it is little wonder they tried to convert the so-called savages. After all, many Christians regard it as unfortunate that our spirits are forced to dwell in wild, smelly, animal bodies. And these "sacred clowns" not only acknowledged but honored the body and passions. The missionaries wanted the farts stifled and the sexual impulses confessed as sin.

The trickster as sacred clown can be found in several other cultures. The priests who led the revelry at Greek Dionysian festivals were a sect of sacred clowns—blessing sex, intoxication, and madness in an attempt to keep pagan spirits strong in the struggle against Apollonian forces of reason. A sacred clown played a part in the solemn Greek pilgrimage from Athens to Eleusis, a route lined with temples. On a bridge over the river Kephissos, a clown waited to make obscene gestures and curse at the pilgrims. We can only surmise the intent, but perhaps the sacred clown was there to humble worshipers and remind them of their humanity on their way to meet the gods.

A slightly different breed of sacred clowns, perhaps more like jesters than tricksters, made their appearance in medieval Europe, where they led the Feast of Fools. This riotous annual ritual took place inside Catholic churches, even under the exalted vaults of Notre Dame Cathedral. A procession of revelers and masqueraders marched into a church, sang obscene songs, told dirty jokes, sprayed the congregation with smelly "holy water," and burned incense made from old shoe leather or cow dung. The church sanctioned this travesty for a while, and sometimes the clergy even participated by electing the leader of the revelers, who was called the Fools' Pope. Eventually the church forced this "mass" into the streets, where the event became known as New Year's Eve.

A similar group of jesters presided over the *festum asinarium*, a strange ritual mass in medieval Catholic churches commemorating Mary's flight into Egypt. During this ceremony asses were led into the church and, after each element of the mass, the congregation responded with donkey sounds. Let us bray?

The rituals of all these sacred clowns seem to be the Western acknowledgment and worship of nature and the animals, both around and within us. Though officially squelched by the one "on high," our wild, natural urges need a place of honor and means of expression. Sacred clowns make no distinction between high and low, the sacred and the profane, and they won't let us forget that we have only recently stood upright and put on garments.

Although we have explored several essential characters and corners of both Eastern and Western spiritual subcultures, a lot of wilderness remains. We have not opened the strange pages of the Bhagavad Gita, with its paradoxical and perhaps allegorical story of one of the gods appearing as a charioteer who tells humans to kill each other in battle. We have left out many Hindu and Sikh sadhus, the teaching of the Gnostics, the writings of Meister Eckhart, and stories of contemporary holy fools such as Krishnamurti, Chögyam Trungpa, and Da Free John. We could continue with tales of holy fools tweaking the nose of the pope or the high priest; arriving in the middle of prayers to dance; playing hide-and-seek all day with children; or sitting alone in a mountain cave, talking only to animals, trees, and the gods. We could go on and on about holy fools, but unfortunately we have work to do. It is time to think.

We now double back and follow the circuitous route of a second trail, which will lead us eventually to another kind of Western crazy wisdom. The trail of Western philosophy takes us through a bumpy field of discourse and treatises, where it is easy to get lost in thought or waylaid by "thinkers" who will try to show us how to use reason to figure out the meaning of life. In spite of the difficulties, Western philosophy is a fascinating journey, and we need not fear, because God will be watching over our progress. Perhaps we can travel more assuredly knowing also that at the end of this second Western trail, at that big roundup in the sky, crazy wisdom waits to bring us back to earth.

CHAPTER FIVE

# Way Out West

The last three thousand years of mankind have been an excursion into ideals, bodilessness, and tragedy and now the excursion is over . . . We have to go back, a long way, before the idealist conceptions began, before Plato, before the tragic idea of life arose, to get onto our feet again. For the gospel of salvation through the Ideals and escape from the body coincided with the tragic conception of human life. Salvation and tragedy are the same thing, and they are now both beside the point.

D. H. LAWRENCE

Most Western culture is the child of either of two gods: Jehovah or Reason—the two dominant conceptions of the Mediterranean world. Our ways of life and thought descended from either the Greeks or the Hebrews. We are the progeny of the Ideas of Plato or the God of Moses; we are raised on the words or the Word, bred as worshipers of signs and symbols.

During that incredibly fertile period from approximately 500 B.C. to 200 B.C., abstract thought must have shimmered off the surface of the Mediterranean Sea and settled into the human mind. On one side of the Mediterranean, the prophets of Judea proclaimed their faith in the word "God." Scholars say this word-god is an example of the Hebrews' great abstract genius; they were the first to worship a name rather than something that could be seen and touched, such as a golden calf. Using this god's "name" in vain or even spelling it out became a sin against the word-god, who became known to some as "He-whose-name-we-never-utter."

Many people, however, could not attach belief so easily to a name, and it wasn't long before Jesus arrived and *the Word was made flesh*. One of Christ's central messages was that the "word" needed to be connected to "being." The divine must in some way be embodied and visualized. Jesus even felt that people would feel more connected to God if they believed they were eating parts of Him. Nonetheless, the Hebrew word-god continued to reign. There is still no image of Him, graven or otherwise, and He is known only through the *words* of the holy book.

## Plato Misses the Point

Meanwhile, on the other shore of the Mediterranean, Greek philosophers proclaimed the supremacy of a different species of abstraction. Beneath the shade of olive trees and stately pillars, Plato, the godfather of thinking, turned Reason itself into a deity and assigned the other positions of his holy trinity to "universal ideas" and "eternal forms." Ironically, Plato built his religion of the mind on the reputation of Socrates, probably the best "thinker" of the time and most deserving of a title as Western crazy wisdom master. The challenge Socrates posed caused the Greek authorities to have him put to death. These were the charges against him:

> Socrates is an evil-doer and a curious person,
> searching into things under the earth and above the
> heaven; and making the worse appear the better
> cause, and teaching all this to others.

It seems probable that Socrates was a perfectly great fool, a master at turning the truth on its head, and that Plato, Socrates' student and unauthorized biographer, misrepresented his mentor's teaching. It is likely that Plato was to Socrates what Paul would later be to Christ, turning crazy wisdom into dogma. We can imagine Socrates as an original trickster of the mind, an artist of logic and antilogic. Like a child who has discovered a new game—reason—and played it well; he showed how it could challenge any truth, even the existence of the gods. He also demonstrated how reason could chase and devour itself. Socrates was the Western Lao Tzu, a master of paradox who stood all knowledge on end and claimed that all he knew was that he knew nothing. Plato with his Laws and Ideals was the Western Confucius, laying claim to knowledge of the highest wisdom for the ultimate good.

> He, O men, is the wisest, who, like Socrates,
> knows that his wisdom is in truth worth nothing.
> *The Apology*

If Plato captured anything of Socrates, it was his methods of working, which turn out to be the familiar techniques of crazy wisdom masters. Socrates wrote nothing down and took no money for teaching. He simply strolled around the agora's porches, talking to whoever gathered around him. He never preached, but held his audience by engaging in dialogue, inquiring with gentle irony into the nature of sure knowledge and beliefs. No doubt many gathered around Socrates to feel his power and integrity as well as to hear his mental ability in action. As his influence grew, Socrates became a threat to the Greek authorities. Finally, he was arrested for opposing Greek imperialism and counseling the youth of Athens to refuse military service and devote their lives to the pursuit of truth rather than wealth. Like Christ, Socrates would not recant or beg for mercy and was martyred for his beliefs. He told his accusers that he would continue his search for truth and asserted: "In another world they do not put a man to death for asking questions: assuredly not." In the end, his attitude toward death reveals Socrates as a true master of crazy wisdom:

> We go our ways—I to die, and you to live. Which is
> better God only knows.

Plato, the father of Western philosophy, sanctified logic and reason as divine powers. Instead of questioning all knowledge as Socrates had done, Plato concluded that reason could acquaint us with the ultimate truth. Eventually, Plato declared that he had figured out that truth, once and for all, and proceeded to enshrine his own ideas:

There are certain ideas of which all other things partake,
and from which they derive their names; that similars, for
example, become similar, because they partake of simi-
larity; and great things become great, because they partake
of greatness. . . .

These abstract "ideas," which Plato discusses in *Parmenides*, are
the ultimate reality. Individual objects, such as a specific chair, are
partially real—real only to the extent to which they partake of the
idea of "chair" or, perhaps, the idea of "chairness." In other words,
the more a chair resembles "chair," the more of a chair it is. At this
point a Taoist would sit down on a particular chair, even if it was only
partially real, but Plato remained standing, gazing into the heavens
for the Ideal Form, that grand piece of intellectual furniture that has
not allowed the Western mind to rest for several millennia.

Plato's statements about "ideas," such as how the good is good
because it partakes of "goodness," are nothing but taut little tauto-
logies. By placing ultimate faith in his mind, Plato tricked himself
into violating the basic rules of logic. Of course, Aristotle formulated those rules later, so maybe Plato just figured he could get away
with it. If only a Taoist or Zen master had wandered into one of Plato's dialogues, the Western world might have been spared some
mental binds, and maybe some physical ones as well. As Plato put
words into Socrates' mouth about the good or the real, a Zen master
would have interjected statements like "Your toga is coming loose"
or "Please pass the dolmas." Maybe someone would have picked up
on the Eastern theme and developed a stream of Western wisdom
concerned as much with being as knowing.

Although many blame Descartes for the mind/body split, Plato
made the first cut. Truth, he believed, is the product of the mind
alone; the needs and desires of the body and senses lead men astray.

The body is the source of endless trouble to us by reason of
the mere requirement of food; and is liable also to diseases
which overtake and impede us in the search after true being:
it fills us full of loves, and lusts, and fears, and fancies of all
kinds, and endless foolery, and in fact, as men say, takes
away from us all power of thinking at all. It has been proved
to us by experience that if we would have true knowledge
of anything we must be quit of the body—the soul in

herself must behold things in themselves: and then we shall attain the wisdom which we desire, and of which we say we are lovers . . .

In Plato . . . there first appears that cleavage between reason and the irrational that it has been the long burden of the West to carry, until the dualism makes itself felt in most violent form within modern culture.

WILLIAM BARRETT

Plato also believed that art can never be a medium for truth. Unlike philosophy and science, which are products of pure intellect, art filters objects through the senses. By devaluing art and poetry, Plato may have been attempting to lift reason above the established Greek gods, with their artistic accompaniment of myth, theater, and ritual. Plato not only severed the body from the mind, he separated the rational from the rest of human experience.

Eventually, Plato's concept of the rule of the mind was narrowed further to become the rule of philosopher-kings, whose authority must be obeyed unquestioningly because they alone know what is real and good. In *The Republic*, as well as in his last work, *The Laws*, Plato lays out his ideal state, complete with caste system, strong standing military, a regimented educational structure for raising perfect citizens, and laws that would deny most free speech and inquiry. Ironically, Plato's perfect society would have put Socrates to death just as the actual Greek system had done. In the end the very structure of Plato's system would have made tyrants of his philosopher-kings.

Plato's writing and thinking can be admired as part of the brilliant first flowering of abstract human reasoning. The difficulty comes with his insistence that reason is the sole and certain means of discovering truth. The refinement of reason has undoubtedly enabled the West to make astonishing achievements in science and technology and to gain phenomenal material benefits. However, this same intellectual power has led to the Western split of mind from body and of humans from the rest of creation. Most crazy wisdom masters would contend that Plato's philosophy directed us down the road to reasonable rack and possible ruin. If we do destroy ourselves, our only excuse and closing line may be (as some jester might say): "Reason made us do it."

# Two Heads Are Better Than One

It would seem that God and Reason are mutually exclusive, each reigning over a separate realm. Over the centuries, however, many Western philosophers have professed belief in both God and Reason at the same time. Some, however, felt compelled to take on the seemingly impossible task of "proving" God's existence through logical argument.

> Most of the propositions and questions to be found in
> philosophical works are not false but nonsensical.
> LUDWIG WITTGENSTEIN

For example, René Descartes, the seventeenth-century father of modern philosophy, attempted to prove the existence of God, but thought it best to prove his own existence first. He concluded that he existed because he could think that he existed. If he did not exist, he would not be able to think of himself as existing. Then he proved the existence of things other than himself, for if they did not exist, he would not be able to think of them either.

> . . . if the objective reality of any one of my ideas be so
> great that I am certain it cannot be in me either formally or
> eminently, and that consequently I cannot myself be the
> cause of it, it necessarily follows that I am not alone in the
> world and that there is likewise existing some other thing,
> which is the cause of this idea. Were no idea of this kind
> to be met with in me, I should have no argument sufficient
> to render me certain of the existence of anything different
> than me.

At this point, a Zen master would have hit Descartes with his staff, confirming the existence of things other than Descartes and his ideas. However, the Zen master would have been of no help to Descartes as he continued on to his supreme idea: his proof that God exists also.

> The only idea that remains for consideration is the idea of
> God. Is there in that idea anything which cannot be regarded
> as proceeding from myself? By the name "God" I mean a
> substance that is infinite, immutable, independent, all-
> knowing, all-powerful, and by which I myself and every-
> thing else, if any such other things there be, have been
> created. All those attributes are so great and so eminent,
> that the more attentively I consider them the less does it

seem possible that they can have proceeded from myself alone; and thus, in the light of all that has been said, we have no option save to conclude that God exists.

Hosanna! We are now believers. That is, of course, if we believe in Descartes's mind as much as he does. Descartes has perfect faith in his ideas, à la Plato, and whatever he can conceive of *must* be real. But his arguments are specious. His ideas prove only the existence of his ideas, not of the things they refer to. He thinks his idea of God must come from God, but in fact his mind may have been praying only to itself.

A few other Western philosophers have proven—at least to their own satisfaction—the existence of a supreme being. They used the power of reason to craft elaborate descriptions of the divine attributes:

> We may also conclude that this supreme substance, which is unique, universal and necessary, having nothing outside of itself that is independent of it, and being a pure consequence of possible being, must be incapable of limitation and must contain as much reality as is possible.
>
> GOTTFRIED WILHELM BARON VON LEIBNIZ

> All ideas, in so far as they are related to God, are true, that is to say, are adequate, and therefore (by the general definition of the emotions) God is free from passions.
>
> BARUCH SPINOZA

The holy fools, both Eastern and Western, might wonder how all this reasoning could have connected the Western philosophers with their God. Indeed, the rational approach seems to separate the thinker from God, by describing something inherently special and distinct. Furthermore, attempting to figure Him out only refutes God's power and mystery. To paraphrase Lao Tzu on the Tao, "The God that can be told is not the eternal God."

The treatises of classical Western philosophers are fascinating displays of abstract thinking. However, from the perspective of modern language philosophy many of these discourses are meaningless, making use of vague words and concepts which refer to nothing but themselves. Moreover, the contents of these philosoph-

The Tao that can be told is not the eternal Tao.

LAO TZU

ical arguments seem irrelevant to contemporary concerns. Perhaps this is simply the fate of all ideas and modes of understanding: All proofs are temporary, and all burning issues eventually smolder and die out. Looking back over Western philosophy from the vantage point of the twentieth century, Ludwig Wittgenstein concluded:

> The results of philosophy are the uncovering of one
> or another piece of plain nonsense and of bumps
> that the understanding has got by running its head
> up against the limits of language.

Classical Western philosophy made reason another Messiah, a divine power incarnated to bring salvation. We can imagine Reason, the deity—a winged, perfectly shaped thought-balloon—lifting Western man off the earth, out of body and nature and into a special niche of creation. Hovering precariously for centuries, we thought and thought and thought some more, but eventually we had to come back down to earth. The crash was inevitable—the fateful blow to the head, the crazy wisdom.

The results of philosophy are the uncovering of one or another piece of plain nonsense and of bumps that the understanding has got by running its head up against the limits of language.
LUDWIG WITTGENSTEIN

CHAPTER SIX

# The Existential Get-Down

I want everything to be explained to me or nothing. And the reason is impotent when it hears this cry from the heart. The mind aroused by this insistence seeks and finds nothing but contradictions and nonsense. The world itself, whose single meaning I do not understand, is a vast irrational.

ALBERT CAMUS

After a long history of brow-wrinkling, brain-twisting, mind-sweating reason, Western philosophy came to its own tentative brand of crazy wisdom. In the eighteenth and nineteenth centuries, Western thinkers bumped up against the bitter conclusion that the intellect could not comprehend the world or its meaning. By the mid-twentieth century, the movement known as existentialism had pronounced the failure of reason and the death of classical Western philosophy.

Existential philosophers wanted desperately to know, name, and secure the world in their minds, but reason let them down. Like jilted lovers, many grew melancholy or bitter and lashed out at the once-exalted human specialty.

Reason failed to offer salvation to the existentialists, but it prevented them from finding solace in God or the church. Belief in God

It was intelligence and nothing else that had to be opposed.

SØREN AABYE KIERKEGAARD

Our reason has driven all away. Alone at last, we end up by ruling over a desert.

ALBERT CAMUS

required a "leap of faith" over reason that few of them could manage, and in church they found only empty words and rituals. The existentialists turned against religion as another sad failure of Western civilization. Nobody tore it apart with more determination than Friedrich Nietzsche.

> It is indecent to be a Christian today. *And here begins my nausea.* I look around: not one word has remained of what was formerly called "truth"; we can no longer stand it if a priest as much as uses the word "truth." If we have even the smallest claim to integrity, we must know today that a theologian, a priest, a pope, not merely is wrong in every sentence he speaks, but *lies*—that he is no longer at liberty to lie from "innocence" or "ignorance." The priest too knows as well as anybody else that there is no longer any "God," any "sinner," any "Redeemer"—that "free will" and "moral world order" are *lies:* seriousness, the profound self-overcoming of the spirit, no longer permits anybody *not* to know about this.

The existentialists practiced crazy wisdom by challenging both God and reason, and thus the Western claim of humanity's special place in creation. We were no longer the chosen ones, watched over like children by a beneficent God our Father, nor was intellect deemed capable of discovering truth or finding higher meaning for our lives. These conclusions, along with the work of Darwin and Freud, shattered the Western psyche. The individual mind and soul—the darlings of Occidental philosophy and religion—were no longer the centerpieces of creation, and it became the grim project of the existentialists to mourn their passing and write the elegies. The despair felt by these late Western thinkers was both personal and collective: regret for themselves and for their culture.

> Forever I shall be a stranger to myself. In psychology as in logic, there are truths but no truth. Socrates' "Know thyself" has as much value as the "Be virtuous" of our confessionals. They reveal a nostalgia at the same time as an ignorance.
>
> ALBERT CAMUS

Existentialists found various ways to escape the torment. Søren Aabye Kierkegaard took the leap of faith—back into the lap of God. Nietzsche saw visions of the awesome mythical Zarathustra, and raved that man must muster the will and strength to create a new world without God. Others—such as Albert Camus and, especially, Jean-Paul Sartre—found temporary consolation in Marxism.

Like tricksters, the existentialists attempted to overturn the moral codes and belief systems of their time—and they too became victims of the resulting confusion. Unlike the Taoist and Zen Buddhists, who found liberation in a life without meaning, many existentialists were driven into severe depression by their inability to find meaning in the world. Without God or reason, these philosophers looked out at an empty, purposeless universe. Despair filled their lives and their literature: *Nausea, Fear and Trembling, The Concept of Dread, No Exit.*

Although most existential philosophers explored the realms of crazy wisdom intellectually, in their own lives many were destined only to become martyrs to this new Western understanding. What existentialists lacked, though some of them yearned for it, was a way out of their minds. A few of them tried the way of the absurd.

## 84

The world can no longer offer anything to the man filled with anguish.

MARTIN HEIDEGGER

With God dead, there remains only history and power.

ALBERT CAMUS

# The Way of the Absurd

In the "absurd" we hear occasional echoes of Taoism. Both describe a nonrational cosmos, indifferent to human concerns as it sweeps everything along on its inexorable course. Confronted with this "absurd creation," Albert Camus wrote of the "absurd man" who must find a different approach to life and another mode of understanding:

> For the absurd man it is not a matter of explaining
> and solving, but of experiencing and describing.
> Everything begins with lucid indifference.

Any Eastern sage would be pleased with Camus' phrase "lucid indifference," which sounds similar to the "just being" of Zen or the deliberate "non-doing" of Taoism. However, unlike the Taoist at

peace with the Tao, Camus himself never made peace with the absurd, and it is widely believed he committed suicide. He was well
aware of his dilemma:

> If I were a tree among trees, a cat among animals, this life
> would have a meaning, or rather this problem would
> not arise, for I should belong to this world. I should *be* this
> world to which I am now opposed by my whole conscious-
> ness and my whole insistence upon familiarity. This ridicu-
> lous reason is what sets me in opposition to all creation. I
> cannot cross it out with a stroke of the pen.

Camus wanted out of his mind and into "being." Instead of his
"insistence on familiarity," he wanted to become comfortable with
unfamiliarity. But no Taoist or Zen master was around to give Camus lessons; there was no tradition in the West to accommodate his
yearnings, no methods to transform his "existentialism" into a way
of life. He was a man of philosophy, and when the thinking game
could not hold him up, he sank.

Of all the existentialists, the nineteenth-century philosopher
Friedrich Nietzsche came closest to forging a new approach to life,
based on a universe without God, morality, or reason. Although
many disagree with Nietzsche's attempts to resolve absurdity, others
would award him the title of crazy wisdom master.

> I live in my own place
> have never copied nobody even half,
> and at any master who lacks the grace
> to laugh at himself—I laugh.
> INSCRIBED OVER THE DOOR
> TO NIETZSCHE'S HOUSE

Nietzsche developed his own unique crazy wisdom philosophy,
which has a great deal in common with both the ideas and styles of
presentation of the Eastern sages. There are moments when
Nietzsche, exploring his wild, anarchistic beliefs, sounds exactly like
an old Taoist holy fool:

> All that is good is instinct—and hence easy, necessary, free. Laboriousness is an objection; the god is typically different from the hero. (In my language: light feet are the first attribute of divinity.)

Nietzsche's divine "light feet" are right in step with the Taoists, but his own heavy boots would not allow him to walk quite so softly. Instead, he felt it necessary to kick apart the foundations of European civilization. With a trickster's chaotic spirit and a jester's skeptical insights, Nietzsche took it on himself to destroy all previous Western thought and history. In this task, he saw himself as the great fool philosopher, a crazy wisdom prophet come to herald the new age.

> It seems to me more and more that the philosopher, as a *necessary* man of tomorrow and the day after tomorrow, has always found himself, and always had to find himself, in opposition to his today: the ideal of the day was always his enemy. Hitherto all these extraordinary promoters of man, who are called philosophers, and who rarely have felt themselves to be friends of wisdom, but rather disagreeable fools and dangerous question marks, have found their task, their hard, unwanted, inescapable task, in being the bad conscience of their time. By applying the knife vivisectionally to the very *virtues of the time* they betrayed their own secret: to know of a *new* greatness of man, of a new untrodden way to his enhancement. Each time they have uncovered how much hypocrisy, comfortableness, letting oneself go and letting oneself drop, how many lies, were concealed under the most honored type of their contemporary morality, how much virtue was *outlived*. Each time they said: "We must proceed there, that way, where today you are least at home."

Nietzsche believed European civilization was sunk in superstition and ignorance, holding onto worn-out myths and ideologies. He called for "revaluation of all values" and for a special race of supermen to arise, face the blank slate, and create a new world. In exhortations such as "Mankind must become better and more evil," we can hear the familiar Taoist sense of irony and paradox. Master Lao and Master Chuang might even have quoted Nietzsche in their disputes with Confucius.

My demand upon the philosopher is known, that he take his stand *beyond* good and evil and leave the illusion of moral judgement *beneath* himself. This demand follows from an insight which I was the first to formulate: that *there are altogether no moral facts*.

Nietzsche had not read Chuang Tzu, but he was certainly one of the few in the West to reach a similar understanding. In a section of *Twilight of the Idols*, subtitled *How the "True World" Finally Became a Fable*, Nietzsche sounds like a Zen crazy wisdom master as he puts forth his version of truth. Nietzsche's first proposition is:

> 1. The true world—attainable for the sage, the pious, the virtuous man; he lives in it, *he is it*.

Nietzsche believed that truth is found in "being" rather than knowing, but like Camus, he had no one to teach him how to *be*. Nonetheless, Nietzsche seemed to understand what is required. In his fifth proposition, he comes a step closer to Zen when he refuses to search for truth, and decides to have breakfast instead.

> 5. The "true" world—an idea which is no longer good for anything, not even obligating—an idea which has become useless and superfluous—*consequently*, a refuted idea: let us abolish it! (Bright day; breakfast; return of *bon sens* and cheerfulness; Plato's embarrassed blush; pandemonium of all free spirits.)

Nietzsche did not believe in truth or knowledge, and he wanted out of the game. Although he was a philosopher, he spoke like a spiritual seeker looking for a different approach to life.

> I want, once and for all, *not* to know many things. Wisdom sets limits to knowledge too.

Like most crazy wisdom masters, Nietzsche saw the human craving for knowledge and significance as our most distressing quality, keeping us grim and out of balance.

Gradually, man has become a fantastic animal that has to fulfill one more condition of existence than any other animal: man *has to* believe, to know, from time to time *why* he exists; his race cannot flourish without a periodic trust in life—without faith in *reason in life*. And again and again the human race will decree from time to time: "There is something at which it is absolutely forbidden to laugh."

Nietzsche was one of the few Western thinkers to question the self-proclaimed importance of the human species. Characteristically, he not only suspected that man's role in history is temporary but called for it to end as soon as possible.

> Man is something that must be overcome. Man is a bridge and not an end.

Nietzsche longed for detachment from his emotional responses to the world. If he had been able to meet with Chuang Tzu, he might have come up with a slightly different version of the new human species that he called for. He might also have found a way to live in closer harmony with his own understanding.

> The advantages of our times: nothing is true, everything is permitted.

At the end of the trail of Western philosophy, we have found some crazy wisdom. However, it remains within the context of the game of reason. Existentialists may have rejected Platonic certainty, but they could not seem to let go of their desire for intellectual salvation. The few who sensed another approach to life were unable to find the Taoist and Zen masters' state of grace. In the end, Jean-Paul Sartre may have best summarized the difficult existential position, as well as the previous two millennia of Western philosophy, with this simple assertion:

> Being has not been given its due.

# The Art of Crazy Wisdom

There is the poet to whom the muse dictates his chants, there is the artist whose hand is guided by an unknown being using him as an instrument. Their reason cannot impede them, they never struggle, and their work shows no signs of strain. They are not divine and can do without their selves. They are like prolongations of nature, and their works do not pass through the intellect.

GUILLAUME APOLLINAIRE, 1905

## The Art of Being

From the first human who picked up a stick to beat out a rhythm on a log or draw an animal's picture in the dirt, artists have given name and form to the mysteries. As agents of the Tao, or Jesus, or the absurd, artists have shown us the latest version of the truth. They have made crazy wisdom dance.

The crazy wisdom artist cuts off one ear to clear the eyes for painting; wails down the walls of oppression with a ram's-horn saxophone; dances until the body becomes spirit; sits in a New York garret or on a Chinese mountaintop and writes poetry to the wind or the next lost generation, tells stories constantly, and sings to us of other truths, crying, "Look! This too is how it is."

Artists employ all the archetypal crazy wisdom disguises: As clowns they transform their bewilderment or wonder into art; as tricksters they reveal our shadow nature, stepping boldly into the realms of sex, chaos, and death; as jesters they parody fashions and beliefs. However, the greatest artists are great fools. As the great fool an artist transforms us, brings us back to our senses by opening our eyes and ears to another reality, or to *this* reality—the world around us that we ordinarily don't see.

> The poet is he who, beneath the named, constantly expected differences, rediscovers the buried kinship between things, the scattered resemblances.
> MICHEL FOUCAULT
> *The Order of Things*

Artists are often agents of crazy wisdom. They speak to a different part of us, bypassing the cloudy filter of reason and the fears and prejudices of the habitual mind. They are visited by the Muses, or tormented by their own passions and demons. By translating their inner turmoil or understanding into art, they challenge the accepted notions of reality and create new ones.

Like Zen, most art does not take well to definition. As Louis Armstrong replied when asked to define jazz, "Man, if you gotta ask, you'll never know."

James Joyce formulated a theory of art that defined the artistic experience as "aesthetic arrest." According to Joyce, art does not have purpose; it exists neither to teach nor to motivate. Joyce called works that evoke desire or disgust propaganda or social criticism. Art, in the purest sense, simply captures rhythms or relationships, and when it works art causes an "epiphany"—the state of "aesthetic arrest." In Joyce's theory, art immerses us in the moment, producing an effect not much different from the Zen master's shout or blow.

> Art is frozen Zen.
> R. H. BLYTH

Albert Camus's existential theory of art also sounds like a Zen master's aesthetic. For Camus, the artist embodies us in the world and the moment: with particulars, with stories, with things.

If the world were clear, art would not exist.
ALBERT CAMUS

If I could tell you what it meant, there would be no point in dancing it.
ISADORA DUNCAN

Aesthetics is for the artists as ornithology is for the birds.
BARNETT NEWMAN

> The true work of art is always on the human scale.
> It is essentially the one that says, "less."

As Camus saw it, art can teach us what science and reason cannot. In opposition to Plato, Camus believes we can know the world through the body and the senses.

> The work of art is born of the intelligence's refusal
> to reason the concrete. It marks the triumph of
> the carnal.

Great artists stop the mind; their work brings a sudden, intuitive revelation that allows the "subconscious" or the "superconscious" to come to the forefront. Like spiritual crazy wisdom masters, artists enlighten us or lighten us up. They teach us how to "be." They give us playthings, plays, play.

> Theater takes place all the time, wherever one is,
> and art simply facilitates persuading one that this is
> the case.
>
> JOHN CAGE

# Meaningless Play

> We have art in order not to perish of truth.
> FRIEDRICH NIETZSCHE

While "the absurd" drove most existential philosophers crazy or left them trembling in their lofts, artists began playing with it, discovering shapes that might be made from the void. At the beginning of the twentieth century, the philosophic-artistic movements of Dadaism, Futurism, and Surrealism turned the absurd into art—"in order not to perish of truth."

> Let's break away from rationality as out of a horrible husk
> and throw ourselves like pride-spiced fruit into the
> immense distorted mouth of the wind! Let's give ourselves

up to the unknown, not out of desperation but to plumb
the deep pits of the absurd.

F. T. MARTINETTI<br>
The Foundation and Manifesto of Futurism, 1908

Like great tricksters, the early-twentieth-century artists decided
to put a grin on the face of the absurd. They sought symbolic representations of a new ethos—a way of honoring "being" itself, even if
its meaning could not be understood, even if it had no ultimate
meaning. Dadaism and Surrealism made acceptance of the absurd a
point of honor for the brave, those who could live with, and even re-
joice in, a godless and purposeless universe. André Breton writes:

> I believe in the pure Surrealist joy of the man who, fore-
> warned that all others before him have failed, refuses to
> admit defeat, sets off from whatever point he chooses,
> along any other path save a reasonable one, and arrives
> wherever he can.

Twentieth-century artists made a complete break with Western
tradition, renouncing previous values and aesthetic standards. Cut
loose from old styles and beliefs, they discovered the freedom, fore-
told by Nietzsche, to create new realities and revel in the energy of
existence. They also had a good time kicking in the windows of old
institutions.

> We will destroy museums, libraries, and fight against
> moralism . . . and all utilitarian cowardice. We are on the
> extreme promontory of ages! Why look back since we
> must break down the mysterious doors of Impossibility?
> Time and Space died yesterday. We already live in the
> Absolute for we have already created the omnipresent
> eternal speed.

F. T. MARTINETTI<br>
The Foundation and Manifesto of Futurism, 1908

The artists of the early twentieth century brought the philosophy
of existentialism to life. They turned solid shapes into liquid ones,
distorted human forms and faces, took apart words and their meanings, and even created new gods.

## Dada and Tao

> The great mystery is a secret, but it's known to a
> few people. They will never say what dada is.
> TRISTAN TZARA

Out of the imagination of some early-twentieth-century artists came a madcap, multidimensional demigod known as Dada, which bears an uncanny resemblance to the Tao. The Dadaist movement was founded in Zurich during World War I by the French poet and self-proclaimed "literary terrorist" Tristan Tzara. Although Dadaist poetry and manifestos often sound like a takeoff of the Tao, we have no evidence that Tzara or other Dadaists were acquainted with Taoist writings. Perhaps a mysterious transmission took place.

> Dada is a quantity of life in transparent, effortless
> and gyratory transformation.
> TRISTAN TZARA, 1918

> Tao never does anything;
> Yet through it all things are done.
> LAO TZU, FIFTH CENTURY B.C.

Dada and the Tao (which *is* pronounced "Dao") seem to do the same dance, perhaps as partners, separated only by time. Even the letters in the names proclaim a relationship. Tao and Dada. Tzu and Tzara. The crazy wisdom likeness goes deeper.

> Logic is a complication. Logic is always false.
> DADA suggests 2 solutions: NO MORE
> LOOKS! NO MORE WORDS! Stop looking!
> Stop talking!
> TRISTAN TZARA

> Those who know don't talk.
> Those who talk don't know.
> LAO TZU

Dada may be a Western twentieth-century name for the Tao. Or else it is not that at all. Maybe it is just Dada.

94

DADA is a virgin microbe
DADA is against the high cost of living
DADA
limited company for the exploitation of ideas
DADA has 391 different attitudes and colours according to
    the sex
of the president
It changes—affirms—says the opposite at the same time—
    no
importance—shouts—goes fishing.
Dada is the chameleon of rapid and self-interested change.
Dada is against the future. Dada is dead. Dada is absurd.
    Long
live Dada. Dada is not a literary school, howl
               TRISTAN TZARA
     "Dada Manifesto on Feeble Love and Bitter Love"

The similarities between the Tao and Dada include the fact that they both appear to be names for everything: the two are both the One. Furthermore, like the Tao, Dada makes no distinctions—no high and low; no holy and profane. Acceptance of either the Tao or Dada may also imply a similar way of living.

    The acts of life have neither beginning nor end.
    Everything happens in a very idiotic fashion.
    That's why everything is the same. Simplicity is
    called dada.

    TRISTAN TZARA

    Approach it and there is no beginning;
    follow it and there is no end.
    You can't know it, but you can be it,
    at ease in your own life.

    LAO TZU

In spite of their similarities, we must remember that Taoism has lasted for centuries and is ranked with the world's major philosophies. Dadaism is just bombast, a flippant artistic statement. Still, there is crazy wisdom in Dada. In a lecture, Tristan Tzara addressed the essence:

I know you're expecting some explanations about Dada. I'm not going to give you any. Explain to me why you exist. You've no idea. You'll say: I exist to make my children happy. But you know it's not really true. You'll say: I exist to protect my country from barbaric invasions. That's not enough. You'll say: I exist because God wants me to. That's a tale to tell the children. You'll never know why you exist, but you'll always allow yourselves to be easily persuaded to take life seriously. You'll never understand that life is a play on words, because you'll never be alone enough to refuse hate, judgements, and everything that needs a great effort, in favour of an even, calm state of mind in which everything is equal and unimportant.

## John Cage and the Music of Sound

John Cage's music, like Tzara's Dada, shows us that everything is equal—and equally unimportant. In 1952 in response to a request for a manifesto on music, Cage wrote:

> instantaneous                    and unpredictable
> nothing is accomplished by writing a piece of music
> nothing is accomplished by hearing a piece of music
> nothing is accomplished by playing a piece of music
>         our ears are now in excellent condition

John Cage is an exemplary crazy wisdom artist who has become one of the twentieth century's most influential cultural figures. His unusual classical music compositions led to the development of "happenings," events in which the audience participates or there is some convergence of art and ordinary life. An author and lecturer, Cage is very articulate about his motivations and techniques. If his art has any purpose, he says, it is to help us "become fluent with the life we are living."

I'm not really trying to say anything in my music. I hope the music becomes an example, an instance that bridges more or less naturally to the absence of music. So that either you have the music or you don't have it and in either case you have sounds. Hopefully, then people can learn to become attentive, with pleasure, to the world of sounds around us that are changing all the time.

Cage denies the significance of "music" and rejects the idea that music is something separate from other sounds. Like a great fool, Cage hears a universe full of music that is inaudible to the rest of us. Since he makes no distinction between good and bad sounds, everything becomes music—a never-ending unfinished symphony. Cage wants to share his music with us, but first we must be liberated from our habits of hearing and shaken loose from our tired ideas about music, art, and, ultimately, life.

> If you develop an ear for sounds that are musical it is like developing an ego. You begin to refuse sounds that are not musical and that way cut yourself off from a good deal of experience.

Cage hears life's continuous music: a modulating concerto of bird songs, car engines, shuffling feet, white noise, commercials, wind, rustling paper—all writing themselves into the random mix. He states:

> My favorite piece of music is the one we hear all the time if we are quiet .

At least one performance of a Cage piano piece produced no "intentional sound" at all: The pianist made a grand entrance and sat down at the piano, but did not once touch the keys during the entire performance. The only "music" was the incidental sound of an auditorium full of people, shuffling, coughing, and whispering. Cage also wrote a composition for instruments that can be found in an ordinary living room, and another for live radios. He is a musical trickster at work, acting in the service of the great fool.

John Cage studied with Zen Buddhist scholar D. T. Suzuki, and both his art and methods of working reflect a deep sympathy with the crazy wisdom of Zen. For instance, Cage says he uses chance operations from the I Ching to help him write his compositions; this technique helps him get rid of "the likes and dislikes of the ego." He wants to get himself out of the way so that the universe can write the music.

> Value judgements are destructive to our proper
> business, which is curiosity and awareness.

Cage's art and ideas deny any distinction between creative process and performance, or between performer and audience. His crazy wisdom shows that life and art are one and the same, perhaps implying that we can make ourselves into works of art by blending more easily into the big picture and becoming more open to the continuously changing dance of creation. In Cage's opinion, the real art is in how we live our lives; once we recognize that, theater happens all around us and music is everywhere.

> There is no such thing as an empty space or an empty time.
> There is always something to see, something to hear. In
> fact, try as we may to make a silence, we cannot. For certain
> engineering purposes, it is desirable to have as silent a
> situation as possible. Such a room is called an anechoic
> chamber, its six walls made of special material, a room
> without echoes. I entered one at Harvard University several
> years ago and heard two sounds, one high and one low.
> When I described them to the engineer in charge, he
> informed me that the high one was my nervous system in
> operation, the low one my blood in circulation. Until I die
> there will be sounds. And they will continue following my
> death. One need not fear about the future of music.

## Verses of Crazy Wisdom

> Man fixes some wonderful erection of his own between
> himself and the wild chaos, and gradually goes bleached
> and stifled under his parasol. Then comes a poet, enemy of
> convention, and makes a slit in the umbrella; and lo! the
> glimpse of chaos is a vision, a window to the sun.
>
> D. H. LAWRENCE

Poets are crazy wisdom's children, and poetry is the medium through which crazy wisdom states its case. The lines of poetry scattered throughout this book are testament to this. As we have seen, many holy fools, both Eastern and Western, express their version of

truth through poetry. Lao Tzu, the preacher of the Book of Ecclesiastes, and the storyteller of the Bhagavad Gita were poets of the
highest order. They wrote the scriptures of crazy wisdom in verse.

Poets often find their visions to be in opposition to their era, and
their poetic voices are shaped by that tension. Throughout Western
history, poets have continually challenged the dominant worldview.
To mainstream religious doctrine they offered alternative mythologies; against the forces of reason and science they mounted the resistance of their own imaginations.

The European Romantic poets of the late eighteenth and early
nineteenth centuries laid down stiff charges against both reason and
religion, if not against God. Lord Byron, William Wordsworth, and
William Blake were among those proclaiming that the Western
mind and heart were out of balance. They saw the cold, objective intellect as the driving force behind the Industrial Revolution, which at
that time was already showing ominous signs of destroying the
natural world. These poets warned that reason and knowledge suf-
focate the "romantic" spirit—the mystical bond between an individual and the rest of creation. The Romantics voice a familiar crazy wisdom theme. In counterpoint to the Age of Reason and the Industrial
Revolution, these poets sang of nature, subjective experience, and
the powers of imagination.

One of the most radical and prophetic voices of the eighteenth
century was that of poet William Blake. He rejected reason's authority in matters of reality, and the church's authority in matters of morality. He constructed his own mythical universe, in which evil is
called Urizen (your reason), and the church is portrayed as the de-
stroyer of energy and joy.

All Bibles or sacred codes have been the causes of the
following Errors:

1. That Man has two real existing principles: Viz: a Body
   and a Soul.
2. That Energy, call'd Evil, is alone from the Body; & that
   Reason, call'd Good, is alone from the Soul.
3. That God will torment Man in Eternity for following his
   Energies.

You dream you are the
   doer,
You dream that action is
   done,
You dream that action bears
   fruit.
It is your ignorance,
It is the world's delusion
That gives you these
   dreams.
   BHAGAVAD GITA

I must Create a System or
   be enslav'd by another
   Man's.
I will not Reason and
   Compare; my business is
   to Create.
   WILLIAM BLAKE

The Errors of a Wise Man
   make your Rule
Rather than the Perfections
   of a Fool.
   WILLIAM BLAKE

Blake received little recognition from his contemporaries and was considered a minor poet or madman by those who read him. Today he is widely quoted and regarded as a visionary. It is the story of many a master of crazy wisdom.

> He has observ'd the Golden Rule
> Till he's become the Golden Fool.
> WILLIAM BLAKE

America's Beat poets confronted the advanced stage of the civilization opposed by the Romantics. Their challenge was to break through the self-satisfied consumerism and reasonableness that held sway over American society from the late 1940s through the early 1960s. In the brash dialect of the streets, the Beats hurled their crazy wisdom verses at the Establishment. They were just a few lonely voices, courageous in their indictment of a society strangled by conformity, a nation blind to its imperial evils. In a poem called "Death to Van Gogh's Ear!" written in 1958, Allen Ginsberg decried the state of the nation:

> Poet is Priest
> Money has reckoned the soul of America
> Congress broken thru to the precipice of Eternity
> the President built a War machine which will vomit and
>      rear up Russia out of Kansas
> The American Century betrayed by a mad Senate which no
>      longer sleeps with its wife

Beat poets drew their inspiration from many sources, but a few—including Gary Snyder, Allen Ginsberg, and Jack Kerouac—were influenced heavily by their contact with Taoism and Buddhism. They began to translate the crazy wisdom of Eastern sages into an American idiom.

> The reason why there are so many things
> Is because the mind breaks it up,
> The shapes are empty
> That sprung into come
> But the mind wont know this
> Till a Buddha with golden
> Lighted finger, hath pointed

To the thumb, & made an aphorism
In a robe on the street,
That you'll know what it means
For there be too many things
In a world of no-thing.
                    JACK KEROUAC

Gary Snyder was deeply influenced by the Taoists and Zen Buddhists. He studied Buddhism for many years in Japan, and later founded a Zen meditation community in the Sierra foothills. Snyder's poetry and regard for nature are both shaped by his Eastern spiritual practices. However, it is in the spirit of the Romantics that he voices his poetic warnings to America and the world about the exploitation of nature taking place in the name of progress and civilization. In the 1960s, long before the environment became a mainstream concern, Snyder was attempting to awaken people to the interdependence of all life and the intrinsic value of wilderness. The lines that follow are from "Revolution in the Revolution in the Revolution."

"From the masses to the masses" the most
Revolutionary consciousness is to be found
Among the most ruthlessly exploited classes:
Animals, trees, water, air, grasses.

The Beat poets, to whom "beat" meant beatitude, were for a couple of decades considered cranks and delinquents by most social and literary critics. Of those Beats who survived the 1950s and 1960s, however, a few have been awarded literary prizes, and their ideas and causes have been acknowledged by mainstream society. If the Beats had lived in an earlier century, they would have been honored only posthumously, like so many poets throughout history, but the speed of twentieth-century cultural transformation revealed them as crazy wisdom prophets within their own lifetimes.

For many people, the definition of poet automatically includes the words "crazy" and "wise." The list of poets who have translated these qualities into verse is long and includes a great chorus of voices. They revel in the energies of existence with no regard for reputation or wealth, challenge the status quo, and offer their verses on the silent mysteries. Throughout history, poets have joined in this chorus to sing their crazy wisdom songs.

Mountains, a moment's earth-waves rising and hollowing;
    the earth too's an ephemerid; the stars—
Short-lived as grass the stars quicken in the nebula and dry
    in their summer, they spiral
Blind up space, scattered black seeds of a future; nothing
    lives long, the whole sky's
Recurrences tick the seconds of the hours of the ages of the
    gulf before birth, and the gulf
After death is like dated: to labor eighty years in a notch of
    eternity is nothing too tiresome,
Enormous repose after, enormous repose before, the flash
    of activity.

ROBINSON JEFFERS
from *The Treasure*

With the poets, we end our exploration of crazy wisdom sources. We have traced these sources through several cultures and many centuries. On the way, we met a wide assortment of holy fools, tricksters, and jesters, philosophers, artists, and poets, and became acquainted with the qualities that unite them. We married the Tao off to Dada, introduced Socrates and Nietzsche to Chuang Tzu, let Coyote dance with Rumi, and made a few other questionable connections, but the bonds seem to be holding. Crazy wisdom lives!

# PART II

# *How to Become Crazy and Wise*

The sacred books of the East are nothing but words.
I looked through their covers one day sideways.
Kabir talks only about what he has lived through.
If you have not lived through something, it is not true.

KABIR

How does crazy wisdom happen? What gyre of gene or bug of brain produces crazy wisdom in an individual? Is it born in the blood, or can it be learned? Where does crazy wisdom get its insights into human behavior and its vast perspectives on the cosmos? If crazy wisdom knows that we don't know, then how does crazy wisdom know *that*?

In the following section, we will attempt to understand the nature of crazy wisdom and the ways in which it develops in individuals. Although it may be impossible to determine exactly how this happens, certain experiences and mental exercises seem to lead to crazy wisdom insights. We will investigate how nature and art affect the process, and how a variety of spiritual techniques drive people "crazy wise." As we explore these methods, we just might develop a little more crazy wisdom of our own.

See, the human mind is kind of like . . .
a piñata. When it breaks open,
there's a lot of surprises inside.
Once you get the piñata perspective,
you see that losing your mind
can be a peak experience.

JANE WAGNER

*The Search for Signs of Intelligent Life in the Universe*

# CHAPTER EIGHT

# The Right Mind

What we need is a good five-cent synthesis.
SAUL BELLOW

Modern science may have discovered the seat of crazy wisdom—the right hemisphere of our cerebral cortex. Recent research has found that the human brain's two hemispheres tend to have separate functions and modes of operation. The left hemisphere seems to be in charge of logic, mathematics, and ordinary language activities, while the right controls kinesthesis, artistic sensibility, and spatial judgment. The left hemisphere is the business center, the place where we work to survive. The right hemisphere is existential, the place where we live and love. The left gets us where we are going; the right puts us in touch with where we are.

Long before we understood the function of each hemisphere, it was recognized that people have at least two modes of understanding. Philosopher Thomas Hobbes called one mode "directed" and the other "free." Indian spiritual teacher Radhakrishanan called one "rational" and the other "integral." French anthropologist Claude Lévi-Strauss referred to one as "positive" and the other as "mythic." A graphic and poetic description of the "two minds" appears in the second-century Indian Buddhist text, the *Lankavatara Sutra*:

May God us keep
From single vision and
Newton's sleep.
WILLIAM BLAKE

The discriminating mind is a dancer and a magician
with the objective world as his stage. Intuitive
mind is the wise jester who travels with the magician and reflects upon his emptiness and transiency.

The left hemisphere is the utilitarian brain—*the opposable thumb of the mind.* It receives and orders information, analyzes the world, gives out names (dog, god, grass, open, gone), and arranges sensory input in familiar patterns. The left hemisphere is an information processor, working bit by bit in a linear, sequential manner.

The right hemisphere's primary function is synthesis, seeing relationships between things and providing an overview. The right hemisphere has been called holistic in its vision and intuitive in its operation. This part of the brain connects the dots . . . but doesn't count them.

One key to understanding the right hemisphere can be found in its association with music and poetry. Some studies have shown that people with left-hemisphere brain damage who have lost most of their language ability can still use words, but only to sing songs that they learned before the damage. Other patients start writing and speaking in poetry for the first time.

The right hemisphere seems to control awareness of the body. Patients with right-hemisphere brain damage are sometimes unable to dress themselves, though their speech and reasoning abilities are intact. Perhaps one of the functions of the right hemisphere is to bring us down from the abstract world of words and ideas and to put us back into our bodies, giving us a sense of our physical presence on the earth.

Our culture's ontological prejudice is obvious from the attitude of medical science toward brain injuries. If only the right hemisphere is damaged and no injury has occurred to language or logic functions, doctors often consider it "minor" brain damage. Perhaps the heavy emphasis on analysis during medical school has left some doctors a bit lopsided, understanding the brain primarily through their own left hemispheres. As Robert Ornstein states in his classic study, *The Psychology of Consciousness,* this lopsidedness has broader and more disturbing implications:

> . . . the development of a hyperanalytic, "rational" science, unchecked by a comprehensive understanding born of intuition, can develop into the destruction of all on the planet.

The left brain is a scientist, the right is an artist.
COLIN WILSON

O to be delivered from the rational into the realm of pure song . . .
THEODORE ROETHKE

Mr. Duffy lived a short distance from his body.
JAMES JOYCE
*Ulysses*

It is obvious that something is not working properly. How else can we explain our mismanagement of resources and our own population, the pollution and destruction of our environment, or the mass murder of our own species? We cannot see the bigger picture and how we fit into it. We are no longer in our bodies; we are not in our *right* mind. Ornstein sees the problem this way:

> A shift toward a comprehensive consciousness of the interconnectedness of life, toward a relinquishing of the "every man for himself" attitude inherent in our ordinary construction of consciousness, might enable us to take those "selfless" steps that could begin to solve our collective problems. Certainly our culture has too severely emphasized the development of only one way of organizing reality.

Perhaps the crises threatening humanity in the late twentieth century arise from simple functional imbalance, an unequal distribution of strength between the brain's left and right hemispheres. Maybe we need a little electrical work, a rewiring of the cerebral circuits. Perhaps exercising the right hemisphere through techniques such as meditation (or development of intuition, or exposure to art, music, and nature) might bring us to true sanity or consciousness, and a more integrated way of living.

Some adventurous cultural anthropologists believe that the recent emergence of mysticism, feminism, and deep ecology are the species' attempt to regain equilibrium. Our survival instinct may be telling us to reawaken our more receptive modes of understanding. Even obsession with sex, drugs, and rock and roll may be seen as an attempt to find relief from the oppression of the rational, controlling mind. A new and necessary mutation may be taking place, attempting to correct the cultural and evolutionary imbalances of the past few thousand years.

There is no way to know what will happen to our species, but while we wait for the verdict, crazy wisdom is hanging out in the right hemisphere. Being on the right side of the brain is a little like being on the Left Bank in Paris: relaxing and watching the passing show, listening to the music on the corner. It's a place to sit around and tell stories and wonder about it all—and most important, to slow down. Call it crazy or lazy, this wisdom may be found only by slowing down and learning the art of being. As Carl Jung explains, this is much more difficult than it sounds:

All Things want to fly. Only *we* are weighed down by desire, caught in ourselves and enthralled with our heaviness. . . . If someone were to fall into intimate slumber, and slept deeply with Things—: how easily he would come to a different day, out of the mutual depth.

RAINER MARIA RILKE

We must be able to let things happen in the psyche. For us, this actually is an art of which few people know anything. Consciousness is forever interfering, helping, correcting, and negating, and never leaving the simple growth of the psychic processes in peace. It would be simple enough, if only simplicity were not the most difficult of all things.

CHAPTER NINE

# Pigments and Pinecones

Crazy wisdom can be awakened through experiences involving art or nature, although in both these realms the process is somewhat mysterious. It *does* seem clear that the transformative qualities of a symphony or sunset engage the nonrational, intuitive mode of understanding.

The experience of art, as discussed earlier, can clear a path for crazy wisdom. Through Joyce's "aesthetic arrest" or Camus's "triumph of the carnal," the artist can bypass reason and give us a different sense of ourselves, embodying us in the world. Art can also offer perspective, showing us the wider context in which we live. The painter or novelist's revelation is both personal and universal, offering a more detached way to view our common experiences, and at the same time giving us a feeling of connection with all humanity. We see that we are all part of the same picture or story, and that life can really be seen as a picture or story.

Nature can also give us the experience, beyond intellectual understanding, of realizing the larger context in which we live. The sky and mountains and oceans are capable of dwarfing or drowning us. Sometimes they take our breath away along with our self-importance. This moment of transcendent understanding was expressed by Robinson Jeffers, whose choice of nature over man was a lifelong poetic theme.

For it's not innocent blank nature made hills look sad and woe-y, it's men, with their awful minds . . .

JACK KEROUAC

The sea's voice worked into my mood, I thought "No
  matter
What happens to men . . . the world's well made though."

Those who live closest to the natural world feel themselves to be
an integral part of the larger web of life. Many native American ini-
tiation rites send adolescents alone into the wilderness, where they
can feel the humbling power of the forces of nature. During this "vision quest," they find a personal spirit guide such as a bird, animal, or
tree, which gives them an intimate connection with the natural
world. Chief Seattle says:

> The perfumed flowers
> are our sisters;
> the deer, the horse, the great eagle,
> these are our brothers.
> The rocky crests,
> the juices of the meadows,
> the body heat of the pony, and man—
> all belong to the same family.

In a similar way, the Taoists and Zen masters listen for the
rhythms of the natural world and adjust themselves to those beats.
Staying in touch with nature's power and mystery reminds them
continually of how little they know and how little they are. Issa's
haiku demonstrates the type of lessons that nature offers on how to
live and die:

> Simply trust
> Do not the petals flutter down,
> Just like that?

Elevating human civilization above the natural world may be the
fatal hubris that will bring the whole show crashing down. By wall-
ing ourselves off into cities and focusing only on the historical concerns of our own species, we have cut our vital link with the rest of
life. Albert Camus vividly assesses our loss in "Helen's Exile":

What imagination could we have left for that higher equilibrium in which nature balanced history. . . . We turn our

backs on nature; we are ashamed of beauty. Our wretched tragedies have a smell of the office clinging to them, and the blood that trickles from them is the color of printer's ink.

We are so caught up in our self-important dramas that we can't smell the poisons in the air or taste them in the water. The Western urban intellectual's long indifference to the notion of a simple, "experiential" understanding of the natural world may turn out to be the gravest rational error of all.

In nature we learn the vital lesson of just being. We feel the perfection of things as they are, and understand what Jesus meant when he said, "Consider the lilies of the field. . . ." Perhaps our culture lacks nothing so much as a sense of this state of being. Alan Watts expressed this sentiment most eloquently in his book, *Nature, Man, and Woman*.

For what we call "nature" is free from a certain kind of scheming and self-importance. The birds and beasts indeed pursue their business of eating and breeding with the utmost devotion. But they do not justify it; they do not pretend that it serves higher ends, or that it makes a significant contribution to the progress of the world.

In this light [of nature] all the weirdly abstract and pompous pursuits of men are suddenly transformed into natural marvels of the same order as the immense beaks of the toucans and hornbills, the fabulous tails of the birds of paradise, the towering necks of the giraffes, and the vividly polychromed posteriors of the baboons. Seen thus, neither as something to be condemned nor in its accustomed aspect of serious worth, the self-importance of man dissolves in laughter. His insistent purposefulness and his extraordinary preoccupation with abstractions are, while perfectly natural, overdone—like the vast bodies of the dinosaurs. As means of survival and adaptation they have been overplayed, producing a species too cunning and too practical for its own good, and which for this very reason stands in need of . . . [a] philosophy which, like nature, has no purpose or consequence other than itself.

The crazy wisdom we gain from both art and nature is like Zen—beyond words and concepts, without purpose or meaning. Art and nature just are, and that is what experiencing them can teach.

........................................

114

# Wonder

*That* the world is, is the mystical.
LUDWIG WITTGENSTEIN

It should be clear by now that an essential ingredient of crazy wisdom is perspective—the understanding born of multiple views and multiple truths. Furthermore, the spark that keeps moving crazy wisdom from point of view to point of view is a basic attitude of doubt. As Voltaire stated, "Doubt is an uncomfortable condition, but certainty is a ridiculous one."

Of course, many see doubt as a negative state, a continual restlessness or frowning skepticism. But on just the other side of doubt lies wonder, the feeling that comes from having an empty head and an open heart. A sense of wonder seems to be another key that unlocks the door to crazy wisdom and keeps it swinging open. Albert Einstein embraced the wonder that plays such a crucial role in all realms of life:

At the moment you are most in awe of all there is about life that you don't understand, you are closer to understanding it all than at any other time.

JANE WAGNER

The most beautiful experience we can have is the mysterious. It is the fundamental emotion which stands at the cradle of true art and true science. Whosoever does not know it and can no longer wonder, no longer marvel, is as good as dead, and his eyes are dimmed.

How wondrously supernatural, and miraculous this! I draw water, and I carry fuel!

P'ANG CHU-SHIH

The Hindu teacher Swami Muktananda was once asked why he didn't work miracles. He replied, "I have no need to work miracles. The circulation of blood through my body is enough."

Holy fools are often awed by the world. Perhaps this comes from knowing how little they know. The mystery is simultaneously humbling and inspiring. Chuang Tzu accepts doubt and playfully wonders what might lie ahead:

How marvelous the Creator is! What is he going to
make out of you next? Where is he going to send
you? Will he make you into a rat's liver? Will he
make you into a bug's arm?

Religions are always after the mystery, trying to put it into faces,
stories, and song. This works for some people. Science is after the
great mystery, too, convinced that it can be made to make sense.
That science will ever solve much of anything is doubtful, but lately
its descriptions of reality are sliding into poetry, sounding more and
more like the wonder of crazy wisdom. In his book *Fearful Symmetry*, theoretical physicist Anthony Zee makes magic out of nearly incomprehensible physical processes:

Use the principle of local symmetry to produce grand
unification, with its inevitable violation of baryon conservation. Include a little CP violation and throw in some
gravity to make it all expand. And, voila, a universe that
produces its own dirt, stars, flowers, and human beings.

Perhaps the ultimate statement of crazy wisdom wonder comes
from a book written in the second century B.C. in India, called *The
Flower Ornament Scripture*. The mystery of existence has never been
expressed in more detail than in this immense Mahayana Buddhist
scripture. The book opens by using the linear, mathematical mind
and then leads us beyond the limits of calculation into mythic realms.
For example, in one sequence the Buddha tries to explain how many
numbers and how many worlds are known to him. The Buddha
talks about quantities that far exceed our present estimate of the
number of atoms in the universe. The Buddha begins calculating like
this: "Ten to the tenth power times ten to the tenth power equals ten
to the twentieth power. . . ." This calculating goes on for several full
pages. We resume near the final summation:

. . . that squared is ten to the power of 25,373,323,152,579,
663,188,831,409,602,560; that squared is ten to the power
of 101,493,292,610,318,652,755,325,638,410,240; that
squared is an incalculable; an incalculable to the fourth
power is a boundless; a boundless to the fourth power is an
incomparable; an incomparable to the fourth power is an

innumerable; an innumerable to the fourth power is an unaccountable; an unaccountable to the fourth power is an unthinkable; an unthinkable to the fourth power is an immeasurable; an immeasurable to the fourth power is an unspeakable; an unspeakable to the fourth power is an untold, which is unspeakably unspeakable; an untold multiplied by itself is a square untold.

Then the Buddha speaks these verses:

> Untold unspeakables
> Fill all unspeakables;
> In unspeakable eons
> Explanation of the unspeakable
>     cannot be finished.

> If untold Buddha-lands are reduced
> to atoms,
> In one atom are untold lands,
> And as in one,
> So in each.

With this vastness ringing through our heart-minds, we will proceed to our own exercise in crazy wisdom.

# CHAPTER TEN

# Working Out with the Holy Fools

Do not give rise to a single thought.
SIXTH CHINESE ZEN PATRIARCH

The holy fools want to drive us out of our minds, knowing that when we get there, the fresh air will do us good. Maybe we will begin to understand that we cannot understand and will relax a little. Only *then* will we begin to understand.

The disciple Hui-K'e asked Bodhidharma, "Please help me to quiet my mind." Bodhidharma said, "Bring me your mind so that I can quiet it." After a moment Hui-K'e said, "But I can't find my mind." "There," said Bodhidharma, "I have now quieted your mind."
CHARLES LUK

Where is the mind? Many Eastern spiritual masters do not consider the "mind" to be located in the skull. They point to the center of the chest, to the dense and complex nerve center just below the sternum, and call it the "heart-mind." Another kind of cognition or recognition may go on in this heart-mind, another way of knowing that requires a name other than knowledge. Using the hyphen as above, we can refer to it as "being-knowledge." Whatever it is called, it is crazy wisdom.

According to Eastern holy fools, the continual buzz in the mind—of facts and figurings, desires and regrets, plans and fantasies—prevents crazy wisdom from being alive in us. Our minds are so full of words that there is no room for wisdom, our psyches so busy "working" that being-knowledge stays far away.

Go ahead. Get your mind to stop and allow you a glimpse into just being—into experiencing this moment without qualifying or thinking about it. You might begin by trying to go for two or three minutes without any thoughts at all. Most people find it very difficult to halt the constant pulse of messages. This kind of experiment is a hint that we are not in charge of our own mental life. A more intensive and thorough investigation of ourselves reveals the shocking extent to which our thoughts and feelings are not under the direction of any free will or independent "self."

Eastern holy fools, who sometimes refer to the mind as "the wild monkey," have invented many exercises to tame it. They created and refined certain techniques of meditation in order to study themselves and discover ways to become free from mental and emotional conditioning.

The West has tended to rely on observational rather than experiential studies of the human condition. We focus our microscopes on cells and subatomic particles, observe rats and chimpanzees and extrapolate to our own situation, or set up experiments in which one group of humans studies another. These methods lead us to what could be called *informative* knowledge, but not *transformative* knowledge—not wisdom. The spiritual teacher Ram Dass describes the difference this way:

> You can either be wise or you can know knowledge. But you can't know wisdom, you have to "be" it. Wisdom has simplicity to it. What the spiritual path offers is a way to come back into balance, to develop our intuition and the wisdom of our heart, so that the intellect is no longer the master, but instead is the servant of our heart . . . the part of us that brings us into unity with ourselves and all other beings.

The practice of meditation involves an intuitive, experiential mode of perception that has nothing to do with reason or knowledge. Meditation seems to activate a special psychic process, only re-

118

The mad mind does not halt. If it halts, it is enlightenment.
CHINESE ZEN SAYING

By definition, human beings do not see or hear. I broke loose from definition.
RUMI

When you try to understand everything, you will not understand anything. The best way is to understand yourself, and then you will understand everything.
SHUNRYU SUZUKI

cently acknowledged and explored by Western science. In *The Psychology of Consciousness*, Robert Ornstein speculates about the effects of meditation:

> The "mystic" experience brought about by concentrative meditation, and other techniques is . . . a shift from the normal, analytic world containing separate, discrete objects and persons to a second mode, an experience of "unity" and holistic perception . . . it is a complementary dimension of consciousness that adds to and can give comprehension to the ordered sequence of "normal" thought.

In most types of meditation, one must first break through the rational, analytic mode of understanding. One way of doing this is to throw the rational mind an impossible question called a koan (in Chinese *kung an*), a riddle meant to short-circuit all logical connections. The method, referred to as "using poison against poison," frustrates the thinking mind until it breaks down. The answer to any koan lies in letting go of the desire to understand it logically. On some level, the answer to any koan riddle is "I don't know." The koan teaches what Alan Watts called "the wisdom of insecurity"— how to live with doubt and even embrace it. With the koan we learn to have questions without needing answers.

Zen practice is said to have 1,700 koans. Three of the most famous are: "What is the sound of one hand clapping?" "If everything returns to the One, to what does the One return?" "Does a dog have Buddha nature?" We could just as well combine the three koans into one and ask "What is the sound of one dog returning to the One?" If you bark, you get thirty blows with the staff.

Other techniques for beginning meditation include the mantra (repetition of phrases or patterns of syllables), visualization (holding images steady in the mind), and concentration on a single object or action, such as one's breath. These practices develop strength and focus of mind, enabling meditators to see through their individual obsessions and confusion to discover what is often referred to as our "true nature." Poet Gary Snyder's Zen Buddhist training led him to understand the process this way:

119

When you set yourself free from life and death, you should know your ultimate destination. So when the four elements separate, where will you go?

KOAN OF MASTER
TOSOTSU ETSU

What was my fundamental face before I was born?

ZEN KOAN

120

Wisdom is intuitive knowledge of the mind of love and clarity that lies beneath one's ego-driven anxieties and aggressions. Meditation is going into the mind to see this for yourself—over and over again, until it becomes the mind you live in.

Meditation is commonly called a "practice," because meditators practice living in this mind—the mind of "clarity." They practice an *ongoing* watchfulness of their mental and emotional life. This practice should not be confused with Western psychology, which studies the individual's personal story. In meditation, one learns to go beyond personality and become aware of the *mechanics* of the mind and emotions. Meditation can teach the *physics* of the psyche—the origin of thoughts and feelings, and how they interact. It can help to free us from our instincts as well as our ideologies. Meditation cultivates equanimity and peace in the mind; it frees us from the psyche's drama, allowing us to just be present in each moment.

Some Eastern holy fools will say that, fundamentally, meditation is a practice of "being." Although this sounds contradictory, it seems that humans do have to *practice* being in order to do it properly. Our tendency is to try to analyze and adjust our environment, as though it were never quite right, or as if we were in constant danger. Meditation practice is an antidote to our desires and fears, a way to allow ourselves to be in the world as it is.

Getting beyond the self is one of the most important results of meditation practice. Once we see the reactive, conditioned nature of our thoughts and emotions, we begin to lose our attachment to them: We no longer identify so strongly with our "personality." Understanding our lack of freedom also gives us empathy for the common predicament of all humanity. From these insights can come a feeling of unity, as well as the great love and compassion that so often guide the holy fools in their responses to the world. Once the "wild monkey" mind has been tamed it can become the "servant of the heart"—a "mind of love and clarity." When there is no "you," it is all you.

If knowledge does not liberate the self from the self, then ignorance is better than such knowledge.

SINA'I

To become a spectator of one's own life is to escape
the suffering of life.

OSCAR WILDE

Meditation might be considered theater. Think of it as a ticket to
step outside yourself in order to get some distance on your own little
drama—to become not only an actor on the world's stage but a member of the audience as well. This process helps us understand our personas as the masks that they are—the archetypes we are cast to portray. As part of the audience we can view the productions we are in as
"plays"—sometimes parodies, and at best musical comedies. For
some, it all looks like the theater of the absurd.

The theater of meditation requires that part of the mind be
trained as an observer, known by various names: the "witness," "the
other," or the "higher self." Climb into the balcony of your consciousness and find a seat. Once you see yourself from up there,
everything begins to look different. Establishing this point of reference is sometimes called getting a "cosmic perspective."

If you are going to practice this theater game, crazy wisdom has
some advice: Give your observer a sense of humor. No need to have
a grim higher self. Just put a wry, bemused smile on the face of your
witness. Your *cosmic* perspective can also be a *comic* perspective. If we
just get some distance, the cosmic and comic become One and the
same. And the joke is on us.

But wait! There is another way of looking at things. Some meditation masters say the way to gain a cosmic perspective is to get out
of those seats in our heads and back *inside* our bodies. They claim that
the best seat in the house is located somewhere near the abdomen.

Perhaps the best advice for gaining cosmic perspective is just to
move. Wherever you are, you can't see *where* you are unless you go
someplace else.

> Journeys bring power and love
> back into you. If you can't go somewhere,
> move in the passageways of the self.
> They are like shafts of light,
> always changing, and you change
> when you explore them.
>
> RUMI

121

We are not free. And the sky
can still fall on our heads.
And the theater has been
created to teach us that first
of all.

ANTONIN ARTAUD

CHAPTER ELEVEN

# Crazy Wisdom on the Road

Those who possess crazy wisdom have an uncommon perspective. They view themselves and the world from odd angles, or from great distances of space and time. Somehow they get the bigger picture and are able to see how all the pieces fit together. We will now try our own exercise in perspective. For this, we borrow methods from Socrates and Chuang Tzu, and begin to turn over a few persistent and puzzling questions that we humans ask about ourselves. This process should loosen attitudes and beliefs and allow our minds to stretch. It's a kind of crazy wisdom workout.

## The Questions

Ever since we became aware of our own existence, humans have asked questions about the meaning of life. Questions like: Who are we? Why are we? Where do we come from? What are we supposed to be doing here? The answers that we have come up with over the centuries are at once silly and sublime, a security blanket for the frightened tribe and elegant examples of imagination. We have invented mythopoetic stories of creation and destruction, heavens and hells. Our answers have given us rationalizations, albeit absurd ones, for the injustices of life and death. Some of these answers have been organized into the world's great religions; others codified and honored as philosophical truths. In the realm of crazy wisdom there are many answers and no answer. As H. L. Mencken wrote:

> Penetrating so many secrets, we cease to believe in
> the unknowable. But there it sits nevertheless,
> calmly licking its chops.

For our exercise in crazy wisdom, we will examine a few of the timeless questions from the contemporary point of view, emphasizing the latest scientific discoveries in many fields. To keep us doubting and wondering, we will also call for the help of some of the crazy wisdom characters we met earlier.

With Coyote in the lead, a Taoist sage on our right and the Jester on our left, followed by a few Zen masters and a pack of clowns, artists, philosophers, and scientists, we now take up our poetry books and walking staffs and begin a journey through the mind of the world, tracking the river of questions to the foot of the tall mountain of answers. Once there we will climb and explore; looking under rocks and behind theories, inside of DNA molecules and spinning subatomic particles; and gazing out over vast vistas of space-time to consider the perennial puzzles of the universe and our place in it.

Throughout this journey of exploration, the members of our group will provide us with commentary and craziness. While we probably won't find the ultimate answers to the ultimate questions, we are not really looking for them anyway. We are looking for another point of view, and everywhere we go gives us that.

The scientists are very important to our journey, as they will provide many of the latest views of ourselves and the universe. Our scientific community includes—to ensure both a micro and macro perspective—a physicist who sees "in depth" and an astronomer who sees "far out." We will also bring along a biologist, a psychologist, an anthropologist, a geologist, and assorted other "ologists"—the truth holders of current culture. The Jester suggests that what we really need is a generalist, an astro-physio-bio-psycho-anthro-geo-pale-ontologist, to synthesize it all. That way, we could save on supplies and overhead. Unfortunately, no such being exists.

Where do we start? Let us imagine that one of our Zen masters, realizing that the first step is arbitrary, simply begins chanting, "Who? Who? Who?" Our journey begins with the most elementary enigma.

## Who Do You Think You Are?

Be humble for you are made of dung. Be noble for
you are made of stars.

SERBIAN PROVERB

Perhaps whales came into
being because nature had a
lot of extra plankton and
squid. What evolutionary
vacuum sucked humans
into existence?

GARY SNYDER

In the beginning—about fifteen billion years ago according to
the latest scientific evidence, give or take a few billion years—there
was a big bang: the great cosmic orgasm. Out of that first fireball
came the spin of atoms and the pattern of molecules, the cooked and
cooling contents of the cosmic soup, blasting away from itself in all
directions with a mighty roar that still echoes in the sea and in our
voices. At the moment of that bang, the forces that brought us to
what we are in this moment were set in motion.

Later—only 3,500 million years ago, give or take a few million
years—a bolt of lightning struck this planet's oozing primal mud
with such force and finesse that it turned chemistry into biology.
This combination of electricity and chemicals started off the multiple mutations that became us, the strange species of protoplasm we
call human—conscious of ourselves and aware that we will die; capable of creating vast mythologies and lilting bridges—spinning
through space on this lukewarm blue-green sphere without any idea
why we are here or what we are supposed to be doing.

Who are we and how do we fit into the bigger picture? And why
do we place such grave importance on our lives and the life of our
species? Has some poorly built survival mechanism made us into
awkward egocentrics and human chauvinists? Looking back on the
long difficult road of evolution, covering three and a half billion
years, what makes us believe we are its final destination?

Let's take a close look at ourselves, individually, standing alone
and naked. You go first. (We call in a physicist and a biochemist for
this examination.) Let's see now—looking closely we find that your
body is made up of approximately 90 percent water. (The Jester calls
the body "the sublime slime.") As we investigate further, we find
that this water, along with everything else in your body, is made entirely of atoms; looking even closer we find that those atoms are almost entirely empty space. Now, if your body is made of atoms, and
atoms are just empty space, then what is holding your clothes on?
Not only does the emperor have no clothes . . . *the clothes have no emperor!* Maybe all of us are just illusions in somebody else's magic act.

At this point, a Zen master smashes our illusory selves with his staff, and through the pain we have to conclude that human beings *are* real, after all. It is even possible that we are the most important reality of all. We know we want to be. We would like to believe that the gear in our brains that we call consciousness has separated us from the rest of creation for a reason. After all, this consciousness—along with the opposable thumb—has given us a tenuous mastery over our environment. What other creature can remove a piece of tree and make chopsticks from it? Which other species buys insurance? Possessing the power to think abstractly and the power to manipulate objects has led us to believe, perhaps rightly, that as individuals *and* as a species, we do have a special place in creation.

Nonetheless, there have always been humans among us who believe that we are not outstanding creatures, and certainly not very smart. A few skeptical jesters have had the combination of audacity and humility to make brilliant cases against their own species, denying that we are the perfect molecular mixture, the cellular summit, the apex of aspiration. They refuse to have such a low opinion of nature as to believe that humans are the best it can do. In *A Mencken Chrestomathy*, the jester H. L. Mencken takes a clear-eyed look at our species' physical attributes.

> All the errors and incompetencies of the Creator reach their climax in man. As a piece of mechanism he is the worst of them all; put beside him, even a salmon or a staphylococcus is a sound and efficient machine. He has the worst kidneys known to comparative zoology, and the worst lungs, and the worst heart. His eye, considering the work it is called upon to do, is less efficient than the eye of the earthworm; an optical instrument maker who made an instrument so clumsy would be mobbed by his customers. Alone of all the animals, terrestrial, celestial or marine, man is unfit by nature to go abroad in the world he inhabits. He must clothe himself, protect himself, swathe himself, armor himself. He is eternally in the position of a turtle born without a shell, a dog without hair, a fish without fins. Lacking his heavy and cumbersome trappings, he is defenseless even against flies. As God made him he hasn't even a tail to switch them off.

If man had created man he would be ashamed of his performance.

MARK TWAIN

Mark Twain also held the opinion that we are an incompetently built species. In "Satan's Letter from the Earth," he makes it clear that our defects are not limited to the physical:

> (Man) . . . is constantly inflicted with a defect . . . the Moral Sense. It is the secret of his degradation. It is the quality which *enables him to do wrong*. Without it, man could do no wrong. He would rise at once to the level of the Higher Animals.

Twain saw the human species as disjointed, out of harmony with itself and the rest of creation. His opinion of *The Damned Human Race* was that we are on the bottom rung of evolution's ladder.

> . . . we have descended and degenerated, from some far ancestor—some microscopic atom wandering at its pleasure between the mighty horizons of a drop of water perchance—insect by insect, animal by animal, reptile by reptile, down the long highway of smirchless innocence, till we have reached the bottom stage of development— nameable as the Human Being. Below us—nothing. Nothing but the Frenchman.

Quite a few psychologists (as well as some holy fools) have added their voices to Mencken's and Twain's, reminding us that for the most part we are "unconscious," barely aware of or in control of ourselves, often ruled by much the same forces as those beings we call "the lower animals." (Coyote looks up from what he is doing and winks.) And one more thing. Even if humans are at the top of the evolutionary ladder, we sure did step on a lot of toes getting here— passenger pigeon toes and the three toes of the three-toed sloth, to name just a few. Since the story isn't over yet, we might well ask who or what will step on human toes on their climb to the top.

An evolutionary biologist might argue that our special human abilities, which we have long considered to be precious gifts from the gods, are just the latest result of the evolutionary crapshoot, nothing but temporary and possibly unsuccessful survival mechanisms. If any of a million conditions had been the slightest bit different, we would not be here, or if we were, it might be as something no one today would recognize as "human."

Nature has no instructions for mankind except that our poor beleaguered humanist-democratic way of life, our fantasies of the individual's high worth, our sense that the weak, no less than the strong, have a right to survive, are absurd.

JOYCE CAROL OATES

Evolution, like history, is more a matter of chance than logic.

STEPHEN JAY GOULD

In the last two centuries we have switched the focus of our investigation of who we are from the creation theory to the evolution theory. We no longer ask what God is like, or why He made us the way we are. Instead, we try to figure out how molecules and cells transformed themselves into consciousness and the opposable thumb. The tentative conclusions we have come up with are somewhat surprising.

Here is one hypothesis, which looks at the last few hundred thousand years of human evolution for an explanation of how we happened to arrive at our current condition. The fact that we are able to read and comprehend the following scenario may be the end result of an ice age—a veritable "blizzard" of evolutionary activity.

Fossil records show that approximately one million years ago, the human brain suddenly began to grow at an unprecedented rate, adding about one cubic inch every hundred thousand years. Then the growth rate doubled, and doubled again, until the brain was growing by *ten* cubic inches every hundred thousand years. Some scientists speculate that the phenomenal growth was triggered by a great ice age, the first in hundreds of millions of years, and thus the first since humans had inhabited the planet. By the time the glaciers were advancing, about eight hundred thousand years ago, humans had already migrated to northern regions of the earth from their point of origin near the equator. The drastic climate change required man to develop many new survival tools, and some scientists speculate that the brain's sudden growth was stimulated by that situation. About one hundred thousand years ago, brain growth stopped and no new gray matter has been added since.

In other words it may be that nothing but ice started the fire in our skulls. Our great energy and ingenuity could simply be the result of being cold; consciousness may be nature's way of shoveling snow! What, then, can we make of the elaborate civilizations and cultures that evolved during the last few hundred thousand years? Perhaps they are side effects of nervous energy left over from our struggle to conquer the elements—energy that continues to find outlets in nuclear bombs and symphonies and skyscrapers full of people writing coded messages to one another. Perhaps war itself is a response left over from a time of competition for sparse resources, a time dominated by our fear of the cold. Maybe that same fear begat the cold war. All that we do today may be the final shivers of an age, not so long ago, when we did not have central heating.

128

In his book, *Timescale*, science writer Nigel Calder offers his own poetic view of how humans fit into the evolutionary scheme:

> In caricatures of Mother Earth, where land masses ran riot, the first lords were colored slime, then upstart worms, then sprawling mammal-like reptiles, all for far longer intervals than humans have existed. In Darwin's paleontological estimation, ours is not so much the era of the risen ape as the Age of Barnacles. Holy mountains turn out to be wreckage of continental traffic accidents, while Chicago and Leningrad sit in the chairs of glaciers gone for lunch. All in all, the refurbished creation myth owes more to Groucho than to Karl Marx. It is a tale of hungry molecules making dinosaurs and remodeling them as ducks; also of cowboys who put to sea, quelled the world with a magnetic needle, and then wagered their genes against a mushroom cloud that knowledge was a Good Thing.

Our most recent scientific discoveries raise great doubts about our lofty place in the cosmic scheme. Compounding those doubts are the current planetary crises—ecological disasters, overpopulation, nuclear weapons—which call into question our ability to survive as a species and, therefore, our claim to a special destiny. The doubts and questions of the current age are deeply disturbing to our individual and collective egos. Are we the Creator's pets or just another complex chemical compound? Is the state of consciousness uniquely human, or is there consciousness everywhere; and if so, did we get the wrong dose? Are we stuck in a transitional time warp, our lives merely a phase like the one between fish and frog, crawling from sea to land in an evolutionary mid-life crisis? Will we need to grow a new kind of eyelid to survive the blinding light to come, or a new type of lung to breathe thicker air? Must we go back to webbed feet to navigate the landscape after the oceans rise? What part of our anatomy will begin to grow and lead us to our next destiny? What sleek new species is waiting to be born from our dilemmas? And meanwhile, what genetic backwater has left us washed up on the shore of this age, gasping for breath, caught between what we were and what we will yet become? What unknowable perfect plan could have designed us like this, floundering between feelings of self-importance and doubt? In the big story of life, who could we be? Scientist Robert Ardrey offers this guess:

We are a tiny little twig of the mammalian tree, an afterthought. Nature was not made for us.

STEPHEN JAY GOULD

We are the missing link.

We need to pause here for a moment. It seems an argument has broken out between a few members of our wandering troupe. Some philosophers and scientists are quarreling over whether we can ever know who we are. A clown, hearing this dispute, tries to solve the problem by simply introducing people to each other. A Zen master is impressed by this solution and bows to the clown. The Zen master then asks, "Isn't it also true that we are what we eat?" On hearing this, the Jester rolls his eyes and says, "If you are what you eat, then why be a vegetable? Why not eat people who are smarter and better-looking than you?" Surprisingly, the Jester does not get hit with a staff for this remark.

In the hope that greater perspective might give us some answers, an astronomer suggests that we head out into space to look at humans from there. We know that the farther away we get from ourselves, the smaller we will look; maybe this will allow us to see the larger patterns. Maybe we will notice some clue to our meaning in the universe.

Of course, to live on a planet is to live in outer space already. Once we get *off* the earth we are able to see that clearly. In fact, one of the best views of earth is from space. Once we get far enough away, we don't see dead animals on the roadsides or beer cans in the rivers or the grimacing faces of city commuters. If we get far enough away, the earth doesn't look dirty. It doesn't even look "earthy." It looks more like a misted marble or a slightly sucked-on, dampish blue gumball.

If we had been monitoring earth from our perch here in space during the past few hundred million years, we might have detected an ominous new development. Up until about one hundred years ago the earth seemed relatively stable. Of course glaciers and continents slowly shifted and the occasional volcano erupted, but nothing too dramatic. The earth was just another cooling hunk of stuff. Then suddenly, at the beginning of the twentieth century, a series of atmospheric disturbances occurred: Waves radiated from the earth—electrical waves, sound waves, light waves—leaping into the sky and around the earth and out into space. Some waves had definite patterns, and anyone on another planet able to detect these might have surmised that intelligent life was transmitting messages. To creatures who could not detect the patterns, it may have looked as if the earth had started decaying.

Also about a hundred years ago, big hunks of solid matter began leaving the earth's surface. Objects in the shape of large birds flew out and back again. Out and back. And as time went on, more and more and bigger and bigger objects came off. Frequent and progressively larger explosions occurred on the earth's surface, sending ever bigger pieces of matter into the air. Soon, big cylinders shot off the planet and orbited around it. In a very short period, the space surrounding the earth, previously empty, became filled with pieces of the earth itself. From anywhere else in space, our planet must have looked as if it had started coming apart.

Could it be that technology is an unwitting euphemism for the process of entropy? Are we simply agents of this planet's disintegration, catalysts for an evolutionary process that takes place without our knowledge or choice?

Looking around the rest of the universe, we realize that the big bang set enormous forces into motion and created huge galaxies of burning stars, each locked into some inexorable course. We see that we are infinitesimal parts of the celestial movement of matter, completely at its mercy. If the cosmos has importance and a purpose, perhaps we can claim the same for ourselves; if it has no larger meaning, we can only assume that we are just along for the ride. If the universe keeps expanding, eventually thinning to nothing, we will go with it. If the universe collapses back on itself (in what scientists call the big crunch) and another big bang starts a new cycle, then we may be reborn, too, in one form or another. In any case, we have no way to escape the hold of physical elements; we are bound to the destiny of all matter.

Physicists agree that we are intimately connected to the cosmos, but they look at this phenomenon from another point of view. Deep inside matter, physicists are finding that each subatomic event is affected by all other subatomic events everywhere in space-time, even when separated by great distances. To describe this interdependence,

Life is a disease of matter.

GERALD FINEBERG

We are, ultimately, the product of primeval forces mediated by the X and Y bosons.

ANTHONY ZEE

physicists claim that reality is "non-local," meaning that the entire universe and everything that happens within it is one interconnected web of occurrence. No autonomy and no separate purpose can exist.

> Leaving us flying like birds into time
>    —eyes and car headlights—
>    The shrinkage of emptiness
> in the Nebulae
> these Galaxies cross like pinwheels and they pass
>     like gas—
>
> ALLEN GINSBERG

The Taoist sage would like to remind us that being part of everything does not make us less, it makes us more. Pointing at the heavens, he quotes the Hindus, who are fond of saying, "Thou art That." Meanwhile, the Jester—a little bored out here in space with no civilization to poke fun at—wants us to move closer to earth. The clowns feel right at home flying around with the furniture in this weightless environment, but a vote is taken and we head back toward home.

As we approach earth from our perch in space, we start to get a better view of all the little creatures that live and die on the surface of the planet. Looking at things from this shorter distance we find that, contrary to what we often assume, humans are not masters of the other forms of life on earth. In *Timescale*, Nigel Calder speculates that plants are earth's real rulers.

> . . . certain cunning plants have taken over the choicest parts of the Earth's surface . . . their apparent passivity is deceptive: they manipulate the animals. [These plants] . . . have recruited battalions of small six-legged and large two-legged animals to serve them. The reproductive self-interest of the plants requires that animals find their flowers attractive, their nectar and fruit tasty. Beside a bed of particularly elegant flowers, a biped stoops in a humble posture, carefully removing any plants except those that have charmed him to their service. Other bipeds swarm in large numbers around the green rectangles in the river valleys.
>
> The master of the planet is now identifiable: it is grass.

Grass first evolved its biped slaves, the human beings, as hunters on the grasslands, and then lured them into the cultivation of special grasses, including wheat, rice, and maize. With unstinted effort, the humans cleared trees and other plants out of the way, and they irrigated the kempt fields for the benefit of grass.

Even if the amber waves of grain are not in charge completely, we are totally dependent on them, and should perhaps honor and pray to the goddesses of grasses more than we have. Maybe we aren't giving due attention to the grasses because we have switched our allegiance to a different master. In *Autogeddon*, Heathcote Williams writes:

> If an alien were to hover a few
> hundred yards above the planet
> It could be forgiven for thinking
> That cars were the dominant life-form,
> And that human beings were a kind of
> ambulatory fuel cell:
> Injected when the car wished to move off,
> And ejected when they were spent.

Perhaps automobiles *are* our new master, intentionally destroying the grasses as they take over the human slave market. Grasses or automobiles, gods or material goods—in the final analysis, as Ralph Waldo Emerson saw, "things are in the saddle and ride mankind." We are not lords of all we survey.

As our group settles back down to earth and feels the pull of gravity again, we really start wondering where our freedom lies. Although most of us admit we are not in charge of the matter and energy of the cosmos or the life of our planet, we still feel we are in control of our own destinies—at least in little ways. A few artists and philosophers in our group insist that they are free and independent, and, furthermore, that they are significant (famous, even immortal) in the larger scheme of things. To answer them, the Taoist master faces the wind, letting his long beard and hair be whipped about by the invisible element, and audibly breaks a little wind himself. With a slightly sentimental shrug, he says, "Our greatest bondage may be to the illusion that we are free."

## FREEDOM'S JUST ANOTHER WORD

The perceptual blind spot that gives us the impression that we are separate from the rest of creation also may have fostered the belief that we are in control, not only of our environment but also of *ourselves*. Debate regarding the truth of this belief used to be primarily a religious matter, known as the "free will/determinism" argument. Disagreement centered on the amount of freedom the Creator had given us to act, or more specifically, to sin or not to sin.

Back when most of Western civilization believed that God was in control of our lives, we often assumed that He could be bribed with a few good deeds or contrite supplications, which left us some degree of choice over our destiny. However, in the twentieth century, science has investigated the free will/determinism question by taking a close look at the biological and psychological makeup of the individual. As the ancient saying goes, self-knowledge is usually bad news.

> Do you think I know what I'm doing?
> That for one breath or half-breath I belong to myself?
> As much as a pen knows what it's writing,
> or the ball can guess where it's going next.
>
> RUMI

What science is discovering about the human condition conforms with much of what holy fools have understood for centuries. It seems to come down to this: Not only are we not in charge of the cosmos or the planet, we are barely in charge of ourselves. This has serious implications for the Western worldview, something Freud realized early in the twentieth century:

> Humanity has in the course of time had to endure from the
> hands of science two great outrages upon its self-love.

The first was when it realized that our earth was not the center of the universe. . . . The second was when biological research robbed man of his peculiar privilege of having been specially created, and relegated him to descent from the animal world, implying an irradicable animal nature in him. . . . But man's craving for grandiosity is now suffering the third and most bitter blow from present day psychological research, which is endeavoring to prove to the ego in each one of us that he is not even master in his own house. . . .

We may never know the extent to which we are free, but it seems safe to say that we attribute to ourselves much more freedom than we actually have. Most people feel they act independently from moment to moment; few even consider the question of the degree to which we control our individual lives, as we have absorbed the assumption of free will so thoroughly. While some acknowledge the large roles conditioning or interdependence play, it is not usually an internalized awareness, and they often forget, when involved in life from moment to moment, the truth of the matter.

Human freedom seems to be severely circumscribed by our fundamental biochemical makeup. Science writer Jon Franklin studied the field of molecular psychology and, in his Pulitzer Prize–winning book, *Molecules of the Mind*, asserts that our belief in free will is itself determined:

> And so, multileveled Mother Nature, wry and cruel but at times strangely benevolent, has inserted a mechanism in the mechanism to prevent that mechanism from fully comprehending its mechanistic nature. Faith itself, in other words, is but mechanism.

Biochemists are reporting that moods and emotions are closely associated with certain chemicals. What we call love, for example, may be understood as the presence of an "excitant amine" known as phenylethylamine, or PEA, in our system. Mice injected with PEA jump up and down and vocalize, while rhesus monkeys exhibit "lip smacking behavior." (Coyote wants to know where he can buy some of this stuff.)

Meanwhile, the latest evidence from biologists indicates that each of us is shackled from birth to a genetically determined future, bound by the chains of the DNA double helix. We are imprisoned in our cells.

Biogeneticists tell us that the DNA molecule is programmed with information that determines how tall we will grow and how strong our teeth will be, what illnesses we are likely to contract, and, to some degree, how long we will live. It is as if we are each born into a spy novel—as the plot unfolds, our identity is gradually revealed. As if that's not enough, our genes provide each of us with a face that we must wear from birth (unless we take drastic measures), whether or not it is considered beautiful. A thick head of hair or a nearsighted squint or lopsided ears—these are features that affect how the world looks at us, and therefore how we look back at the world. (The clowns glance at each other and start to laugh.) On the physical level, at least, we are not *free* to be ourselves; we are *forced* to be ourselves.

Our belief in freedom is also challenged seriously by recent brain research revealing that humans actually have three distinct brains: what might be called a reptilian brain, a mammalian brain, and the new cerebral cortex, or "human" brain. Although we make maximum use of our reptilian and mammalian brains, experiments show we use our new, human brain at about 15 percent capacity. To add insult to this insult, writer and educator Joseph Chilton Pearce speculates that 15 percent is used only to rationalize the reactive behavior of our reptilian and mammalian brains. Humans have the unique ability to make up excuses for ourselves as we go along. (Coyote winks again.)

In *Galapagos*, Kurt Vonnegut looks back at our world from a million years in the future, by which time it is obvious that today's brains did not work very well:

> Apologies for momentary brain failures were the staple of everybody's conversations: "Whoops," "Excuse me," "I hope you're not hurt," "I can't believe I did that," "It happened so fast I didn't have time to think," "I have insurance against this kind of thing," and "How can I ever forgive myself?" and "I didn't know it was loaded," and on and on.

135

Did you know the RNA/DNA molecule can be found throughout space in many galaxies . . . only everybody spells it differently?

JANE WAGNER

Contemplating the mechanism of our own minds and gazing morosely on the chemical action and reaction that equate with consciousness and personality, we seem directed toward the dark conclusion that free will is but a concept designed, like Santa Claus or God, to shield us from the unacceptable truth. The truth, we are terrified of learning, is that we are chaff in the wind. . . .

JON FRANKLIN

Someday the brain's evolution may provide us with a more comprehensive or different type of self-awareness, which will allow us the freedom to act instead of just reacting. We may need to become conscious in a more profound sense of the word before we can be free. As the poet Robert Bly states:

> The reptile brain has embodied itself in the outer
> world in the form of a tank which even moves like
> a reptile. A "saint" is someone who has managed to
> move away from the reptile and the mammal
> brains and is living primarily in the new brain.

From another angle, psychologists tell us that individual freedom is completely circumscribed by our early upbringing. As infants, we ingest our parents and then spend the rest of our lives trying to digest them. We eat them whole, from their genes to their judgments. We eat their values, their fears, their moods, their worldviews; even if we rebel against them, they shape that rebellion. Their voices continuously echo inside of us. We never leave home.

Psychologists tell us that we are stuck inside personalities which are almost completely formed in our earliest years, long before we could decide who we wanted to be. Considering humanity's lofty view of itself, we might find the Freudian viewpoint especially humbling—much of who we are depends on how we were potty-trained. Is it possible to break loose somehow from our deepest, earliest conditioning?

So many strings tie us to the past, to people, to politics; there are so many ways to view conditioning and so many ways to take it apart. Volumes have been written about how we are programmed to conform to the values and fashions of the society into which we are born. Even the strong identification some people have with "freedom" and "individuality" may be merely a product of a particular set of cultural values. Adding another dimension, geological anthropologists (or anthropological geologists) talk about "geographic determinism"—the hypothesis that our perception of reality is shaped, at least partially, by the mountains or the flatlands that surround us.

Cosmic, geological, biological, psychological, cultural, political—so many forces shape us. And we haven't even mentioned the possibility of past lives influencing the present one, the most important factor in many Eastern philosophies of who we are. So why *do*

A person is never himself
but always a mask; a person
never owns his own person,
but always represents
another, by whom he is
possessed. And the other
that one is, is always
ancestors. . . .

NORMAN O. BROWN

What I most want
is to spring out of this
    personality,
then to sit apart from that
    leaping.
I've lived too long where I
    can be reached.

RUMI

we have the profound conviction that we are free and independent beings who shape and control our own destinies? Can we make a case for some degree of individual autonomy or personal freedom? Our Taoist sage offers a paradoxical answer from Chuang Tzu, his favorite source:

> Let your mind wander in simplicity, blend your spirit with the vastness, follow along with things the way they are, and make no room for personal views—then the world will be governed.

Most members of our group are intrigued with this question of human freedom. A few clowns stick out their tongues and bop each other, trying to prove they are free by acting spontaneously, until a philosopher points out that this is their normal behavior, and thus predictable. In the melee, a Zen master gets bopped by mistake; he claims that he demonstrates his freedom by choosing not to *react* to the blow. He gets bopped again, this time intentionally. Meanwhile, an artist who is hungry for new scenery points out that we are going around in circles and getting nowhere. The Taoist sage remarks, "We are getting nowhere only because we think we are going somewhere in the first place." Hearing this, a clown asks innocently, "Well, if we aren't going somewhere, then why are we here?" At this, everyone bursts into great laughter.

> Life is too important a thing ever to talk seriously about it.
>
> OSCAR WILDE

## Why Are We Here?

> The meaning of life is that it stops.
> FRANZ KAFKA

Contemporary street wisdom informs us that "Life's a bitch and then you die." This could be the first line of a couplet ending with the line: "And nobody knows the reason why." What *is* the meaning of this life we live?

Existential uncertainty is difficult if not impossible for many people to live with. Knowledge is our survival mechanism, and we have a nervous biological craving to know just what is going on. We want certainty, especially about the meaning of our lives, and if we can't find certainty in knowledge, then many will turn to blind faith. In *Waiting for Godot*, Samuel Beckett makes it clear that blind is really the only kind of faith there is.

> VLADIMIR: What are we doing here, that is the question. And we are blessed in this, that we happen to know the answer. Yes, in this immense confusion one thing alone is clear. We are waiting for Godot to come . . .

We can't accept that life is nothing more than the moments between birth and death. That would be absurd! Our existence—our suffering—must have some greater significance, and if the universe won't tell us what it is, then we will have to make something up. Enter the multitude of gods and religions. (Choose one of the above.)

In this secular era, many old gods have been replaced with ideologies, or "isms," or nation-states, or even lifestyles. If we can't discover the one supreme reason for existing, we create relatively satisfying earthbound purposes: a utopian future, or "freedom," or "progress," or "the children," or "all the gusto." We also have Joseph Campbell's view:

The believer is happy, the doubter wise.

GREEK PROVERB

> I don't believe life has a *purpose*. Life is a lot of protoplasm with an urge to reproduce and continue in being.

Maybe that's all we're here to do: "Go forth and multiply." Just be and beget and be and beget and be and beget, until some cosmic catastrophe ends it all. Or maybe one great truth or purpose does exist for which all of us are living or should be living, and we just don't know it yet. One day we may discover we were put here to develop the best possible basketball team for the intergalactic tournament, or to serve as hosts for microbes that are the Creator's true chosen ones. Or maybe we are part of someone's experiment to determine whether we can figure out why we are here, and our confusion, like that of rats in a maze, is the whole point.

Perhaps someday the one *true* god or goddess will appear and say, "Nobody got my name right." Or maybe *all* deities exist but none of them are "good," and they take no interest in whether or not we are good. Could it be that all these years we have been good only for goodness' sake? Maybe all of our questions will be answered one day. Maybe they won't. Gertrude Stein claims she has already found the answer:

> There ain't no answer.
> There ain't going to be any answer.
> There never has been an answer.
> That's the answer.

But this raises another question. If we aren't meant to know, then why this "why?" Another damn "why!" Why why why? What kind of joke is this? Why do we carry the "why" chromosome? Where will our questions lead us?

> God made man because he loves stories.
> YIDDISH SAYING

Let's assume that we *are* here to provide stories. Here is a good one. Once upon a time, in fact only a few hundred years ago, most Westerners believed that humans lived on a planet that was located at the very center of the universe. Then a great scientist named Galileo figured out that the earth circles the sun, and therefore the *sun* must be the center. The Catholic church, believing that humans had been specially created, and therefore that the earth had to be the center of the universe, forced Galileo to recant. This took place back in the 1630s, but the Church did not forgive Galileo until 1979. By then, astronomers and physicists had discovered that the sun itself is a relatively small star located on the edge of a relatively small galaxy in a cosmos that includes billions of galaxies filled with uncountable billions of stars. The Vatican absolved Galileo, but made no further pronouncement as to the center of the universe.

So, where *is* the center of the universe? And where are we in relation to it? Have we been pushed into the wings? Is the earth just a backdrop for a truly meaningful drama happening thousands of galaxies away, and humanity merely a crowd of extras spinning around the lead characters who play their parts on center stage—light-years from earth?

Like any crazy wisdom story, this one has yet another twist. Astronomers have recently found that the big bang sent everything in the universe moving away from everything else uniformly in all directions, so that, in fact, every single point in the universe can be considered the center. "That's you, baby!" the Jester says, laughing. "You are still the center of the universe, just as you always believed and hoped you would be!"

The clowns puff out their chests, obviously proud, but a physicist stands up and clears his throat to get our attention. Holding up a picture of Albert Einstein for effect, he reminds us that since the discovery of space-time, it is impossible to locate ourselves in space (*where* we are) unless we simultaneously locate ourselves in time (*when* we are). Where and when are one. This may mean that, as many of us have suspected, maps and clocks are unreliable.

Our group agrees that the time has come to look at time. But first, all of us must synchronize ourselves in the moment. Is everybody ready? **Be here now!** Whoops, you missed it. Don't worry; the here and now will certainly come around again. Next time you may be better prepared.

## Time Out

Read not the Times, read the Eternities.
HENRY DAVID THOREAU

One way crazy wisdom gets crazy and wise is by playing with time—going into the past or the future to see what the present looks like from a different angle. Travel broadens. Time travel changes everything.

Humans today divide their lifespans and their history into segments: millennia, centuries, decades, years, months, hours, minutes, seconds. However, according to the laws of physics, fixing *any* firm date, including today's or New Year's Eve's, is impossible. Time, after all, is relative to space, and both may be relative to something else. Nonetheless, people need to know when rent is due, how long the egg has been boiling, and whether they are wearing the appropriate costume for this decade. For practical reasons, we need to set our watches and use this year's calendar. However, the popular

There was a young lady named Bright
Whose speed was much faster than light.
She went out one day
In a relative way,
And returned the previous night.

ANONYMOUS

saying "Your time is what you make it" may be true in more ways than one. Whether your life is long or short depends entirely on your expectations and your concept of time.

For example, scientists keep finding evidence that indicates the universe is older than previously thought, and our own lifetimes seem to shrink in comparison. On the other hand, we still live a long time compared to the mayfly, whose life lasts only a day. What if the weather is bad that particular day? A mayfly's whole life could be rained out. Even within our own species, there is great variation. Consider that, compared to people in the East, people in the Western world measure time and history almost as though they were mayflies.

## The Time of Your Lives

> The world was created on 22nd October, 4004 B.C. at 6 o'clock in the evening.
>
> JAMES USHER
> *Archbishop of Armagh, 1581–1656*

> [Heaven and earth] and man was created by the Trinity on the 23rd of October, 4004 B.C., at nine o'clock in the morning.
>
> DR. JOHN LIGHTFOOT,
> *Vice Chancellor of the University of Cambridge, in 1859, correcting by 15 hours Bishop Usher's estimate of two centuries earlier*

Western belief systems have stuck us firmly in the limited spectrum of recorded human history, with very little breathing room. The Judeo-Christian tradition claims that the universe is just a few thousand years old, which does not give life much of a past, and leaves no room at all for dinosaurs.

Judeo-Christian history lends current human affairs a significance far beyond that allowed by the vast timetables of other cultures. The eternal cycles or endless renewals essential to Asian and Native American mythology are absent from Western belief. Biblical texts make no mention of past worlds or worlds to come. We are told that Jehovah made the world in a week, that earth is the only world there has ever been or ever will be, and that human history is the primary measure of time.

Eastern cosmologies include beliefs of endless cycles and worlds upon worlds upon worlds. Hindus measure time in divisions called *yugas*, four of which make up one *mahayuga*, which covers a period of 4,320,000 years. One thousand *mahayugas* make up one *kalpa*, or complete "world system." (A world system can be thought of as the time between two big bangs.) In the Hindu cosmology, one "world system" is equivalent to just *one day* in the life of their supreme deity, Brahma. One hundred years of these "days," or 311,000 billion human years, completes the supreme deity's lifespan. However, according to the Hindu text, the *Brahmavaivarta Purana*, not even Brahma, the creator, can lord it over time: "Brahma follows Brahma; one sinks, the next arises; the endless series cannot be told."

Similarly, the Buddhist concept of time is beyond human comprehension. The Buddha offers a graphic picture of this vastness. He describes a granite mountain seven miles high and seven miles wide. Every one hundred years a crow with a silk scarf in its beak flies over the mountain, brushing the top of the peak. The time it takes for that scarf to wear down the mountain completely makes up one world cycle. Then, of course, comes another granite mountain. Make room for the crow, Sisyphus.

In the previous chapter we watched the Buddha calculate the incalculable number of atoms in the universe. This measurement system can also be applied to time. Depending on one's calculations, either three, seven, or thirty-three incalculables will occur before the end of time. Presumably, how an incalculable compares to an infinity is still being worked out.

Anthropologist-philosopher Mircea Eliade claims that all of these Eastern concepts of time result in a "metaphysical depreciation of human history." Vast incalculables are humbling in two respects: Not only are time and the universe much bigger than us, we can't even figure out *how* much bigger.

With the big bang theory, which places the age of the universe at about fifteen billion years, Western science is just beginning to peek into the possible vastness of time. Astrophysicists are now hypothesizing the big crunch, during which our universe will collapse into a single particle and then, possibly, explode in another big bang. When the Dalai Lama, the Tibetan Buddhist leader, was asked what he thought of the big bang theory, he replied, laughing, "Oh yes, we know about that. But it's not just *one* Bang. It's Bang, Bang, Bang!" It could be that the West is finally coming to its own version of the ancient Eastern worldview: the cyclical, repeating nature of time and universes. The difference is that our understanding of these cycles will be through the language of black holes and curved space, rather than through visions of granite mountains or of Lord Shiva, who creates and destroys world systems with each step of his dancing feet.

Our crazy wisdom group is resting. Coyote begins howling at the moon, but we can't be sure which of the infinity of moons he howls at, or what world system it belongs to. Meanwhile, a few astrophysicists are feverishly trying to figure out if Asian cosmology could fit into their current theories. Our scientists are concerned that, if Eastern "incalculables" turn out to be real, a lot of mathematicians will be out of jobs and a considerable number of Nobel Prizes may need to be returned.

One puzzled physicist asks the Taoist sage how, without infrared tracking devices and radio telescopes, the ancient Eastern sages came to their understanding of time and world cycles. The Taoist answers, enigmatically of course, "By paying attention." At this point, the Zen master interjects, "The only instrument that tells time accurately is the stomach. When we get hungry, it's time to eat; beyond that, all this talk makes little difference." The Jester, who is beginning to like these Zen sayings, jumps up and raises his hand to give the Zen master a high five, but the Zen master hits him with his staff instead and shouts, "It makes a big difference!"

Oriental and Occidental ideas of time create distinctly different attitudes toward life. The Judeo-Christian worldview, with its single universe, gives each of us just this one lifetime to get it right. At the end, we are led to believe, we will be judged on how well we performed, and rewarded or punished for all eternity. What a heavy burden! One or two mistakes and we are doomed forever, unless of course we are one of God's chosen, who will be forgiven all sins. Pray that you pray to the right deity! In the West, even those who don't actively believe in the Judeo-Christian mythology are deeply influenced by it. Most of us live as though this lifetime were the final exam, the first and last chance.

I used to believe in reincarnation, but that was in a past life.

PAUL KRASSNER

In the West we hear, "You only go around once in life so reach for all the gusto." The Truth in Advertising Council should have required the beer manufacturer who used that slogan to *prove* that we only go around once. A great percentage of the world's population doesn't believe it.

Both the Hindu and Buddhist views of life are much more open-ended. In these belief systems, humans are given many lifetimes to achieve perfection and salvation. In fact, in Hinduism everyone is destined to rebirth after rebirth until each person finally has the experience of *moksha*, or enlightenment and can leave the rebirth wheel. In other words, in the Hindu system, we are all saved eventually. If you are tired of the go-round and want to get off sooner, you work harder, but everyone and everything makes it someday. Making it means that you dissolve into emptiness and return to the uncreated, unconditioned state—the uncarved block, the void, the blankness of perfect peaceful nothing.

But wait! This Eastern cosmology with its multiple lifetimes and eventual salvation is not all good news. According to Eliade, philosophy that believes in rebirth:

terrorizes man and compels him to realize that he must begin this same evanescent existence over and over again, billions of times, always enduring the same endless sufferings. And the effect of this is to exacerbate his will to escape, to impel him to transcend his condition as an "existent" once and for all.

The Buddha said that the tears one individual sheds throughout a cycle of lifetimes could fill all the rivers, lakes, and oceans on earth. For people who believe in reincarnation, the idea of many more lifetimes looms over them, an appalling proposition, perhaps somewhat akin to the Western concept of an eternity in purgatory. East or West, take your pick. If it isn't one thing, it's another.

According to most Eastern mythologies, we can be reborn in different forms and in other realms of existence: as a *deva* (angel) in a heavenly realm, or as a hungry ghost in a universe of terrible suffering. In these systems, human birth is considered precious, because it is as humans that we can best understand our predicament and work toward our liberation from the wheel of rebirth. In addition, human incarnations are rare. A Buddhist parable asks us to imagine that on one side of the world a blind turtle is set loose into the seven seas, while, on the other side of the world, a wooden yoke is set to float freely on those same seas. The chance of the blind turtle surfacing with its head through that yoke is the same slim chance we have of being reincarnated as humans.

145

A few members of our group have begun telling each other what they want to be in their next lives. The Jester, half serious, asks a Zen master, "Is it possible I could be reincarnated in a place with no government?" The Zen master smiles and replies, "With your karma you will probably be reborn as the vice-president." Meanwhile, a few of the scientists who have been conferring come forward with a statement, possibly hoping to reclaim the high ground from the Asian sages. They contend that Eastern cosmologies still talk as if time is an absolute that goes in one direction. They conclude with the words of one of their own masters, Albert Einstein, who wrote:

> People like us, who believe in physics, know that
> the distinction between past, present, and future is
> only a stubbornly persistent illusion.

Now wait a minute—if there is any such thing. Are all our concepts of time, Eastern and Western alike, nothing but fantasy? If no past, present, or future occurs, does that mean we won't get old and die? If time in the conventional sense doesn't exist, maybe we can all relax—there are no deadlines to meet and we are instantly immortal. If there is no distinction between present and future, then maybe you, the reader, are reading this word at the same time it is being written. (If so, please think of a good sentence to follow this one.)

"Be here now!" The Zen master tries this again, but of course everybody misses it, except for one clown who claims to have seized the moment and now offers to show it to anyone who wants to see. Meanwhile, most of our group members seem to have lost their bearings and appear dizzy or confused. The Taoist master explains that it is common to feel this way after looking deeply into the mysteries of space and time. After discovering that there is no center to the universe, no central standard time, no East, no West, no now, no then—we are left with no place from which to get our bearings. We are bound to become dizzy, if not crazy and wise. For clarification, the Taoist sage recites from Chuang Tzu:

> There is no end to the weighing of things, no stop to time, no constancy to the division of lots, no fixed rule to beginning and end. Therefore great wisdom observes both far and near, and for that reason recognizes small without considering it paltry, recognizes large without considering it unwieldy, for it knows that there is no end to the weighing of things. It has a clear understanding of past and present, and for that reason it spends a long time without finding it tedious, a short time without fretting at its shortness, for it knows that time has no stop. It perceives the nature of fullness and emptiness, and for that reason it does not delight if it acquires something nor worry if it loses it, for it knows that there is no constancy to the division of lots. It comprehends the Level Road, and for that reason it does not rejoice in life nor look on death as a calamity, for it knows that no fixed rule can be assigned to beginning and end.

Could it be that we just can't know anything? Many in our group are coming to this conclusion, if they weren't there when we started. A biologist who is convinced of our ignorance points out the irony in the fact that we have labeled our species "Homo sapiens," the man who is wise. However, a few other scientists feel this label is too modest. They are impressed with a recent, and utterly serious, movement in the scientific community to rename our species "Homo sapiens sapiens," the man who is *very* wise. Hearing this the Jester laughs and says, "If we were really wise we would reclassify ourselves as just humans, period. Then we wouldn't have so much to live up to." The scientists, whose reputations and livelihoods ride on this issue, hold their ground. Although we may not understand the ultimate meaning of life, they assert, we *are* smart enough to learn the laws of nature and how the universe works. At this, the Taoist master smiles and says, "This belief continues in each new generation, in spite of a long, long history of mistakes."

# What Do You Know?

Thou knowest no man can split the atom.
JOHN DALTON
*British chemist and physicist responsible for the modern conception of*
*atomic theory, 1803*

Heavier-than-air flying machines are impossible.
LORD KELVIN
*British mathematician, physicist, and president*
*of the British Royal Society, 1895*

Looking back on the history of "knowledge," it becomes clear that it changes every century and is different in each civilization. Still, most people believe that what *they* know about the world is true. For example, people once *knew* that the world was flat, that the sun went around the earth, and that space was fixed and absolute and filled with something called "ether." Indeed, it seems something of a miracle that we have managed to survive our own ignorance. For example, Johann Hartmann, a seventeenth-century chemistry professor, was highly regarded in his time for his medical knowledge:

> For epilepsy in adults I recommend spirit of human
> brain or a powder, to be compounded only in
> May, June and July, from the livers of live green
> frogs.

In spite of being "wrong," many ideas seem to have worked just fine for the people who knew them to be true. When the world was flat, nobody sailed out too far. When the sun rotated around the earth, people still harvested their crops in the right season. Religious beliefs don't seem to have affected human destiny any more than scientific ones. When Zeus rather than Jehovah ruled the heavens, life was about the same: a mixture of joys and sorrows. The quality of life may not have much to do with knowledge or belief.

Perhaps the quest for any kind of certainty is doomed to failure. Taoists and Dadaists and good historians would bow to that. Now even scientists tell us that there is no fixed, objective knowledge— nothing is independent of our subjective observations. In the end,

Knowledge is fashion.
ROBERT HARDIN

there may be no "objective" truth, only "projective" truth. What we find always depends on what we are looking for; what we look for depends on who we are and what we think we need to know. The questions are always part of the answer.

Some crazy wisdom critics say our quest for knowledge is futile, although relatively harmless. Others contend that our desire to know has outlived its value as a survival mechanism and is getting in the way. The radical doubters and hard-line curmudgeons assert that our search has been disastrous all along.

## Adam and the Apple and the Atom and the Eve of Destruction

> So when the woman saw that the tree was good for food, and that it was a delight to the eyes, and that the tree was to be desired to make one wise, she took of its fruit and ate; and she also gave some to her husband, and he ate.
>
> *Genesis 3:6*

> Curiosity killed the cat.
> **FOLK SAYING**

At best, knowledge has always been double-edged—both a blessing and a curse. The biblical story says that the pursuit of knowledge got us kicked out of the Garden of Eden. If Eve hadn't wanted to know what was going on, she wouldn't have eaten of the tree of knowledge. Today we might be in Paradise still, wandering blissfully in naked innocence, passing time by naming things, and enjoying the fruits that give no knowledge but sure taste good.

Our desire for certainty may be born from pride and fear, from our belief that we *can* know everything and our insecurity when we don't. So we keep searching for the elusive key that will unlock the fundamental mysteries. In the twentieth century, scientific materialism has led us to look for answers inside matter itself, as if by taking apart the world we could find a clue to the secrets of creation. The scientists split matter open; and they split it open again. And again. And when they finally got to the atom they split *that* open, too. Inside the atom they *did* find the essence of all matter . . . and, lo and behold, it was energy! The tremendous, unspeakably pure power of the cos-

*The seeker is that which is being sought.*
BUDDHIST SAYING

*So great is the confusion of the world that comes from coveting knowledge!*
CHUANG TZU

mos was hiding there inside the smallest of all things, holding matter together with an intricate and unimaginable force. There was knowledge inside the atom—just as there was knowledge inside the apple—and by discovering it, we may have angered the gods again. In our urgency to know, we have once again dared to steal the fire, the hidden sacred knowledge that could drive us even farther from the garden, and perhaps banish us from the planet forever. Of course, it might have been worse. As the old joke says, the only thing worse than finding a worm in an apple is finding only half of a worm.

The knowledge we obtained from eating the apple in the Garden of Eden was the knowledge that divided up the universe and separated us from creation. However, the knowledge acquired from splitting the atom showed us that, at the most rudimentary level, all things are one. We are back where we started—before the Fall.

In splitting the atom, physicists found that matter and energy are interchangeable, which destroys the categories of both matter and energy. Now the two can't be separated; we are left with matter-energy, a reality held together by the dash. Space-time requires the same dash. Some people write the Almighty's name with a dash: G–D. Maybe the dash in the middle is the key to everything. Maybe it's a minus sign.

Ultimate knowledge may exist in the dash itself, in the joining together of all realities, the understanding that the Taoists' "ten thousand things" of this world are actually one. Inside the dash, our logic and language cannot survive, but it may be the place where crazy wisdom lives. We know that all things require their opposite: dark is necessary to light, death is necessary to life, now needs then, yin is always getting ready to yang, and down is up and down simultaneously. To accept paradox is to accept what appears to be the fundamental law of nature and rule of life. It might be that you *can* have your cake and eat it too, but you can't have your cake and eat it too. Or, as physicist Neils Bohr put it:

> A great truth is a truth whose opposite is also a
> great truth.

Most crazy wisdom masters understand that truth, like everything else, keeps changing. Our philosophies are continually overturned, and our scientific conclusions are reversed or shown to be only partially true. Descartes had truth for his era, but now we blame him for the mind/body split. Newton was absolutely right about his

149

There are no facts, only interpretations.
FRIEDRICH NIETZSCHE

All truths are only half truths.
ALFRED NORTH WHITEHEAD

universe, but not about other universes. Einstein's theories are being revised. Change may be the only constant in the universe. Truth is a verb.

Our Zen masters have stopped chanting and are teaching some of the clowns how to meditate. The scientists are playing volleyball with the philosophers, and the Jester is sitting under a tree, staring into the distance. Coyote is nowhere to be found. Everybody in our crazy wisdom group seems tired. The Taoist sage explains what has happened. "The difficulty is that most of us are not content to just walk and look, we want to know everything. Another difficulty is that we not only don't know how *not* to know, we don't know how to know."

# Think About It

The more the critical reason dominates, the more impoverished life becomes. . . . Over-valued reason has this in common with political absolutism: under its dominion the individual is pauperized.

CARL JUNG

Where do you think thinking has gotten us? Would we even be here if we didn't think, or to put it another way, would we have become extinct if we didn't think? Maybe we'd be "ex-thinkt." Descartes believed he wouldn't be here if he didn't think. He claimed, "I think, therefore I am." Perhaps he should have said, "I think, therefore I *think* I am."

We are caught in a traffic jam of discursive thought.

CHÖGYAM TRUNGPA

Of course we cannot, and do not wish to, dispense with the thinking process altogether, but we might learn how to use it better, and especially how to shut it off when appropriate. So much thinking is obsessive and habitual, a waste of energy, an extraneous feedback loop in the nervous system that is about as useful as the appendix. Do we really need the repetitious and gratuitous grinding of words and images, the chewing of mental cud? Furthermore, "critical reason," with which we constantly judge ourselves and the world, can be an alienating mode of thinking, tiresome and even painful.

Kurt Vonnegut takes a different stance from many when he claims that thinking is ineffective not because it is obsolete but because it is overdeveloped and possibly too advanced. In *Galapagos*, he looks back from the future to find:

> The mass of men was quietly desperate a million
> years ago because the infernal computers inside
> their skulls were incapable of restraint or idleness;
> were forever demanding more challenging
> problems. . . .

Vonnegut blames the problem on our "oversized brains," which do not fit our needs and circumstances. In *Wampeters, Foma, and Granfalloon*, he says, "The human brain is too high powered to have many practical uses in this particular universe." And again in *Galapagos*, "There was no end to the evil schemes that a thought machine that oversized couldn't imagine and execute."

Not only is thinking dangerous, it is highly overrated as a pastime. Many spiritual crazy wisdom masters suggest that you try "non-thinking" sometime. It feels good. It even feels wise. Some people think that non-thinking is "empty-headed." Quite true, the masters say, and don't knock it if you haven't tried it.

The jester Jonathan Swift didn't think much of thinking too much. In *Gulliver's Travels*, he describes strangely familiar creatures called Laputans:

> Their heads were all reclined either to the right, or the left;
> one of their eyes turned inward, and the other directly up to
> the zenith. I observed here and there many who employed
> servants, with a blown bladder fastened like a flail to the end
> of a short stick, which they carried in their hands. In each
> bladder was a small quantity of dried peas or little pebbles.
> With these bladders they now and then hit the mouths
> and ears of those who stood near them, of which practice I
> could not then conceive the meaning; it seems, the minds of
> these people are so taken up with intense speculations, that
> they neither can speak, nor attend to the discourses of
> others, without being roused by some external sensation
> upon the organs of speech and hearing; for which reason,
> those persons who are able to afford it always keep a flapper
> in their family, as one of their domestics, whose job it is,

151

Our meddling intellect
Misshapes the beauteous
    form of things:
We murder to dissect.
WILLIAM WORDSWORTH

when two or more persons are in company, gently to strike
with his bladder the mouth of him who is to speak, and
the right ear of him to whom the speaker addresseth
himself.

Through the characteristics of Laputans, Swift satirized the
British of the early eighteenth century. Surely, today we are much
more advanced in our ability to communicate.

> Listen within your ear. Speak without forming
> words. Language turns against itself and is likely to
> cause injury.
>
> RUMI

## A Word by Any Other Name

> The confusions which occupy us arise when
> language is like an engine idling, not when it is
> doing work.
>
> LUDWIG WITTGENSTEIN

Some modern crazy wisdom critics have tracked down the
thinking disease to words themselves—what author Colin Wilson
calls "the mind parasites"—the buzzing insects in the brain. (The
Jester asks, "Is that what's bugging you?")

The fall from grace was a fall from the actual into the symbolic
life. In fact, it may have been the *word* "apple" that got stuck in Ad-
am's throat. We seem to have become entranced by our ability to give
names to creation, until we no longer understand that the word is not
the thing. Wittgenstein illustrates the problem this way:

> How do I know that this color is red? It would be an
> answer to say: "I have learnt English."

Modern language philosophers and linguists investigate how we
deceive ourselves with our sophisticated system of signs and symbols. They explain how our belief in the reality of words, especially
abstractions such as "love" or "democracy," creates misery and confusion. Words that refer to vague emotional states or lofty political

And the Lord said, Come
ye therefore, let us go
down, and there confound
their tongue, that they may
not understand one anoth-
er's speech.

*Genesis*

ideals can trigger responses that are completely inappropriate to a specific situation. Words that refer to nothing in particular and have no inherent meaning can affect us as surely as a blow to the head.

Oliver Sacks, who studied aphasics, realized that they could perceive, beneath language, a deeper truth communicated by a speaker's emotional and physical presence. Indeed, Sacks noted, "one cannot lie to an aphasic. He cannot grasp your words, and so cannot be deceived by them. . . . "

Holy fools claim that language abstracts us from the world, keeping us from direct, or intuitive, perception. Many spiritual seekers say that language, with its subject/object relationships—one thing supposedly acting on another in simple cause and effect—entangles us in the illusion of separateness. The grammar of our language misses the interconnectedness, the oneness. The poet Rumi, though words were his medium, nonetheless believed that words hide reality:

> Do you know a word that doesn't refer to something?
> Have you ever picked and held a rose from R, O, S, E?
> You say the NAME. Now try to find the reality it names.
> Look at the moon in the sky, not the one in the lake.
> If you want to be free of your obsession with words
> and beautiful lettering, make one stroke down.
> There's no self, no characteristics,
> but a bright center where you have the knowledge
> the Prophets have, without books or interpreter.
>
> RUMI

A Buddhist aphorism cautions us against missing the moon because we focused on the finger pointing at it. We might also take care not to miss the moon by assuming that today's moon is the same as yesterday's moon. The moon, too, is a process.

Our language behaves as though reality were solid. On the simplest level, it positions a subject and an object, which we think of as "real," on opposite sides of a verb, which we think of as less than real. Perhaps the Hopi language reflects more closely the laws of nature. For the Hopi, the nouns *are* verbs; it is inherent in the language that everything is interacting or in process. Many physicists also tell us that action is all there is. Nonetheless, our language keeps piling up static "things," leaving us stuck under the illusion of solidity.

Repeating a word again and again shows that in itself, without a use in a situation, it becomes meaningless.

LUDWIG WITTGENSTEIN

O, swear not by the moon, the wandering moon, that monthly changes in her circled orb.

SHAKESPEARE

Language is a virus from outer space.

WILLIAM BURROUGHS

Of course many people insist that language is essential, that we couldn't survive without it. However, we should notice that the rest of the universe is able to talk to us without words. If we don't understand, perhaps it is because we don't know how to listen. Here are a few last words about words. Listen.

> One word less.
> One. Wordless.

Language is a tailor's shop where nothing fits.
RUMI

In the silence that follows, our crazy wisdom characters begin to disperse. The Taoist master wanders off toward some misty mountains, while the Jester heads back to the city to look for work. The clowns have decided to join the circus. The Zen masters sit down to meditate, agreeing that the here and now is as good as any spacetime. The scientists pack up their notes; they have decided to become socially responsible by studying the greenhouse effect. A few philosophers want to go back to school to learn a trade. Meanwhile, Coyote is heard in the nearby bushes, taking part in some boisterous and energetic activity. He no doubt will be able to take care of himself. As the dust settles, we come upon a poem by Pablo Neruda, titled "Flies Enter a Closed Mouth," a perfect epitaph for our questions and wanderings:

> Why, with these red fires, are the rubies ready to burst into flame?
>
> Why is the heart of the topaz
> yellow with honeycombs?
>
> Why is it the rose's vagary
> to change the color of its dreams?
>
> Why did the emerald freeze
> like a drowned submarine?

And why does the sky pale
in the starlight of June?

Where does the lizard buy
fresh paint for its tail?

Where is the subterranean fire
that revives the carnations?

Where does the salt get
that look of transparency?

Where did the coal sleep
before it woke to its darkness?

And where, where does the tiger buy
the stripes of its mourning, its markings of gold?

When did the honeysuckle first
sense its own perfume?

When did the pine take account
of its fragrant conclusion?

When did the lemons learn
the same creed as the sun?

When did smoke learn how to fly?

When do roots talk with each other?

How do stars get their water?
Why is the scorpion venomous
and the elephant benign?

What are the tortoise's thoughts?
To which point do the shadows withdraw?
What is the song of the rain's repetitions?
Where do birds go to die?
And why are leaves green?

What we know comes to so little,
what we presume is so much,
what we learn, so laborious,
we can only ask questions and die.
Better save all our pride
for the city of the dead
and the day of the carrion:
there, when the wind shifts
through the hollows of your skull
it will show you all manner of
enigmatical things, whispering truths in the
void where your ears used to be.

After yet another round of perennial questions, we have once again come up with the perennial blanks. Like Chuang Tzu or Socrates, when we look at all sides of our questions we are led in a circle and never arrive at a definitive edge or place of certainty. As we travel out into space-time or inside matter-energy, things appear different at every point along the way. After seeing so many perspectives the multiple realities blur and dissolve before our eyes, and we end up right back where we started, confirmed in the knowledge that we know nothing. After exploring these processes and perspectives of crazy wisdom and, hopefully, gaining some of our own, we are finally prepared to enter into the here and now: the quickly disappearing moments of the twentieth century.

PART III

*Crazy Wisdom
in the Twentieth
Century*

What a fine comedy this world would be if one did
not play a part in it.

DENIS DIDEROT

The forces of change are having a great romp through the twentieth century, overturning cherished beliefs and behavior and causing the planet itself to wobble in its orbit. In the past one hundred
years, the human species has experienced an unprecedented explosion of information and inventions, nothing less than revolution in
our evolution. In a burst of speed, humans have invented fantastic
tools and toys and awesome terrors that have transformed the land-
scapes of our psyches and continents—an ice age's worth of change
in less than a century. Within a minute of historical time we have
redesigned the surface of our planet and redefined ourselves.

In just a few brief decades, the prevailing ways of life have been
transformed from religious to secular, rural to urban, and industrial
to technological. The airplanes and automobiles, the radios, movies,
televisions, and computers have scrambled cultures and customs
worldwide. Every god and every flag in every corner of the planet
has been challenged by the knowledge, if not the direct intervention,
of the gods and flags from other regions.

Nothing remains as it was; no one is left untouched. Fortunately,
in this time of tremendous upheaval, crazy wisdom is flourishing
again and, speaking here through the jester Woody Allen, wants to
let us know that:

> More than at any time in history mankind faces a
> crossroads. One path leads to despair and utter
> hopelessness, the other to total extinction. Let us
> pray that we have the wisdom to choose correctly.

We once had an Iron Age; after a series of intervening ages, we
now live in the Age of Irony. The rapid changes of the last hundred
years show us that there may be no such thing as progress; that for
every step forward, we take at least one step backward. Maybe we
don't even know forward from backward. In this time of great
change, some have begun to see humanity as nothing more than a
species of clowns, wobbling precariously on a shaky rung of the
evolutionary ladder, wondering if this support system will hold us,

wondering whether the ladder is even leaning against the right wall. And nobody appears qualified to clear things up for us, unless, of course, God is waiting for the auspicious year 2000 to show his or her face. In the meantime, we seem to be on our own.

In a standard twentieth-century cartoon image, a dignified man wearing top hat and tails walks along jauntily, self-assured and proud. He is about to slip on a banana peel. We can put our entire civilization under that top hat; we feel proud of our progress, certain of our direction, convinced of our understanding, and . . . whoops! "Hey, what about the ozone layer? Who knew about this greenhouse effect? Overpopulation? Nuclear waste? Why didn't somebody tell us that this might happen?" That banana peel could have been left by Coyote, or maybe it's the contemporary equivalent of the fool's cliff. In our wondrous and dangerous world, both congratulations and condolences are in order, because Dickens's words on the French Revolution still apply today: "It was the best of times, it was the worst of times, it was the age of wisdom, it was the age of foolishness. . . ."

In these difficult days, the fact that crazy wisdom should arise to offer perspective and tell us not to take it too seriously is natural and necessary. As we venture into this exploration of the twentieth century, we rely heavily upon the Jester's ability to cut through the public relations mumbo jumbo produced by politicians and priests. We also call on the Trickster to remind us that our roots lie in the dark, unpredictable world of nature. (It is essential that Coyote come along even though he always brings trouble and a strange smell wherever he goes.) And of course, we count on the wisdom of the great fool, the sage who sees the unity and perfection of all things, including the planet's possible destruction. As for the clowns, well, that's us, holding a steering wheel that is disconnected from the car, and just noticing the tidal wave of polluted water cresting over our heads. As we make our way through the floods and fires of the contemporary scene, we might remember that clowns usually manage to survive. Crazy wisdom reminds us to look occasionally at the big picture— and cultivate the ability to let go.

160

Matter first appeared $10^{-38}$ seconds or so after the Big Bang, and will all disappear maybe $10^{+40}$ seconds from now.

SHELDON GLASHOW

# CHAPTER TWELVE

# Looking Forward to Looking Backward

In order to get a better view of the twentieth century, we will move forward to the year 2000, and then take a look back. The year 2000 is a promontory, a great watershed of history. No doubt it will be a time for human reflection and assessment, resolution and prediction. It should also be the wildest New Year's Eve party ever experienced.

The year 2000 will not only be the end of the century, it will also be the millennium. Imagine the media blitz. Surely, a TV documentary entitled "The Millennium: A Long Look Back" will begin with the narrator's line: "Yes, ladies and gentlemen, and what a millennium it has been . . ." There will be millennium sales ("$1,000 off everything in our store!"), advertising hooks ("Millennium, the deodorant that lasts . . ."), and thousands of impossible warranties and promises for the unforeseeable future. Meanwhile, magazines and television specials will review one thousand years of everything—food, sex, weapons, women's wear, you name it. Every industry will comment on its "progress" over the last millennium, and the majority of human endeavor will be proclaimed an astounding success.

And why not? Consider, for example, that the Chinese perfected the use of gunpowder only around 1000 A.D. In the last thousand years, improvements on that single invention have matched anything our species has accomplished. Also in the year 1000, the Indian mathematician Sridhara recognized the importance of zero, a break-through in our understanding of numbers. The zeros have increased exponentially since then, until we can no longer conceive of what the many zeros represent, nor can we actually count what we can calculate. Nonetheless, the growth in the number of zeros has convinced us that we are getting somewhere.

We certainly have learned a lot in the last millennium. A thousand years ago, most people believed the earth was flat, stationary, the center of the universe, and only about 5,000 years old. They did not know about other galaxies, gravity, evolution, cells, molecules; in fact, they did not understand very much at all. Will we seem as ignorant to humans in the year 3000?

Of course, some things never change. According to historical records, the approach of the last millennium caused widespread fear of the world's imminent end, the last judgment. As far as we know, it didn't occur. Today that good old millennial fever is heating up again. Fundamentalists shout apocalyptic passages from holy books and point to signs that foreshadow the end of days and the return of this or that messiah. Their fervor centers on the auspiciously round-numbered year 2000. Incorrigible, we humans! We are probably impressed by all those zeros in the date, which signify—as Sridhara discovered a millennium ago—nothing.

# The Sensational Senseless Century

When we look at the events of these last hundred years, it seems as though history moved in slow motion for the millennium's first nine hundred years. We are in a different age of civilization than those humans who lived in the last century and thus can see ourselves in a very different light. Way back in 1900, people had a limited picture of the universe and our place within it. Although we no longer believed that the sun revolved around the earth, it was commonly accepted that the Milky Way was just about the entire universe. One galaxy! It wasn't until almost midcentury that we began to discover billions of other galaxies full of billions of other stars.

Around the year 1900, the planet's metabolism seemed to accelerate. People and ideas had moved relatively slowly before the turn of the century, but then everything began to speed up. Henry Ford built his first car in 1893 and the Wright brothers took their first flight in 1903. In 1899 the first magnetic sound recording was made, and in 1900 R. A. Fessenden transmitted human speech via radio waves. In 1900 no one could have predicted that, less than seventy years later, rockets would take humans to the moon and orbiting satellites would transmit both sound and moving pictures to all areas of the earth. The twentieth century exposed everyone to everyone else. Cultural diversity was devastated, and innocence became nearly impossible.

The first year of the twentieth century saw the detonation of an intellectual bomb—an explosive herald of the "real" bombs that followed in midcentury. It happened in December 1900, when Max Planck formulated quantum theory and started a complete revolution in our understanding of the way in which the universe works. Quantum mechanics eventually undermined the accepted concept of linear cause and effect as well as the notions of scientific objectivity and absolute truth. At the most basic level, quantum theory finds the world to be unpredictable and unknowable. The discovery that energy comes in bundles (quanta) also led to the creation of the atomic bomb.

In 1900 we did not have the birth control pill or know how to create new species of life through genetic engineering. The nature of DNA was not discovered until 1953. In 1900 no antibiotics existed. In 1900 we did not even know how to make plastic. In 1900 nobody could have imagined today's Los Angeles. In 1900 not one person believed in rock and roll.

It was in the auspicious year 1900 that Sigmund Freud first published his *Interpretation of Dreams*. No one's dreams have been viewed in the same way since, and we have created some exceptional new nightmares. Back in 1900 it would have been impossible to imagine that during the next hundred years, humans would kill nearly one hundred million other human beings. But then, in 1900 only one and a half billion people inhabited the earth. Few people could have foreseen that (in spite of all the killing) the population would nearly double by the year 1950, and then double again by 1988! Some enterprising mathematician recently calculated that the weight of human bodies will exceed the weight of the planet itself by the year 3500 if the population continues to increase at the current rate.

## The All Too-Human Century

While the human population has increased threefold in this century, industrial production has increased by a factor of fifty. Four-fifths of all that industrial growth has come since 1950. Experts say the enormous amount of pollution caused by this burst of productivity is heating up the planet's atmosphere and threatening civilization. At the beginning of the century nobody would have thought that humans could create such an impact on the environment. It would have been as impossible to imagine the total eradication of the planet's rainforests as to conceive of a bomb that could destroy all life on earth. As the poet Gary Snyder writes in *The Real Work*:

> The last eighty years have been like an explosion.
> Several billion barrels of oil have been burned up.
> The rate of population growth, resource extraction,
> and destruction of species is unparalleled. We live
> in a totally anomalous time.

By almost any standard of comparison, the twentieth century appears out of proportion to the rest of history, and it is the exponential increase in the size, speed, and consumption levels of the human population that has made the difference. In *The End of Nature*, Bill McKibben writes:

> In the course of about a hundred years, our various
> engines and industries have released a very large
> portion of the carbon buried over the last five
> hundred million years. It is as if someone had
> scrimped and saved his entire life and then spent
> everything on one fantastic week's debauch.

Only in the twentieth century have humans begun to seriously threaten the evolution of life on earth. In the second half of the century, we discovered that the growth of our civilization was destroying the habitat of other forms of life and threatening many species with extinction. In the early 1970s the United States started keeping the Endangered Species List, which reads like a *Who's Who* of the animal world. The list contains the names of many hundreds of species of fish, bird, and animal life, including the grizzly bear, the Asiatic lion, the African gorilla, the chimpanzee, the jaguar, the cheetah, the leopard, 13 species of monkey, 5 species of wolf, 11 species of deer, 4 species of rhinoceros, 7 species of otter, 3 species of kangaroo, 8 species of whale, 3 species of dove, 8 species of crane, 5 species of duck, 3 species of hawk, 4 species of owl, 12 species of parrot, 20 species of pheasant, various storks, pelicans, falcons, and eagles, 3 species of alligator, 11 species of crocodile, 15 species of turtle, the Indian python, and a multitude of amphibian and fish species. The list of endangered plant and insect life is equally long. In 1990, experts estimated that *thousands* of species of plant, insect, and animal life become extinct every single year, primarily due to the destruction of the planet's forests. When a species becomes extinct it is taken off of the endangered list. Humans have not yet placed themselves on that list, since it is presumed that only having too *few* members of a species is what endangers it—not too many.

## The Rise and Fall and Rise and Fall and Rise . . .

> We learn from history that we learn nothing from history.
>
> GEORGE BERNARD SHAW
> *The Revolutionists Handbook*

The twentieth century has seen the rise and fall of several major empires, as political boundaries have been rearranged over and over again, in record time. At the beginning of the century, Europe was the center of power in the world, with Britain, France, Holland, Portugal, and Spain claiming dominion over all the continents. By the First World War, the European empires had begun to disintegrate, and as we near the end of the century they have been reduced to nothing but minor players in the geopolitical scheme. Only a few decades ago, the British were proud to say, "The sun never sets on the British Empire." Almost all that is left are those few chilly little islands, and one might now be correct in saying that the sun hardly ever rises on the British Empire.

The European empires survived for several hundred years, but in the twentieth century the process of rise and fall speeded up. Russia gained and lost a vast hegemony within several decades. In half a century Germany conquered half a continent and then lost it—twice. In the middle of the century, the United States became a superpower, and near the end of the century saw its sphere of influence be-

A nation never fails but by suicide.
RALPH WALDO EMERSON

gin to shrink. And just as the imperial sun set on the islands of Britain in the first half of the century, it rose on the islands of Japan during the second half.

Looking back from the year 2000, we see an almost rhythmic pattern of empires rising and falling throughout history: the Mesopotamian, Babylonian, Egyptian, Persian, Mongolian, Mayan, Aztec, Greek, Roman, and Ottoman empires, many Chinese dynasties, and smaller hegemonies too numerous to mention. Along with the crown and the keys to colonial treasures, it seems that each new empire inherits a blueprint for its rise and fall. The blueprint requires that the empire be established by brute force, or a combination of force and economic power, often in the name of a particular deity or as the herald of a new political theory and a better standard of living for all. Guided by racism and feelings of superiority, the empire inevitably exploits colonized peoples and resources, causing resentment and eventually revolt; this leads in turn to control problems for the empire, followed by military overextension. The difficulties abroad seem to happen concurrently with both a decadence at home fostered by too much wealth and a breakdown of imperial civilization as the conquered cultures begin to infiltrate the homeland. All this ends in disintegration of the empire, marked by devastation for many, both at home and in the colonies, and culminating in the imperial nation becoming a colony of someone else's empire. Looking back at history, Oswald Spengler concludes that this decline and fall is inevitable:

> Here, then, I lay it down that *Imperialism*, of which petrifacts such as the Egyptian empire, the Roman, the Chinese, the Indian, may continue to exist for hundreds or thousands of years—dead bodies, amorphous and dispirited masses of men, scrap-material from a great history—is to be taken as the typical symbol of the end. Imperialism is Civilization unadulterated. It is not a matter of choice—it is not the conscious will of individuals, or even that of whole classes or peoples that decides. The expansive tendency is a doom, something daemonic and immense, which grips, forces into service, and uses up the late mankind of the world-city stage, willy-nilly, aware or unaware.

Looking back at the twentieth century, we find that at least the last half of it could be called "the American century," as the United States took over many of the former European colonies with Coke

---

The essential cause of Rome's decline lay in her people, her morals, her class struggle, her failing trade, her bureaucratic despotism, her stifling taxes, her consuming wars . . .

WILL AND ARIEL DURANT

and movies and dreams too rich ever to be fulfilled. After only a few brief decades, it very well may be the United States' turn for the inevitable slide. In fact, U.S. power may have actually reached its apotheosis in 1969, when an American astronaut hit a golf ball across the surface of the moon, a nonchalant act that symbolized greatness as well as, perhaps, the pride that goeth before. The United States seems to have been hitting into the rough ever since. Maybe America will be immune to the dictates of history and the fate of all previous empires and superpowers, but it is best not to count on it.

Since it is such a common thing, losing an empire certainly brings no shame on a people. Individual citizens may even find it to their advantage. When there is no longer any need to spend most of the national treasury on the military to protect an empire or sphere of influence, the mother country can use its resources for housing, education, and health. As the *Tao Te Ching* says:

> When there is Tao in the empire
> The galloping steeds are turned back to fertilize the
> ground by their droppings.
> When there is not Tao in the empire
> War horses will be reared even on the sacred mounds
> below the city walls.

A major decline in U.S. productivity and consumption could be seen as a boon to the ecological health of the North American continent: a chance for the nation to take a few breaths and figure out how to clean up the air and water and how to dispose of nuclear and toxic wastes. An economic decline may be a proper adjustment in the larger balance of nature, and perhaps better for everyone in the long run. Many Americans might even welcome the opportunity to slow down and relax a little. It is not so easy being a citizen of a superpower.

Looking back from the year 2000, the Jester or a holy fool might also remind us that at the end of an empire there is really nothing to fear but fear itself. After all, Rome didn't decline in a day. During the collapse of the Roman Empire, many Romans didn't even notice it was happening. A few centuries after the trouble subsided, the Romans started calling themselves Italians and they seem to be doing fine today.

If decline is to be America's fate, accepting it without too much struggle would be the best approach. In the past, the world's great powers have stubbornly tried to hold on to their status and glory,

167

No power on earth is stronger than the United States of America today, and none will be stronger than the United States of America in the future.

RICHARD M. NIXON

bringing about prolonged wars and great suffering. If we could learn from the mistakes of the past, we might rewrite the blueprint for the decline. Perhaps the safest way to get down from the big imperial mountain is to walk, not fall.

> Tribe follows tribe and nation follows nation
> like the waves of the sea.
> It is the order of nations, and regret is useless.
> Your time of decay may be distant but it will surely come,
> for even the white man, whose God walked and talked
>     with him
> as friend with friend, cannot be exempt from the common
>     destiny.
> We may be brothers after all. We will see.
>                                   CHIEF SEALTH, 1855

In the twentieth century, all aspects of life, from the biological to the political, have been transformed in ways that we have yet to assimilate. Centuries-old belief systems and behavior patterns are disintegrating as the rate of change approaches the speed of light. As we watch cultural and political movements rise and fall before our eyes, it feels as though we are living through many lifetimes. This phenomenon *should* make history transparent, offering us great perspective and wisdom, but it doesn't immediately appear that this is happening. The speed of change tends to leave us feeling as though we have no ground to stand on, as if we fly through the universe homeless and lost. Considering our situation, we might recall the ancient Chinese curse: "May you live in interesting times."

From the vantage point of the year 2000, we might conclude that our collective consciousness and conscience have not kept up with our information-gathering and tool-making abilities. Too many humans have developed knowledge without wisdom, skill without heart, left brain without right, yang without yin. We know how to *do*, but not how to be.

Maybe the retrospectives at the end of the century and millennium will provide us with a vital consciousness-raising experience, but crazy wisdom knows enough history to be suspicious of such great expectations. The year 2000 *will* probably provide good amusement and, if we're lucky, offer at least a minimal exercise in crazy wisdom. Oswald Spengler's *Decline of the West*, though written in the first half of the century, offers us good advice as we approach the millennium:

A century of purely extensive effectiveness—let us say frankly an irreligious time which coincides exactly with the idea of the world-city—is a time of decline. True. But we have not *chosen* this time. We cannot help it if we are born as men of the early winter of full Civilization, instead of on the golden summit of a ripe Culture, in a Phidias or a Mozart time. Everything depends on our seeing our own position, our destiny, clearly, on our realizing that though we may lie to ourselves about it we cannot evade it.

CHAPTER THIRTEEN

# Scientific Proof That Crazy Wisdom Does and Does Not Exist

Of all the twentieth century's twists, none has altered our perspective more than the revolutions in science and scientific theory. Genetic and evolutionary biologists provide us with a radically new, and less than flattering, picture of ourselves. Astronomers show us a universe of a size beyond our comprehension, and to add insult to insult, they tell us that the universe seems to be disintegrating. And while physicists have found that reality is not what it appears to be, they haven't yet been able to tell us what it actually is.

In the twentieth century, one of crazy wisdom's favorite personas is that of the mad scientist. Dressed in a white lab coat, hair disheveled, eyes bulging behind thick glasses, crazy wisdom does its magic act in research labs and think tanks, making things appear and disappear and revealing paradox at every turn. In its new guise as "science," crazy wisdom has more credibility these days than it's had since the flowering of Taoism, many centuries ago.

For centuries spiritual crazy wisdom masters have believed that consciousness, or "mind," is the essential ingredient of any reality. Modern physicists seem to confirm this idea by showing that, contrary to popular belief, we can alter reality, at least on the subatomic level, simply by observing it. For example, experiments show that an electron can be both a particle and a wave at the same time, depending on how we look at it, and, perhaps, on whether we look at all. Some physicists posit that particles exist *only* when an observer is present. In fact, one of the most widely accepted explanations of quantum physics, the Copenhagen interpretation, states categori-

Anyone who is not shocked by quantum theory has not understood it.

NIELS BOHR

cally: "There is no reality in the absence of observation." Although these descriptions of the subatomic realm may not apply in the universe we can perceive, physicists have not yet drawn the exact line between the two. Therefore, let us assume for a moment that quantum theory works on all levels.

O.K. There is no reality in the absence of observation. If a tree falls in the forest and nobody is there to hear it, the falling tree does not make a sound because there is no tree in the first place. If there is no reality in the absence of observation, then if everyone closes their eyes simultaneously and ignores reality, it will go away. Crazy wisdom says, "Let's give it a try!" Unfortunately, someone will always peek.

Further into the Copenhagen interpretation, these scientists hedge their bets by stating their understanding of quantum mechanics in another way: "There is no *deep* reality." The Jester heartily agrees, reminding us that in the late twentieth century all realities are relatively shallow.

One of the most bizarre attempts to explain quantum phenomena is the theory of multiple realities. (Images may arise of an Eastern deity with many faces and arms.) This theory is based on the belief that there are many versions of reality occurring simultaneously. Specifically, it postulates the existence of a number of parallel universes, which never intersect, and whose physical laws may differ radically. This theory is, thus far, one of the best explanations for the fact that subatomic events seem to have many possible outcomes, each independent of the others. In other words, every experiment has many results, every question has many answers, and *all of them are true*. According to this theory, scientists can eat their cake and have it too! Nonetheless, parallel universes have implications that are difficult for anyone to accept. In his book *Quantum Reality*, Nick Herbert quotes scientist Bryce DeWitt's reaction to the theory:

> I still vividly recall the shock I experienced on first encountering this multiworld concept. The idea of $10^{100+}$ slightly imperfect copies of oneself all constantly splitting into further copies, which ultimately become unrecognizable, is not easy to reconcile with common sense. . . .

It is easier for most scientists to accept the wave/particle paradox, which states that an electron can be both a wave and a particle at the same time. Some scientists try to explain it this way: "Everything that has already happened is particles. Everything that has yet to hap-

171

Reality is the leading cause of stress amongst those in touch with it.

JANE WAGNER

We all agree that your theory is crazy, but is it crazy enough?

NIELS BOHR TO WOLFGANG PAULI

pen is waves." The present is created as soon as we notice it, and the future is waving to us, waiting for us to wave back. We shouldn't be too surprised when waves and particles, seemingly so different, turn out to be one and the same. After all, the ground beneath our feet in no way resembles the thin vapors drifting through the galaxy. Nonetheless, our planet was formed from such gases, and will eventually dissolve back into them. From waves to particles, from vapors to forms: as above so below, and so inside matter-energy.

For the past decade or so, scientists have also talked about "antimatter," claiming that an entire universe of this antimatter exists—a sort of mirror image of our familiar universe of matter. Of course, any Taoist sage knows that everything requires its opposite in order to exist, so why should matter be any different? However, we now have to ask ourselves not only "What is the matter?" but also "What is the antimatter?" And more importantly, "What does the antimatter have against the matter?" The Taoist sage reminds us that the essential question still remains: "Does it matter?"

Nobody knows how to fit the pieces of the new scientific discoveries together yet. Currently, the theoretical wizards are busy looking for a comprehensive model that will unite the latest information regarding particles, forces, and formulae under one umbrella theory that explains how all the phenomena of the universe work. Can there be such a theory? Will they find a single sentence or an equation that will sum it all up? A few years ago scientists called the object of their quest the Grand Unified Theory, or GUT. They have now changed its name to the Theory of Everything, or TOE. From the GUT to the TOE? Perhaps they have lowered their sights.

One of the latest and best hopes for the Theory of Everything is the "superstring theory," which claims that the fundamental building blocks of matter are not particles but strings. (Violins to accompany the material melodrama?) Physicists who support this theory claim that all strings are exactly the same, but that the patterns in which they vibrate are different, causing them to be manifested in the world as different forms. (Waves into particles?) If uniform strings are all there is to reality, then mystics must be correct in saying that all things are one. Or as the hippies used to say, "Everything is everything."

The superstring theory also supposes that we have a *ten dimensional universe*—nine dimensions of space and one of time—and it describes that universe in terms of the Planck scale, which is *ten trillion trillion times smaller* than the atomic scale. (No one has yet come up with a good analogy to describe how small that is.) The idea that there are invisible dimensions to reality is most fascinating. Scientists speculate that only three dimensions of space expanded along with the universe after the big bang. The other six dimensions remained curled up and are hidden from us. Maybe we are lucky. It could be that much harder to find our car keys or our niche in the world if we had to deal with six more dimensions.

Even if the superstring theory is true, at least one unanswered question remains: Who is pulling the strings? Physicists claim this is not their area of concern. Crazy wisdom suspects that in any Theory of Everything there will always be some loose ends.

If you find it hard to keep up with all the new scientific break-throughs, you might find solace in the "hundredth monkey" theory. Although widely disputed, it claims that if enough members of a species learn something new, a point of saturation is reached where-upon the entire species will begin to understand it spontaneously. Biologist Rupert Sheldrake formulated a hypothesis that may explain how this hundredth monkey phenomenon works. He claims that new behaviors or concepts can spread through a species sponta-neously, due to a vibratory process called "morphic resonance." Practically speaking, this means that if we just relax and wait awhile, enough people will read up on the idea of morphic resonance, and we won't have to. Sometimes it is okay to let ourselves be monkey num-ber one hundred one. Crazy wisdom says, "Let's take turns."

173

> You are not thinking. You are merely being logical.
> NEILS BOHR TO ALBERT EINSTEIN

## Science Becomes Mythology

> Neither science nor rationality are universal mea-sures of excellence. They are particular traditions, unaware of their historical grounding.
> PAUL FEYERABEND

For millennia, humans have believed in things they could not see: gods and ghosts and spirits galore. Think of Plato's Ideal Forms, the Buddha's Nirvana, the Christian vision of God and His Heaven. Indeed, often we imbue these invisible realms and phantoms with more reality than the things we *can* actually see and touch. Over the centuries, shamans and high priests have told us about the spirits who spoke only to them, and most of us believed their stories, no matter how fantastic. Now we believe the scientist-shamans who tell us of strange, invisible worlds far beyond ordinary perception and comprehension. Even scientists themselves admit they haven't seen the subatomic realms—only traces that indicate they exist—and yet we have faith in their descriptions.

Science may have finally moved into the realm of myth or poetry. Its theories read like mystical visions, its equations are a new system of hieroglyphs. Perhaps contemporary scientists are simply giving us new symbols for the incomprehensible mysteries of the universe. We will certainly enshrine the Grand Unified Theories in our holy books of science, where they will be honored as another chapter in the saga of our attempt to understand the universe. However, we should be aware that the latest scientific "truths" correspond to our sensory perception of reality no better than the biblical version of truth. Science is just another set of names for the unknowable.

Perhaps someday we will worship the forces and elements that are being discovered today. After all, the core of any religion is stories about the beginning and end of creation, and scientists are now writing a new scripture.

Every human society has established a description of how the universe began, and now physicists and astronomers have their story. In the beginning, they say, there was a "singularity": one particle that contained the entire universe, so small that nobody could even see it. As physicist John L. Castri explains in *Paradigms Lost:*

> You might object that it seems to go well beyond the bounds
> of credulity to imagine that the whole universe could be
> compressed into a volume far less than that of an atom,
> since the energy density must have been intolerably large.
> But remember, according to quantum theory energy
> and time are *conjugate* variables, so we can get large amounts
> of energy into a small volume if the time is short enough.

Why not? That sounds at least as plausible as the idea that a Creator with a white beard formed the heavens and the earth in seven days.

Physicists and astronomers are writing a new version of Genesis at last. "In the beginning we were all one particle." What a cozy, egg-like image: all of us tucked in with all other life, and with the oceans and mountains and stars and galaxies. All packed together inside that one little particle. (It must have been a very, very heavy little particle.)

Atoms are not things.
WERNER HEISENBERG

For millennia mankind has believed that nothing can come out of nothing. Today we can argue that everything has come out of nothing. Nobody needs to pay for the universe. It is the ultimate free lunch.
PAUL DAVIES

Almost two thousand years, and no new god!
FRIEDRICH NIETZSCHE

And so it came to pass (probably) that all things were *too* together, and it became just too hot and cramped and steamy and wildly intense inside that one particle, so that eventually and suddenly there occurred a great coming apart, a tremendous explosion . . . **and it was called the big bang**. Out of that one particle came everything that now and ever did exist, including the great forests and oceans and bicycles and lawyers and pizzas and lint and billions of huge galaxies full of stars. Amen! What a wondrous, miraculous story these scientists have come up with! But what about the end of the story? According to theoretical physicist Anthony Zee:

> Everything will decay into a cloud of pions and positrons.

Science, our current picture of reality, may well be seen by people in the future as quaint or even silly; they may view our faith in physics as equivalent to believing in Santa Claus or a sun god. It's not that the latest scientific discoveries are "wrong." On the contrary, our "new scientific paradigm" is probably the perfect description of reality for *our* evolutionary situation. Today's science may even be a bridge to a new and "necessary" way of ordering our lives. Nonetheless, we should understand that this new scientific paradigm might eventually become the old scientific paradigm. The latest science is not the last word.

Awareness of the tidal nature of scientific "truth"—each wave superseded by another—caused Albert Camus great frustration. He wanted not only spiritual certainty but scientific conclusions as well:

> You describe this world to me and you teach me to classify it. You enumerate its laws and in my thirst for knowledge I admit that they are true. You take apart its mechanism and my hope increases. At the final stage you teach me that this wondrous and multi-colored universe can be reduced to the atom and that the atom itself can be reduced to the electron. All this is good and I wait for you to continue. But you tell me of an invisible planetary system in which electrons gravitate around a nucleus. You explain this world to me with an image. I realize then that you have been reduced to poetry: I shall never know. Have I the time to become indignant? You have already changed theories. So that

science that was to teach me everything ends up in a
hypothesis, that lucidity founders in metaphor, that uncertainty is resolved in a work of art.

As an artist and truth seeker, Camus understood the mythopoetic nature of the new scientific realities. It is interesting to note
that the most intuitive and revolutionary modern scientists—Bohr,
Einstein, Heisenberg, Bohm—have also been aware that they were
working in many realms at once, not just the scientific. Consider this
comment from Neils Bohr, the father of quantum mechanics:

> When it comes to atoms, language can be used only
> as in poetry.

In honor of Dr. Bohr, crazy wisdom offers this poem, found in
a newspaper article:

> Antiprotons are so small that one quadrillion—
> that's 1,000,000,000,000,000—would occupy
> a space 30,000 times smaller than the period at the
> end of this sentence.

In reality, twentieth-century science has taken us nowhere, period. In a sense, we are right back to 500 B.C., when a Greek named
Democritus (sounding just like some modern theoretical physicists)
wrote:

> By convention sweet is sweet, by convention bitter
> is bitter, by convention hot is hot, by convention
> cold is cold, by convention color is color. But in
> reality there are only atoms and the void.

Democritus must be forgiven for thinking that atoms are real; he
did not have the atom-smashing machines and lasers which have allowed today's physicists to discover that the solidity of atoms, too, is
myth. In the end, only the void may be "real," and even that is questionable. Neurophysicist Karl Pribam claims that the universe may
be most like a hologram—perhaps you can step right through the
walls of reality if you know the secret word. Many holy fools would
claim that all reality comes from the mind at work. It's all illusion,
just a shadow play.

At the same time that Democritus of Greece was looking into the atomic nature of things, Gautama the Buddha, in India, realized that even atoms (which were called *kalapas*) could be broken down into smaller units. The Buddha constructed a new word (*asti-kalapa*) to refer to *sub*atomic particles. Furthermore, he taught that *trillions* of transformations in these subatomic particles happen in the blink of an eye. Today, scientists have isolated subatomic changes that do indeed take place trillions of times a second. How did the Buddha figure that out? Could he have slowed his mind down to the point that he actually saw events occurring in trillionths of a second? Impossible—unless, of course, the Buddha had developed mental power equivalent to an atom-smashing machine and laser camera.

Perhaps science does not adequately replace our former stories. Many critics believe that by reducing everything to matter and energy, science has robbed us of spirit and mystery. In *A Selection from Phoenix*, D. H. Lawrence, sounding a bit like Coyote howling at the moon, made one of the most eloquent objections to science's objectification of the world.

I77

The universe is made up of stories, not atoms.

MURIEL RUCKEYSER

> The Moon! Artemis! the great goddess of the splendid past of men! Are you going to tell me she is a dead lump? . . .
>
> She is not dead. But maybe we are dead, half-dead little modern worms stuffing our damp carcasses with thought-forms that have no sensual reality. When we describe the moon as dead, we are describing the deadness in ourselves. Do we imagine that we, poor worms with spectacles and telescopes and thought-forms, are really more conscious, more vitally aware of the universe than the men in the past were, who called the moon Artemis, or Cybele, or Astarte? Do we imagine that we really, livingly know the moon better than they knew her? . . .
>
> Do you think you can put the universe apart, a dead lump here, a ball of gas there, a bit of fume somewhere else? How puerile it is, as if the universe were the back yard of some human chemical works! How gibbering man becomes, when he is really clever, and thinks he is giving the ultimate and final description of the universe! Can't he see that he is merely describing himself, and that the self he is describing is merely one of the more dead and dreary states that man can exist in? When man changes his state of being, he needs an entirely different description of the

universe, and so the universe changes its nature to him entirely.

Is our description true? Not for a single moment, once you change your state of mind: or your state of soul. Our state of mind is becoming unbearable. We shall have to change it. And when we have changed it, we shall change our description of the universe entirely. We shall not call the moon Artemis, but the new name will be nearer to Artemis than to a dead lump or an extinct globe. We shall not get back the Chaldean vision of the living heavens. But the heavens will come to life again for us, and the vision will express also the new men that we are.

Before we leave the universe of modern science, crazy wisdom wants to remind us of Heisenberg's uncertainty principle and Einstein's theory of relativity, the two swords of modern science that undercut the whole science game. The uncertainty principle says that we can't really know subatomic reality, because it changes when and according to how we try to measure it. In addition, the theory of relativity claims that all measurements and judgments depend on the observer's position and velocity. In other words, neither scientist nor subatomic reality can be pinned down. The observer and the observed seem to be locked in an eternal dance with each other, both unable to stop long enough for a clear picture to be taken. There can be no objectivity, no absolute truth in science. We can't know reality because we are inside of it . . . *we are it.* Together wherever we go.

In this late age of civilization, as our previous myths and religions grow old, science has arisen to take their place, offering new names for the same old cloud of unanswered questions. The new scientific paradigm presents a shimmering, unknowable reality full of mysterious quarks and pions and gluons and antiprotons and strong and weak forces, leaving us, in the end, with uncertainty, except for the probability that we still don't know anything. So now, let us go to church—the latest version.

## The First Church of Science

Saint Isaac and Albert's Cathedral. The circular ceiling is a large revolving planetarium. It displays a continuously accurate view of the heavens to the very limit of astronomical exploration, billions of light-years away.

The mind precedes all things, the mind dominates all things, the mind creates all things.

GAUTAMA THE BUDDHA

In the cathedral's alcoves stand holograms of the Saints of Science, each captured at the moment of revelation: Heraclitus stands in his ever-changing river; Galileo looks through his telescope at the stars; Euclid holds his ruler and triangle; Newton poses, a ripe apple on his head; Einstein stands in front of a curved mirror, sticking out his tongue; Schrodinger has his cat on his shoulder; Heisenberg looks uncertain.

The chapel's stained-glass windows portray scenes from the story of evolution. Present-day *homo sapiens* is presented as we first enter the church; as we move down the aisle toward the altar, we move backwards through time. The last window before reaching the altar shows a one-celled organism.

On pedestals flanking the altar sit two giant statues—replicas of a hydrogen and a helium atom. Across the sanctuary wall, electrified models of other atoms (enlarged of course) spin in their orbits, crashing into each other, and exploding in flashes of light, giving churchgoers a sense of the dynamic reality of charged particles.

Where the Christian crucifix or Ark of the Torah is normally found stands the sacred symbol of the First Church of Science—an emblem of six white dots on a black field, a representation of the six known quarks. The Holy Sextet: Up, Down, Top, Bottom, Strange, and Charmed. The basic reality. AMEN. The black field represents the emptiness from which everything sprang, or the black hole from which it emerged, or perhaps the "dark area," the first cause—the mystery that remains to be solved.

We enter the church during a service. Each member of the congregation, dressed in a white lab coat, recites the liturgy—hydrogen, helium, lithium, beryllium, boron, carbon, and so on, through the periodic table. Then, the supplicants bow their heads and pray that the Theory of Everything will soon make itself known. Finally, the congregation will chant the First Church of Science's own Hail Mary, its Shema Yisreel, its great mantra—atom ah hum, atom ah hum, atom ah hum . . .

CHAPTER FOURTEEN

# Art Now

No more masterpieces.
ANTONIN ARTAUD

The twentieth century's most radical literary and artistic movements have tended to overturn one another in rapid succession,
meeting Artaud's injunction. The revolution took various names as
it proceeded: Cubist, Futurist, Suprematist, Constructivist, Syn-
chromist, Modernist, Dadaist, Surrealist, Abstract Expressionist,
Existentialist, Situationist, Beat, Psychedelic, Pop, Op, New Wave,
and _____ (fill in the blank with the name of tomorrow's movement). Modern artists challenged tradition, disregarded previously
accepted ideals of morality and beauty, dissolved distinctions and
categories, and refuted reason at every turn. Art in the twentieth century has been a defiant exhibition of crazy wisdom.

The twentieth-century artistic movements revolted against cultural certainty. It was a revolt with great historical precedent—the
Taoists against the Confucians, the early Christians against the Romans, the Romantics against the Age of Reason—a struggle perhaps
as old as our "two brains." In the twentieth century the struggle was
between the artist/humanist and the rationalist/materialist: two cultures, two minds.

Twentieth-century art has often made a direct statement against
the materialism and militarism of the times. Artistic protests ranged
from Picasso's contorted, suffering images in *Guernica* to Jimi Hen-

DADA is the voluntary
destruction of the bourgeois
world of ideas.
DADAIST SLOGAN

drix's screaming guitar version of the U.S. national anthem to the two female performance artists, one American and one Vietnamese, who tied themselves together with a twelve-foot rope for an entire year. This century has seen especially murderous acts orchestrated in the name of the greater glory of humanity, and many artists have gone to the barricades, trying to get our attention in order to expose the deceit of the governments and profiteers and to offer alternatives to the barbarity.

Artists have confronted this difficult century, attempting to be heard over the exploding bombs and the constant babble of commercialism. They have stood naked before us, revealing their own nightmares, which share the common terrors of the spirit in a time of darkness.

> The confusion is not my invention. . . . It is all around us and our only chance is to let it in. The only chance of renovation is to open our eyes and see the mess. . . .
>
> SAMUEL BECKETT

# Make It New

> We are not Gothic or Rococco people; we have to reckon with the hard cold facts of a *late* life, to which the parallel is to be found not in Pericles' Athens but in Caesar's Rome. Of great painting or great music there can no longer be, for Western people, any question.
>
> OSWALD SPENGLER

The twentieth century follows a long history of Western culture, and the traditional artistic forms seem stale or irrelevant. Gertrude Stein wrote, "A rose is a rose is a rose," explaining that she wanted to give the word "rose" back its potency, to let us smell the flower when we read the word. Only by making it into a chant could she bring the word back to life. Stein said, "It is doubly hard to be a poet in a late age."

Many artists have felt the twentieth century to be a late age. The language is tired, the beliefs halfhearted, the stories either too old or

181

The novel cannot live in peace with the spirit of our time: if it is to go on discovering the undiscovered, to go on progressing as novel, it can do so only against the progress of the world.

MILAN KUNDERA

Moloch whose mind is pure machinery! Moloch whose blood is running money! Moloch whose fingers are ten armies! Moloch whose breast is a cannibal dynamo! Moloch whose ear is a smoking tomb!

ALLEN GINSBERG

The simplest surrealist act consists of going down into the streets revolver in hand, and shooting at random.

ANDRÉ BRETON

not old enough. There is no ritual, only spectacle; no mythology, only fashion.

Twentieth-century artists needed to find new languages, new styles, and new realities to revive the artistic statement. In an age of instantaneous communication and mass production, they had to be absurd, surreal, and revolutionary, over and over again. As images and information were expanding exponentially, art, in order to remain art and not become fashion, had to stay one step ahead. As each new form of expression arose it had to be buried ried immediately. As Jean Cocteau said, "The only work of art which succeeds is that which fails."

## Art Who?

> A painting is a flat surface with paint on it.
> MOTTO OF CONSTRUCTIVISM

Turning inward, art began to question itself. Artists moved away from the perceivable world and any attempt to interpret or represent it. Since the absurdities of twentieth-century life inevitably kept pace with the artists' wildest experiments, there was nothing left for art to do but take itself apart, showing the fraudulence inherent in trying to capture reality and the impossibility of saying anything at all.

As a means of reevaluating art, some artists made art their subject. They purged their work of any relationship to the world, hoping to purify their vision and get down to what they considered to be "the basics." While the physicists of the time reduced their world to subatomic particles, artists pared theirs down to line, color, shape, rhythm, and timbre—the quantum particulars which precede meaning and lie behind all perception. With God dead, the symbols of physics and geometry moved to the center of the canvas. Wassily Kandinsky saw those symbols as representing a new ethos:

> The impact of the acute angle of a triangle on a circle produces an effect no less powerful than the finger of God touching the finger of Adam in Michelangelo.

Twentieth-century painters turned to pure color or simple geometric shapes or, as in the work of Jackson Pollock, seemingly random splashes and swirls of paint. On stage, the theater of the absurd

---

182

One should either be a work of art or wear a work of art.

OSCAR WILDE

The idea of content in art is today mainly a hindrance, a nuisance, a subtle or not so subtle philistinism.

SUSAN SONTAG

My work is a matter of fundamental sounds. If people get headaches among the overtones, they'll have to furnish their own aspirin.

SAMUEL BECKETT

dispensed with beginnings, middles, and ends, and jumbled the sequence and meaning of words as well. Avant-garde jazz and classical music dissected old harmonies and rhythms, invoking the pure sounds that exist outside of melody or form. Art began to be primarily about the materials of art—the elementary interaction of the senses with waves of light and sound.

## The Kulture of Kitsch and Camp and Collage

> I really feel sorry for people who think things like soap dishes or mirrors or Coke bottles are ugly, because they're surrounded by things like that all day long, and it must make them miserable.
>
> ROBERT RAUSCHENBERG

Some twentieth-century artists were great tricksters, engaged in dissolving all distinctions and categories until there was no more holy or profane, no beautiful or ugly, no "highbrow" or "lowbrow." The result was an artistic movement that rejected the very idea of art itself.

Marcel Duchamp set the tone in 1914 when he began selling ordinary objects as art, pieces which he called "readymades." Duchamp once went into a hardware store, bought an iron rack used for drying bottles, and simply signed his name to it, transforming the rack from a useful consumer product into a "work of art." Another time, he bought a snow shovel, signed it, and called it, "In Advance of the Broken Arm." Collage artists like Robert Rauschenberg picked up where Duchamp left off, using everyday objects such as newspaper clippings and automobile tires as ingredients in their work. John Cage put the sounds of everyday life into his music. Andy Warhol presented the familiar image of a soup can label or a media personality and repeated it until we saw it, like Gertrude Stein's rose, in a new way—perhaps as the icon of the religion of materialism.

> The whole point of Camp is to dethrone the serious.
>
> SUSAN SONTAG

Like great fools, these artists took on the twentieth century with innocence and wonder, and sometimes with a deep sense of the absurd. Like clowns and jesters, they saw everything in the world as an object for either play or ridicule.

From this crazy wisdom perspective sprang new art forms. These included "cut-ups," novels and poems produced by randomly combining bits from various printed materials, and "found poetry," whole excerpts taken verbatim from sources such as newspapers, medical texts, and government speeches. Music was written by consulting oracles such as the I Ching or astrology. The era was filled with art at random, "found art," art everywhere, art, art, art. The artists were playing with the cluttered landscape, selecting from the growing quantity of images and consumer goods, and shining spotlights on them. In the process, they showed us our perceptual prejudices as well as our milieu, our "civilization." Susan Sontag interpreted the new aesthetic this way: "The art of our time is noisy with appeals for silence."

In a sense, the kitsch artists were like Zen masters, pointing to the ordinary and connecting us to our everyday environment. Their art was non-art, a glorification of the mundane, a Western form of haiku. With the adoption of a crazy wisdom perspective, all the world becomes a stage and everything in it is art.

The outrageous contortions of art in the twentieth century may have stemmed from a species survival mechanism kicking in. The brash splashes and assemblages in visual art, the dissonant crashes and honks of music, the theater's absurdity, poetry's howls and chants—perhaps the artists' revolution as a whole arose from an instinctive need to revive the experiential and the intuitive, to reclaim the right brain, mythic understanding, revelry and rebellion, crazy wisdom. As Lawrence Ferlinghetti writes:

> Chaplin is dead but I'd wear his bowler
> having outlived all our myths but his
> the myth of the pure subjective
> the collective subjective
> the Little Man in each of us

184

Everyone will be famous for fifteen minutes.

ANDY WARHOL

# CHAPTER FIFTEEN

# And Then God Said, "Let There Be Crazy Wisdom . . ."

All great truths begin as blasphemies.
GEORGE BERNARD SHAW

The twentieth century has been a rough time for God, as well as for God's creatures. In the 1960s the cover of an issue of *Time* magazine posed the question "Is God Dead?" The Jester just laughed and said, "Of course God is not dead. He's just having a midlife crisis."

As we move into this subject matter, crazy wisdom would like to point out that even if all gods and goddesses are only figments of our imagination, it doesn't mean that they are not "real." They are at least as real as we are. Furthermore, it is more likely that *all* belief systems are true than that just one of them is true. Every god and goddess helps to define and to refine us; therefore, each is our "creator." Each religion gives the solace of a "higher meaning," a place to rest our questions and our heads. Whether we worship the sun or the Son, we always worship life itself; we worship ourselves.

Distancing ourselves from our beliefs is difficult. However, in the past few centuries, anthropology and mass communications have revealed a vast array of gods and religions, and this should shed some light on all belief systems, including our own. Let's step back for a few minutes and walk that thin twentieth-century line between blasphemy and a healthy, humorous skepticism.

Irreverence is my only sacred cow.
PAUL KRASSNER

We keep thinking of deity as a kind of fact, somewhere; God as a fact. God is simply our own notion of something that is symbolic of transcendence and mystery. The mystery is what's important.
JOSEPH CAMPBELL

# The Hundred Thousand Names of G–D

The Ethiopians say that their gods are snub-nosed
and black, the Thracians that theirs have light
blue eyes and red hair.

XENOPHANES

According to the Judeo-Christian tradition, a male god named
Jehovah created the heavens and the earth and everything else in just
six days. The Bible says that God looked at His creation and "saw that
it was good." Some crazy wisdom observers think this could be the
first recorded use of irony.

For a different creation story, we go to a Bantu tribe in Africa,
whose creator is named Bumba. In the beginning Bumba was alone
except for darkness and water. Suddenly, he was smitten with ago-
nizing stomach pains, and he vomited out the sun, the moon, and all
living creatures. That sounds plausible. The universe is the product
of a stomachache.

If you happened to be from the central region of southwest Africa, you would probably believe in the sky-god Ndjambi, whose
name can be spoken or written only on special occasions. Hopefully,
this is one of them.

Meanwhile, goddesses are returning to the West. If we're lucky,
they will arrive in time to save us from further subjugation at the
hands of mythological machismo. Crazy wisdom followers may enjoy praying to the ancient female Chinese creator named Nu-gua,
who formed the first human beings from yellow clay. She also invented the flute. Nu-gua sounds like a sweet, playful deity. It would
be nicer to crawl into Nu-gua's lap for some Great Mother nurturing
than to beg mercy or await judgment from a wrathful, jealous,
"thou-shalt-have-no-other-gods-before-me" male deity, whose
name we shall not utter. As Joseph Campbell pointed out,

> In our religion everything is prosaic, and very, very
> serious. You can't fool around with Yahweh.

If God lived on earth,
people would break out all
His windows.

HASIDIC SAYING

That fear first created the
gods is perhaps as true
as anything so brief could
be on so great a subject.

GEORGE SANTAYANA

## The Breasts of the Beatitude

Every year, millions of Hindu pilgrims go to Madurai, the holiest city in southern India. They go to visit the two-thousand-year-old Shree Meenakshi Temple, a complex which stretches for a quarter of a mile and features two enormous towers, sculpted from top to bottom with images of myriad Hindu gods and goddesses. This temple celebrates a strange, miraculous legend.

Shree Meenakshi, the daughter of a Pandayan king, was born with three breasts. The king was told that her third breast would disappear when she met the man she was fated to marry. This miracle occurred when Shree Meenakshi met the deity Lord Shiva. So, they married, and now live happily ever after. To ensure their happiness, Brahman priests perform a ceremony at the temple every night. They take Lord Shiva and his lingam (a stylized phallus) into Shree Meenakshi's bedchamber. Observers say the priests who perform this ritual today seem distracted; perhaps because this conjugal mating has taken place each night for nearly two thousand years.

Most Westerners would consider such a religious ceremony primitive. Hindus pray to phalli, as well as to statues of monkey and elephant gods, deities with multiple arms and faces, and fire-breathing goddesses who wear necklaces of skulls. Every day, millions of people offer flowers, incense, and adulation to these images. Meanwhile, in the West, many people have no image to which they can address their spiritual yearnings. Their notion of a first cause or higher power is a vague concept such as "cosmic consciousness" or a scientific theory like evolution. Both idols and ideas can both serve as links to the spiritual, but abstractions seem to hold less mythic power. They do not embody the mystery. To fire our imagination and connect us to the wonder of all the forms that cosmic consciousness has taken, it may be more inspiring to bow down to a monkey idol or place a garland over a large stone phallus. In the specific lies the universal.

Strange as it may seem, many people with access to information about others' gods still believe that theirs is the *only* god—the only valid god, or good god, or the only god that can save people. Religions still try to convert people to their brand of deity, to swap a false god for the right one.

In the summer of 1985, when Pope John Paul visited the Republic of Central Africa, he appeared at a gathering of tens of thousands

187

Say it, no ideas but in things.

WILLIAM CARLOS WILLIAMS

DEFINITION: God is the shortest distance between zero and infinity. In which direction? one may ask. We shall reply that His first name is not Jack, but Plus-and-Minus. And one should say: ± God is the shortest distance between 0 and infinity, in either direction.

ALFRED JARRY

of people. In full papal regalia, he celebrated communion, and when he was finished symbolically eating the body and drinking the blood of his god, he gave a speech, telling the Africans to stop practicing voodoo. As Cole Porter once asked, "Who do that voodoo . . . ?"

Through the ages, one of the jester's favorite pastimes has been lampooning gods and religions, and poking a little fun at the seriousness of most beliefs and rituals. Ever since humans first decided that a creaturelike creator controlled things and cared especially for us; ever since the first prayer or sacrifice was sent up in the hope that something would be sent back down, crazy wisdom jesters have been busy laughing and spreading doubt.

The twentieth century has fostered some particularly inspired irreverence. For instance, writer Philip Wylie observed that "if Jesus came back today, he would be killed again. But this time he would probably be electrocuted. And from that moment on, people would start wearing little electric chairs on chains around their necks." Lenny Bruce attempted to deflate religious chauvinism and hypocrisy with "bits" like this:

> You and I know what a Jew is—someone who killed our Lord, Jesus Christ. I don't know if we got much press on that in Illinois—we did this about two thousand years ago—two thousand years of Polack kids whacking the shit out of us coming home from school. There should be a statute of limitations for that crime. Why do you keep breaking our balls for this? Alright, I'll confess . . . my family did it. I found a note in my basement. It said:
> "We killed him.
> signed,
> Morty."

As we saw earlier, Mark Twain had some bitterly humorous disagreements with Jehovah and Christianity. One passage, however, written in a more somber tone, stands out as one of the most complete indictments ever made against any god and the life which that god created.

> The first time the Deity came down to earth, he brought life and death; when he came the second time, he brought hell.

## 188

Pope John Paul would be more popular if he called himself Pope John Paul George and Ringo.

PAUL KRASSNER

Do not take the Buddha for the Ultimate. As I look at him, he is still like the hole in the privy.

LIN-CHI (RINZAI)

Life was not a valuable gift, but death was. Life was a fever-dream made up of joys embittered by sorrows, pleasure poisoned by pain; a dream that was a nightmare-confusion of spasmodic and fleeting delights, ecstasies, exultations, happinesses, interspersed with long-drawn miseries, griefs, perils, horrors, disappointments, defeats, humiliations, and despairs—the heaviest curse devisable by divine ingenuity; but death was sweet, death was gentle, death was kind; death healed the bruised spirit and the broken heart, and gave them rest and forgetfulness; death was man's best friend; when man could endure life no longer, death came and set him free.

In time, the Deity perceived that death was a mistake; a mistake in that it was insufficient; insufficient, for the reason that while it was an admirable agent for the inflicting of misery upon the survivor, it allowed the dead person himself to escape from all further persecution in the blessed refuge of the grave. This was not satisfactory. A way must be contrived to pursue the dead beyond the tomb.

The Deity pondered this matter during four thousand years unsuccessfully, but as soon as he came down to earth and became a Christian his mind cleared and he knew what to do. He invented hell, and proclaimed it.

Now here is a curious thing. It is believed by everybody that while he was in heaven he was stern, hard, resentful, jealous, and cruel; but that when he came down to earth and assumed the name Jesus Christ, he became the opposite of what he was before; that is to say, he became sweet, and gentle, merciful, forgiving, and all harshness disappeared from his nature and a deep and yearning love for his poor human children took its place. Whereas it was as Jesus Christ that he devised hell and proclaimed it!

Twain's statements may seem outrageous, but if humans must be tested and judged, why shouldn't the gods? Unfortunately, few gods seem to have a sense of humor, or much perspective on themselves. Despite being gods, they just can't seem to see the bigger picture. H. L. Mencken would like us to have a little sympathy for them. Looking back through history from the perspective of the twentieth century, he realized that just as every dog has its day, so

189

does every god. In "Memorial Service," Mencken asks for a moment of silence for those gods who have passed away.

Where is the grave-yard of dead gods? What lingering mourner waters their mounds? There was a time when Jupiter was the king of the gods, and any man who doubted his puissance was *ipso facto* a barbarian and an ignoramus. But where in all the world is there a man who worships Jupiter to-day? . . .

. . . Tezcatilpoca was almost as powerful: he consumed 25,000 virgins a year. Lead me to his tomb: I would weep, and hang a *couronne des perles*. But who knows where it is? Or where the grave of Quitzalcoatl is? . . . Or Xiehtecutli? Or Centeotl, that sweet one? . . . Or all the host of Tzitzimitles? Where are their bones? Where is the willow on which they hung their harps? In what forlorn and unheard-of hell do they await the resurrection morn? Who enjoys their residuary estates? Or that of Dis, whom Caesar found to be the chief god of the Celts? Or that of Tarves, the bull? Or that of Moccos, the pig? . . . Or that of Mullo, the celestial jack-ass? There was a time when the Irish revered all these gods. . . . But to-day even the drunkest Irishman laughs at them.

But they have company in oblivion: the hell of dead gods is as crowded as the Presbyterian hell for babies. Damona is there, and Esus, and Drunemeton, and Silvana, and Dervones, and Adsalluta, . . . and Mogons. All mighty gods in their day, worshiped by millions, full of demands and impositions, able to bind and loose—all gods of the first class, not dilettanti. Men labored for generations to built vast temples to them—temples with stones as large as hay-wagons. The business of interpreting their whims occupied thousands of priests, wizards, . . . bishops, archbishops. To doubt them was to die, usually at the stake. Armies took to the field to defend them against infidels: villages were burned, women and children were butchered, cattle were driven off. Yet in the end they all withered and died, and to-day there is none so poor to do them reverence. . . .

Mencken might have remembered that our relationship with the gods is reciprocal: people choose another god only when they are themselves no longer a chosen people.

Quickly, before lightning strikes us, we offer Jack Kerouac the last word on god.

No,—what is God?
The impossible, the impeachable
Unimpeachable Prezi-dent
Of the Pepsodent Universe
But with no body & no brain
no business and no tie
no candle and no high
no wise and no smart guy
no nothing, no no-nothing,
no anything, no-word, yes-word,
everything, anything, God,
the guy that ain't a guy,
the thing that can't be
and can
and is
and isn't

We must not judge God from this world. It's just a study that didn't come off. It's only a master who could make such a blunder.

VINCENT VAN GOGH

CHAPTER SIXTEEN

# Crazy Wisdom Reads the News

Heaven and earth are impartial;
They see the ten thousand things as straw dogs.

TAO TE CHING

We have explored the back pages of twentieth-century news-papers—the science, art, and religion sections—and now it is time to move to the front page, the headlines. Mostly they chronicle colossal mismanagement, ignorance, and bad behavior.

The social and political events of our time substantiate some of crazy wisdom's most controversial claims. The two world wars, the scores of little wars, the holocausts and genocides—should have killed off most of our illusions about our special intelligence or our status as children of a benevolent deity.

Indeed, war was the primary motivation for most of the centu-ry's technological advances. Over the belligerent past hundred years, the fear response forced us into the habit of working overtime to in-vent and build new weapons. Now momentum itself has overtaken us, and we can't stop producing—neither guns nor butter, products nor pollution. The assembly line's controls are stuck in the "on" po-sition, and we may have lost our capacity to manage the proliferation of just about everything, including ourselves. In twentieth-century wars, as usual, everybody loses. War wins.

Twentieth-century progress is best exemplified by the nuclear arms race, the one enterprise to which our leaders and thinkers have

Why did they call it World War I, unless they knew it was the first of a series.

PAUL KRASSNER

Technological progress is like an axe in the hands of a pathological criminal.

ALBERT EINSTEIN

devoted the most resources, energy, and attention. This race is like a voodoo horror realm or Dantean hell, a limbo in which we are forced to plan our own suicides endlessly, and to prepare to kill ourselves in a searing, flesh-melting blast.

Shortly after the nuclear arms race began, both the United States and the Soviet Union had the capacity to kill everyone on the planet; the addition of more and more weapons came to be known as "overkill." The Jester finds this consolation in overkill: Chances are, the second time they kill you it won't hurt as much, because you'll already be dead.

As the century progressed, bombs grew bigger and more powerful. During World War II, the Allies dropped a total of *only* two million tons of high explosives, including the two atomic bombs on Japan. Then in Vietnam, the United States alone dropped almost *four times* that amount. Now we have the hydrogen bomb, a nuclear device that makes the original atom bomb look like a firecracker. It has never been tested on cities and people, so we don't know exactly what would happen, but a *single* hydrogen bomb can have the explosive power of twenty-four million tons of TNT, which is *three times* the explosive power of all the bombs dropped during the Vietnam War. Three Vietnams in one bomb. Or twelve World War IIs in one bomb. We now have many hydrogen bombs of this size.

For years the Pentagon called its official military strategy Mutual Assured Destruction, or MAD. The reasoning behind MAD was that if they kill all of us, we will kill all of them; and if we kill all of them, they will kill all of us. With overkill in the equation, official logic was: If they keep building bombs, then we must keep building bombs, because we wouldn't want them to be able to overkill us more than we can overkill them. Thus is peace preserved.

In 1980, after twenty-five years of MAD, the Pentagon under President Ronald Reagan began to consider the possibility of conducting a "limited" nuclear war. In accordance with this new idea, our official nuclear policy was changed from Mutual Assured Destruction to Nuclear Utilization Targeting Strategy, or NUTS. Now, it is doubtful that those acronyms occurred by chance. The Pentagon admitted, and even seemed to snicker, that it was going from MAD to NUTS.

Meanwhile, smaller nations also began to build nuclear devices. The Indian government chose a fascinating secret code to report the results of the first test of their nuclear weapon. When the bomb exploded successfully, top-level Indian officials were informed that "the Buddha is smiling." There is some dark crazy wisdom in that code.

In spite of *glasnost* and the apparent end to the cold war, the possibility of nuclear holocaust remains. Calling on the chaotic trickster element deep inside us, we might look for the brighter side of nuclear destruction, and see if we can find a few good things to say for it.

First of all, nuclear war would provide a certain cosmic closure, since, as far as we know, we all *started* with a big bang. In addition, everyone knows that a bullet with his or her name on it exists somewhere out there; a twenty-megaton hydrogen bomb just happens to be *one* bullet engraved with *everybody's* name. That bomb, acting as the great equalizer, would bring all classes, races, and religions together in one brilliant flash of shared destiny. The added consolation to death by nuclear war is that we won't be missing anything when we're gone. *The Guinness Book of World Records* will be closed.

The reverse side also has a reverse side.
JAPANESE PROVERB

# The Next News

Nature, once a harsh and feared master, now lies in subjection, and needs protection against man's powers. Yet because man, no matter what intellectual and technical heights he may scale, remains embedded in nature, the balance has shifted against him, too, and the threat that he poses to the earth is a threat to him as well.
JONATHAN SCHELL

As the century draws to a close, news of war, and of the nuclear arms race in particular, is slowly losing its premier position in the headlines and is being replaced by news of global warming, deforestation, and other threats to the environment. It seems inevitable that without the cold war, heat will become the major threat to human survival. The heat of our civilization, created by the burning of energy to fuel excessive speed and greed, threatens to destroy us. Ironically, the fear of "nuclear winter" is giving way to concern over what might be called "pollution summer." Little doubt remains that saving the planet—the forests, the oceans, the atmosphere—will demand humanity's full attention in the twenty-first century. The balance of nature will become far more important than the balance of power. Nonetheless, the environmental crises will continue to undermine our claims of special intelligence and mastery over the forces of nature. The problems have developed over time, but humanity has been slow to catch on.

We were shocked to learn that human activity is altering the planet's atmosphere. We release so much carbon dioxide and methane gas that it prevents heat from escaping and causes global temperatures to rise. This is called the "greenhouse effect." Basically, we have given the planet a fever. The increasing heat could eventually devastate agriculture worldwide, and cause what scientists refer to as "biomass crashes" and "ecosystem deaths." In addition, the rising temperature might melt the polar ice caps, resulting in another great flood. (Remember, God promised He would never again destroy civilization with a great flood, but He didn't say we couldn't do it on our own.)

On the other hand, it is possible that we've been doing the right thing by polluting. Some scientists say we were due for another ice age, and we may be warming the atmosphere just in time to neutralize the cold spell. Who can know? Then again, we may overheat by destroying the ozone layer, which protects us from the sun's ultraviolet rays. There is this consolation: if we are going to cook ourselves, at least we have a choice of methods—quick frying in nuclear war, microwaving if the ozone disappears, or poaching in the greenhouse effect.

Scientific evidence for the atmospheric crisis is accumulating, and more voices are raising the alarm. In *The End of Nature*, Bill McKibben writes:

> The idea of nature will not survive the new, global
> pollution—the carbon dioxide and the methane
> and the like. This new rupture with nature is differ-
> ent both in scope and in kind. . . . We have
> deprived nature of its independence, and that is
> fatal to its meaning.

Nonetheless, we drive ourselves and our cars and power plants ever faster, burning up our limited supply of the dark carbon, pouring our wastes into the air. All this is done in the name of making safe and comfortable homes for ourselves, when in fact we are probably destroying the only home we have. John Seed, editor of *World Rainforest Report*, writes:

I've studied all the statistics quite intensively for the last 10 years, and it's quite clear that, unless we fundamentally change within our lifetimes, no future generations of human beings will be able to save us. None of the conservation efforts that are taking place now, even multiplied by a factor of 10 or even 100, will be enough to stop the deterioration of the biological fabric out of which we, and all life, have been created.

Species extinction, forest destruction, water and air pollution, nuclear and toxic chemical contamination—these stories will no doubt dominate the headlines of the twenty-first century. In response, a crazy wisdom perspective is likely to emerge as the next version of truth. The "Gaia hypothesis" and "deep ecology," two philosophies that express the unity of all creation, may direct national policy as well as our day-to-day lives. Both have attracted a lot of interest lately, and have even earned some support from the scientific community.

The Gaia hypothesis is based on the theory that our planet functions as a single organism. All matter, living and nonliving, is inexorably linked; we cannot damage any part without damaging the whole. Similarly, deep ecology proposes that humans are neither separate from, nor more important than, the rest of nature. The deep ecologists believe in protecting nature, not for the purpose of human survival, but for the sake of life itself. They trace their ideas and inspiration to Taoists, Zen Buddhists, native Americans, Romantic poets, and early American transcendentalists, proclaiming once again the unity of all things and "being" itself as a state of grace. In *Deep Ecology*, John Seed writes that with unity

Alienation subsides. The human is no longer an outsider, apart. As your memory improves, as the implications of evolution and ecology are internalized and replace the outmoded anthropocentric structures in your mind, there is an identification with all life. Then follows the realization that the distinction between "life" and "lifeless" is a human construct. Every atom in this body existed before organic life emerged 4,000 million years ago. Remember our childhood as minerals, as lava, as rocks?

And while it is true that "human nature" revealed by 12,000 years of written history does not offer much hope that we can change our warlike, greedy, ignorant ways, the vastly longer fossil history assures us that we *can* change. We *are* that fish, and the myriad other death-defying feats of flexibility which a study of evolution reveals to us. A certain confidence (in spite of our recent "humanity") is warranted. From this point of view, the threat of extinction appears as the invitation to change, to evolve. The change that is required of us is not some new resistance to radiation, but a change in consciousness. Deep ecology is the search for a viable consciousness.

As humanity moves on to new crises, no doubt many will look for a scapegoat for our environmental situation. Who is responsible for the threats to our life-support system? It may be impossible to find a culprit. No one could have known, for instance, that using chlorofluorocarbons would eat away the ozone shield. We assume that former President Richard Nixon's close friend Robert Aplanalp, who made his fortune in aerosol sprays, had no idea his product would contribute to one of the most threatening environmental crises since Noah's time. (The Jester says, "The family that sprays together gets ultraviolet rays together.") Nor could Henry Ford have predicted the environmental destruction and political havoc that would result from mass production of automobiles. Had he foreseen the end results of his ingenuity—the highway deaths, pollution, oil crises, and degradation of landscape and habitat by freeways— would he have started up that mindless machine, the assembly line? After Hiroshima, Albert Einstein said of his life's work, "If I had known they were going to do this, I would have become a shoemaker."

In spite of the way we're destroying the rain forests and poisoning the oceans and atmosphere, despite the extinction of millions of plant and animal species, and the fact that we humans have killed over one hundred million of our own kind in the last century—in spite of all this, many crazy wisdom masters would still say that there is no evil in the world, only ignorance. It is really nobody's fault. As a Tibetan Buddhist adage recommends: "Roll all blames into one."

# PART IV

## *Conclusions*

# CHAPTER SEVENTEEN

# Crazy Wisdom Does the Dance of Death

Of all mindfulness meditations,
That on death is supreme.
**BUDDHA**
**THE PARINIRVANA SUTRA**

Death, where is thy sting-a-ling-a-ling?
**DOROTHY PARKER**

As we come to the end of this crazy wisdom story, we come to death. Or else death finally comes to us. Everybody and everything dies. In some very real sense, crazy wisdom has been talking about death all along: the death of knowledge and truth, beliefs and philosophies; the death of art forms and political institutions, nations and empires; the death of gods and goddesses, even the death of planets and galaxies and universes. It is appropriate that we join crazy wisdom in this last dance.

Each of us and all of our offspring will disappear from earth. In a few billion years the sun will explode, and with that fiery event surely the earth will be destroyed. The Pyramids and the Eiffel Tower and the World Trade Center will be gone, and all copies of the Bible will have burned up. You may be thinking that by then, with luck, humans will have emigrated from this planet into a more stable solar system. We still have to remember that, according to current astronomical understanding, the entire universe is in either of two

How do I know that loving life is not a delusion? How do I know that in hating death I am not like a man who, having left home in his youth, has forgotten the way back?
CHUANG TZU

processes: expanding into nothingness, or slowing down expansion, which eventually will cause it to collapse back into a single particle. Whatever occurs, not even Shakespeare will survive.

What do we fear when we fear death? The loss of our "selves"? According to the holy fools there is no self; all we have to lose are our illusions. Death is simply a way of ending this painful separation, a way of dissolving back into the flow, a homecoming. Crazy wisdom says, "We have nothing to fear from death but nothing—and nothing is nothing to fear at all."

> Death is just infinity closing in.
> JORGE LUIS BORGES

Perhaps the most tragic aspect of death is that we fear it so much. Recent research shows that people who are resuscitated medically, literally brought back from the dead, aren't too happy about the revival. Apparently they enjoyed being dead; they say it's very peaceful. As Mark Twain commented, "All say, 'How hard it is that we have to die'—a strange complaint to come from the mouths of people who have had to live."

Death is crazy wisdom's best friend and most important teacher. When we get to know our own death and ask it to move in with us, all things assume their proper perspective. Rumi puts it this way:

> Why fear grief
> when Death walks so close beside?
> Don't fear the General
> if you are good friends with the Prince.

Eastern holy fools have developed many ways to become friendly with death. Most meditation practices can be understood as a rehearsal for death, an exercise in letting go of each moment. When death arrives we might then be ready to let go of the last moment of life. Some Hindu and Buddhist yogis meditate at graveyards and cremation grounds to become intimate with the processes of decay and transformation. Tibetan monks blow ceremonial horns made from human femurs and eat out of bowls carved from human skulls. In these actions, they partake of life in the face of death, thereby becoming more intimate with both.

From the perspective of life, which is the only perspective avail-

I'm not afraid of dying. I just don't want to be there when it happens.
WOODY ALLEN

The happiness of the drop is to die in the river.
AL-GHAZALI

able to us, death is nothing to fear. Crazy wisdom tries to explain it this way: If life is a joke, death is the punch line. If life is a tragedy, death means the show is over and we can leave for home. If we have many lives, as believed in the East, then we must also have many deaths, so we might as well get good at dying. Also, some sages say that only by learning how to die do we finally learn how to live. What a deal! Two lessons in one!

But wait. As usual, there's a catch. Those same sages will also tell us that once we learn how to live and die, we are finally allowed off the rebirth wheel. In other words, just when we get it right the game is over. Oh well, that's life.

> "The thing to do when you're impatient," he proceeded, "is to turn to your left and ask advice from your death. An immense amount of pettiness is dropped if your death makes a gesture to you, or if you catch a glimpse of it, or if you just have the feeling that your companion is there watching you."

In this excerpt from *Journey to Ixtlan*, the sorcerer Don Juan tells Carlos Castaneda to keep death over his left shoulder. To do this, it helps most of us to have an image that represents death. Some people visualize the grim reaper (usually with a smiling skull). You may wish to picture nuclear bombs, the sleek modern symbols of death. For your death and dying practice, the Pentagon has conveniently listed their nuclear weapons according to size, and then given each one a cute name, offering a personal touch. There are bombs called Juliette and Hotel. Crazy wisdom's favorite, a relatively small bomb with the explosive equivalent of 50,000 tons of TNT, is named Golf. Whenever we get lost in pettiness and need to pause for perspective, we can visualize the Golf bomb over our left shoulders. "Hello, Golf," says crazy wisdom. "Fore!" That should clear the mind of confusion and allow us to play on through.

Every form is subject to transformation. That is the law of nature. And so each of us goes from womb to world to tomb to worms, just as our species travels from waves to caves to graves and, some would say, back to the start again. Every ending is also a beginning and death surely leads somewhere. We do know that without death for comparison there would be no such thing as life.

Crazy wisdom wonders why this moment of transformation

203

The birth of a man is the birth of his sorrow. The longer he lives, the more stupid he becomes, because his anxiety to avoid unavoidable death becomes more and more acute. What bitterness! He lives for what is always out of reach! His thirst for survival in the future makes him incapable of living in the present.

CHUANG TZU

has such a poor reputation, so much so that the thought of dying evokes fear and sorrow. The very word "death" has become laden with negative connotations. Death. It sounds so sudden and final. Perhaps we should give it another name. This new name should refer to the transition of the spirit, the aura, the essence that we often call a person's "energy." Since we usually think of the spirit in terms of light, let's look at "light" as a metaphor. We might imagine that when we cease to exist, our light fades into the surrounding shadow, or, conversely, that our shadows fade into the surrounding light, depending on whether our view of life is bright or dim. Instead of calling this transformation death, we can now call it the "dissolve." It's still the big "D," but to dissolve implies only that one has lost one's outlines. We dissolve into that place where there is only darkness, or into pure, eternal light. "We will all dissolve someday"; "She is sick and dissolving." After all, that *is* how we leave. We just fade from sight and from memory, and the show goes on.

# Death Poems and Epitaphs

A crazy wisdom tradition among poets, artists, and Zen monks in Japan is to write a "death poem" as one approaches the final moments. It is considered cheating to write the death poem before one is quite sure that death is imminent, since the poem is a final test of one's attitude toward death, a testament to one's level of spiritual attainment. On their deathbeds, the masters are fearless, in full control of their artistic powers, and ready with wry perceptions of crazy wisdom.

From one basin
to another—
stuff and nonsense.
ISSA

Bury me when I die
beneath a wine barrel
in a tavern.
With luck
the cask will leak.
MORIYA SEN'AN

This must be
my birthday there
in paradise.
JOSEKI

My old body:
a drop of dew grown
heavy at the leaf tip.
KIBA

All conditioned things are impermanent. Work out your own salvation with diligence.
THE BUDDHA'S
LAST WORDS

BENJAMIN FRANKLIN'S
EPITAPH:
The Body of B. Franklin,
Printer,
Like the Cover of an Old
Book,
Its Contents Torn Out And
Stripped of its Lettering and
Gilding,
Lies Here
Food for Worms,
But the Work shall not be
Lost,
For it Will as He Believed
Appear Once More
In a New and more Elegant
Edition
Revised and Corrected
By the Author.

Till now I thought
that death befell
the untalented alone.
If those with talent, too,
must die
surely they make
a better manure?

**KYORIKU**

Though I should live
To be a hundred,
The same world, the same cherry-
blossoms;
The moon is round,
The snow is white.

**TAIYA TEIRYU**

205

A few days before his death, Zen teacher Kozan Ichikyo called his pupils together and ordered them to bury him without ceremony, forbidding them to hold services in his memory. He wrote the following poem on the morning of his death, laid down his brush, and died sitting upright.

Empty-handed I entered the world
Barefoot I leave it.
My coming, my going—
Two simple happenings
That got entangled.

While living
Be a dead man,
Be thoroughly dead—
And behave as you like,
And all's well.

ZEN MASTER BUNAN

It is customary and auspicious for Zen monks to die while sitting in meditation. Chinese Zen Master Chihhsien asked his disciples, "Who dies sitting?" They answered, "A monk." Then he asked, "Who dies standing?" His disciples answered, "Enlightened monks." Chihhsien then took seven steps and died standing up.

In *Oriental Humor*, R. H. Blythe tells of an even more impressive exit: Zen monk Teng Yinfeng asked his followers if anyone had ever died upside down. When they told him it had never been seen or heard of, Teng stood on his head and died. A great closing act for a great fool.

WILLIAM BUTLER YEATS'S
EPITAPH:
Cast a cold eye
On life, on death.
Horseman, pass by!

CHAPTER EIGHTEEN

# The End Is Also
# the Middle

And I am not a demigod,
I cannot make it cohere.
EZRA POUND
*Canto XVI*

It may not be wise to draw any conclusions from what's been said in this book, but it would be crazy not to try. In any case, there are several good quotations left that might go nicely into a summary. So, let us begin to conclude. As Groucho Marx might say, "Hello . . . I must be going."

The torch of doubt and chaos, this is what the sage steers by.
CHUANG TZU

We have heard many different voices singing variations on the crazy wisdom themes, and the most common refrain is that we can't be sure about much of anything. As soon as we become too certain of our understanding, the trickster arises to switch the shape of things or reveal another layer of reality. According to crazy wisdom, truth's name is transformation.

We are here and it is now. Further than that all human knowledge is moonshine.
H. L. MENCKEN

Crazy wisdom points out that everything we know, everything we believe, and everything we are is destined to evolve or dissolve into something else. Life transforms from microbe to monkey to man. Man raises a flag, only to have it lowered and another one unfurled in its place. As we move from culture to culture and paradigm to paradigm, today's conventional understanding continually overturns yesterday's. Gods come and go, and new scientific and artistic movements arise to show us truth and beauty from different angles. Meanwhile, the universe continues on toward a destiny about which we can only speculate. In *The Universe and Dr. Einstein*, Lincoln Barnett offers a current story about the end of the world:

> The sun is slowly but surely burning out, the stars are dying embers, and everywhere in the cosmos heat is burning to cold, matter is dissolving into radiation, and energy is being dissipated into empty space. The universe is thus progressing toward an ultimate 'heat death,' or as it is technically defined, a condition of 'maximum entropy.' When all system and order in the universe have vanished, when randomness is at its maximum, and entropy cannot be increased, when there is no longer any sequence of cause and effect—in short, when the universe has run down, there will be no direction to time, there will be no time. And there is no way of avoiding this destiny.

From the Eastern crazy wisdom masters who talk of our existence as lasting less than the blink of an eye in a universe measured by "incalculables" to the evolutionary biologists and astrophysicists who put us in our place in the latest stories of life-matter-energy, the voices of crazy wisdom caution us against imputing too much importance to ourselves or to our species. The clowns still trip over their shoelaces and their pride, while the tricksters rub off the thin veneer of our dignity and civilization to reveal the raw, original design. And, of course, jesters forever arise to mock our latest ridiculous fashions and solemn beliefs, reminding us not to be so full of ourselves that we can't see ourselves. Mark Twain punctured human pride like a master:

> Man has been here 32,000 years. That it took a hundred million years to prepare the world for him is proof that that is what it was done for. I suppose it is. I dunno. If the Eiffel Tower were now representing the world's age, the skin of paint on the pinnacle-knob at its summit would represent man's share of that age; and anybody would perceive that that skin was what the tower was built for. I reckon they would, I dunno.

Many of the voices of crazy wisdom have told us that what we call reason is not that reasonable at all. Holy fools have explained their suspicion of the rational mind and tried to disabuse us of our persistent urge to categorize and analyze, while psychologists and biochemists find that the mind is deeply conditioned, even mechanistic, in its functioning. Some holy fools insist that the most truly reasonable faculty—what we might call "consciousness"—has not yet developed in us. Indeed, we have only to look at history for proof of how unreasonable our species can be in the name of reason.

The very existence of crazy wisdom implies that another kind of intelligence might arise once we accept our ignorance and our limitations. A better balance of doing and being may be possible in our minds and lives. It is likely that we do not yet understand how to understand. As Jean-Paul Sartre said, "Everything has been figured out, except how to live."

Throughout this book, we have heard holy fools and mad modern scientists talking about the unity of all things. They tell us that, while distinctions and separations may be of some practical use, in essence they are nothing more than illusions. According to crazy wisdom, reality rests easier in the center of the paradox, in the slashes and dashes that join all things together: matter-energy, space-time, particle-wave, either/or, this/that, us/them.

Life itself is paradox: both meaningful and meaningless, important and insignificant, a joke and a yoke. These mutually exclusive qualities exist simultaneously, just as wave *and* particle do in the subatomic world. For all practical purposes, life is many things at once. Poet Robert Frost captures this understanding with a line he wanted engraved on his tombstone:

I had a lover's quarrel with the world.

If there is any central message in *Crazy Wisdom*, it is simply that we need not take ourselves quite so seriously. If all things are constantly transforming and will eventually die, then perhaps the best way to live is not by holding on, but by *letting go with all our might*— letting go of our impossible craving for certainty or significance; letting go of our demands on the universe for perfect happiness and everlasting life. Our only option may be to learn what Alan Watts called "the wisdom of insecurity" and to discover that which Camus sought—a way to be comfortable with unfamiliarity. We are then free to leap with Chuang Tzu into "the boundless" and make it our

He who knows he is a fool is not the biggest fool; he who knows he is confused is not in the worst confusion.

CHUANG TZU

The most fundamental of divisions is that between the intellect, which can only do its work by saying continually 'thou fool,' and the religious genius which makes it all equal.

WILLIAM BUTLER YEATS

Students achieving oneness will move ahead to twoness.

WOODY ALLEN

home. Accepting uncertainty as our philosophy might allow us to honor each other's stories more, delighting in all the bizarre and wondrous interpretations of the mystery. We might also show more tolerance for those who appear to be fools, and for those who speak truths we don't wish to hear.

Trying to draw a moral from the crazy wisdom story might be especially crazy, but if we must, the moral is that it is time to slow down and relax; to learn less of doing and more of being. Given the brevity of our existence and the fact that we don't know what it means or what we are supposed to be doing here, perhaps our only recourse is to learn how to be in the moment with what is before us. This sentiment has been expressed in different ways by many sages, most often in the simplest of terms:

A rabbi whose congregation does not want to drive him out of town is not a rabbi.

HASIDIC SAYING

> Don't worry, be happy.
> MEYER BABA

> What, me worry?
> ALFRED E. NEUMAN

These few words may sound too simplistic to those for whom reality implies difficulty and complexity. Nonetheless, many holy fools have emphasized simplicity of thought and living as the path to harmony and, therefore, the ultimate human virtue. Some modern crazy wisdom masters—jesters, tricksters, and holy fools alike—tell us that slowing down may actually be progress, and that just sitting still may be one of the most useful of all activities. To elaborate on these sentiments and close this book, we leave you with the statement of a poet, Pablo Neruda, offering us the final words of crazy wisdom.

### KEEPING QUIET

Now we will count to twelve
and we will all keep still
for once on the face of the
earth,
let's not speak in any language;
let's stop for a second,
and not move our arms so much.

It would be an exotic moment
without rush, without engines;
we would all be together
in a sudden strangeness.

Fishermen in the cold sea
would not harm whales
and the man gathering salt
would not look at his hurt hands.

Those who prepare green wars,
wars with gas, wars with fire,
victories with no survivors,
would put on clean clothes
and walk about with their brothers
in the shade, doing nothing.

What I want should not be confused
with total inactivity.
Life is what it is about; . . .

If we were not so single-minded
about keeping our lives moving,
and for once could do nothing,
perhaps a huge silence
might interrupt this sadness
of never understanding ourselves
and of threatening ourselves with
death.

Perhaps the earth can teach us
as when everything seems to be dead in winter
and later proves to be alive.

Now I'll count up to twelve
and you keep quiet and I will go.

# References

## Part I

page 3.  Chuang Tzu. *The Complete Works of Chuang Tzu*, translated by Burton Watson. New York: Columbia University Press, 1968, p. 302.

3.  Dowman, Keith. *Masters of Enchantment: The Lives and Legends of the Mahasiddhas*. Rochester, VT: Inner Traditions International, 1988.

3.  *Everything You Know Is Wrong*. Title of record album by the Firesign Theater. 4 or 5 Crazee Guys Publishing Company, 1974.

4.  Ecclesiastes 2:12. *The New Oxford Annotated Bible*. Revised Standard Version. New York: Oxford University Press, 1962.

4.  Zen saying, as stated in a talk by Alan Watts.

4.  *The Ten Principle Upanishads*. Translated into English by W. B. Yeats and Shree Purohit Swami. New York: Collier Books, 1937, p. 20.

5.  Waley, Arthur. *The Way and Its Power*. New York: Grove Press, 1958, pp. 171, 193.

5.  Zen koan. As cited in *Zen Buddhism*, edited by William Barrett. Garden City: Doubleday Anchor, 1956, p. 100.

5.  Beckett, Samuel. Quoted in *Irrational Man*, by William Barrett. New York: Anchor Books, 1962, p. 283.

5.  Franklin, Jon. *Molecules of the Mind*. New York: Dell Publishing, 1987, p. 259.

6.  Campbell, Joseph. *The Power of Myth*. New York: Doubleday, 1988.

6.  Abu Said. As quoted in *The Way of the Sufi*, by Idries Shah. New York: E. P. Dutton and Co., 1970, p. 219.

7.  Rogers, Will. As quoted in *The 637 Best Things Anybody Ever Said*, selected and compiled by Robert Byrne. New York: Ballantine Books, 1988, p. 116.

7.  Milarepa. *The Hundred Thousand Songs of Milarepa: Volume One*, translated by Garma C. C. Chang. Boulder: Shambala, 1977.

7.  Merton, Thomas. *The Way of Chuang Tzu*. New York: New Directions, 1965, p. 150.

8.  Tolstoy, Leo. *War and Peace*, translated by Rosemary Edmonds. New York: Viking Penguin, 1957.

8.  Campbell, Joseph. *The Power of Myth*.

8.  Allen, Woody. *Side Effects*. New York: Ballantine Books, 1981, p. 81.

8.  Spengler, Oswald. *The Decline of the West: An abridged edition* by Helmut Werner. New York: Alfred A. Knopf, 1962, p. 19.

9.  Yiddish proverb. *The Joys of Yiddish*, by Leo Rosten. New York: Pocket Books, 1970, p. 314.

9.  Koestler, Arthur. *Janus: A Summing Up*. New York: Random House, 1979.

9.  Yiddish proverb. *The Joys of Yiddish*, p. 107.

page 10. Valery, Paul. *The Collected Works in English*. Princeton: Princeton University Press, Bollingen Series, 1970.

10. Jung, Carl. *The Portable Jung*. Edited by Joseph Campbell. New York: Penguin, 1971.

10. Kabir. *The Bijak*. Translated by Linda Hess and Shukdev Singh. Albany, CA: North Point Press, 1983, p. 113.

11. Baudelaire, Charles. *Intimate Journals*, translated by Christopher Isherwood. San Francisco: City Lights, 1983, p. 61.

11. Nietzsche, Friedrich. *The Gay Science*, translated, with commentary, by Walter Kaufmann. New York: Vintage Books, 1974, p. 74.

11. Kabir. *The Bijak*, p. 112.

12. Dillard, Annie. *Teaching a Stone to Talk*. New York: Harper and Row, 1982, p. 15.

12. Rumi. As quoted in conversation with Shams Kairys.

13. Ojibway saying. Found inscribed on a postcard.

13. Flaubert, Gustave. *Dictionary of Accepted Ideas*. New York: New Directions, 1954.

13. Avatamsaka sutra. Translated by Thomas Cleary. Boston: Shambala, 1987.

13. Herbert, Nick. *Quantum Reality: Beyond the New Physics*. New York: Anchor Press, 1985, p. 17.

13. Casti, John L. *Paradigms Lost*. New York: William Morrow and Co., 1989.

14. Freud, Sigmund. *The Interpretation of Dreams*. New York: Avon Books, 1965.

14. Zen Master Dogen. As cited in conversation with Jack Kornfield.

14. Blake, William. *The Essential Blake*. Selected by Stanley Kunitz. New York: Ecco Press, 1987, p. 91.

14. Rumi, Jelaluddin. From "Moses and the Shepherd" in *This Longing: Poetry, Teaching Stories, and Selected Letters*. Versions by Coleman Barks and John Moyne. Putney, VT: Threshold Books, 1988, p. 22.

15. Vonnegut, Kurt. *Wampeters Foma and Granfalloons*. New York: Dell Publishing Co., 1976, p. 162.

15. Shuryu Suzuki. As quoted in *Zen To Go*, compiled and edited by Jon Winokur. New York: New American Library, 1989, p. 80.

15. Wilde, Oscar. *The Wit and Wisdom of Oscar Wilde*. New York: Dover, 1959, p. 209.

16. Long Chen Pa. Saying printed on decorative poster.

17. Thoreau, Henry David. *Walden*. New York: New American Library, 1980.

18. Pynchon, Thomas. *Gravity's Rainbow*. New York: Viking Penguin, 1973.

19. Hillman, James. *The Dream and the Underworld*. New York: Harper and Row, 1979, p. 180.

20. Chaplin, Charlie. As quoted in *The 637 Best Things Anybody Ever Said*, p. 131.

20. Santayana, George. *Soliloquies in England*. New York: Charles Scribner, 1922.

20. Freud, Sigmund. "Wit and Its Relation to the Unconscious," in *The Basic Writings of Sigmund Freud*. New York: Modern Library, 1966, p. 633.

page 21. Wagner, Jane. *The Search for Signs of Intelligent Life in the Universe*. New York: Harper and Row, 1986, p. 26.

21. Bruce, Lenny. *The Essential Lenny Bruce*. New York: Bell Publishing Co., 1970.

21. Rogers, Will. Delivered in radio address.

21. Wilde, Oscar. *The Wit and Wisdom of Oscar Wilde*, p. 210.

21. Orwell, George. As quoted in *The Oxford Book of Aphorisms*, chosen by John Gross. Oxford: Oxford University Press. 1987, p. 279.

22. Shakespeare, William. *King Lear*. Baltimore: Penguin Books, 1958, p. 59.

22. Swift, Jonathan. *Gulliver's Travels and Other Writings*. Boston: Houghton Mifflin Company—The Riverside Press, 1960, p. 441.

23. Twain, Mark. *Letters from the Earth*. New York: Harper and Row, 1962, pp. 31, 33, 180.

24. The Marx Brothers. *Flywheel, Shyster, and Flywheel: The Marx Brothers' Lost Radio Show*. New York: Pantheon Books, 1988, p. 324.

24. Joyce, James. *Finnegans Wake*. New York: Viking Press, 1939, p. 580.

25. Hoffman, Abbie, in conversation.

25. Iktomi. As quoted in *The Trickster*, by Paul Radin. New York: Schocken Books, 1972.

26. Radin, Paul. *The Trickster*. New York: Schocken Books, 1972, p. 168.

26. Yaqui legend. As quoted in *Coyote's Journal*. Berkeley: Wingbow Press, 1982.

26. Blackfoot myth. From *The Trickster* by Paul Radin.

27. Jung, Carl. From *The Trickster* by Paul Radin, p. 207.

27. Maidu Coyote story. Adopted from the book *The Way We Lived* by Malcolm Margolin. Berkeley: Heyday Books, 1981, p. 149.

28. Jaeger, Lowell. "Why Dogs Smell Each Other's Butts," from *Coyote's Journal*. Berkeley: Wingbow Press, 1982.

30. Shakespeare, William. *A Midsummer Night's Dream*. New York: Penguin Books, 1971.

30. Blake, William. *The Complete Poetry and Prose of William Blake*. Berkeley: University of California Press, 1982, p. 36.

31. Rumi, Jalaluddin. *We Are Three*. Athens, GA: Maypop Books, 1987, p. 13.

31. Bronowski, Jacob. *The Ascent of Man*. Boston: Little, Brown and Company, 1973.

31. Blake, William. *The Complete Poetry and Prose of William Blake*, p. 37.

36. Shah, Idries. *The Way of the Sufi*, p. 246.

36. Jesus of Nazareth. From "The Gospel of Saint Thomas," in *The Secret Book of the Egyptian Gnostics*, by Jean Doresse. Rochester, VT: Inner Traditions International, Ltd., 1988, p. 358.

36. Cox, Harvey. *The Feast of Fools*. New York: Harper and Row Perennial Library, 1972, p. 169.

37. Vitray-Meyerovitch. *Rumi and Sufism*. Sausalito, CA: Post-Apollo Press, 1987, p. 26.

page 37.  Third Zen Patriarch. From pamphlet distributed by Alan Clements, re-printed from a translation by The Zen Center, Rochester, New York.

37.  Jesus of Nazareth. Luke 18:25. *The New Oxford Annotated Bible.*

38.  *The Dhammapada.* Translated by Irving Babbitt. New York: Oxford University Press, 1936, p. 59.

38.  Chuang Tzu. *The Complete Works of Chuang Tzu,* translated by Burton Watson, p. 357.

38.  Jesus of Nazareth. Luke 17:24. *The New Oxford Annotated Bible.*

39.  Hanh, Thich Nhat. *The Heart of Understanding: Commentaries on the Prajnaparamita Heart Sutra.* Berkeley: Parallax Press, 1988, p. 1.

39.  Nietzsche, Friedrich. *The Portable Nietzsche.* New York: Viking Press, 1954.

39.  Zen Master Hakuin. As quoted in *The Book* by Alan Watts. New York: Vintage, 1972, p. 117.

39.  Gandhi, Mohandas K. *All Men Are Brothers.* Ahmedabad, India: Navajivan Publishing House, 1960.

39.  Gandhi, Mohandas K. *Gandhi on Non-Violence.* New York: New Directions, 1964, p. 25.

40.  Gandhi, Mohandas K. *All Men Are Brothers,* p. 160.

40.  Gandhi, Mohandas K. *Gandhi on Non-Violence,* p. 9.

40.  Gandhi, Mohandas K. As quoted in *Gandhi the Man,* by Eknath Easwaran. Petaluma, CA: Nilgiri Press, 1973, p. 152.

41.  Gandhi, Mohandas K. *All Men Are Brothers,* p. 215.

41.  Ibid.

41.  Gandhi, Mohandas K. *Gandhi the Man,* p. 102.

41.  Yeats, William Butler. *Selected Poems and Two Plays.* New York: The Macmillan Company, 1962, p. 91.

43.  Zen Master Hakuin. As quoted in *Psychotherapy East and West* by Alan Watts. New York: Vintage, 1961, p. 166.

44.  Chuang Tzu. *The Complete Works of Chuang Tzu,* p. 47.

44.  Lao Tzu. *Tao Te Ching.* Translated by D. C. Lau. London: Penguin Books, 1963, Chapter 2.

45.  Chuang Tzu. *The Complete Works of Chuang Tzu,* p. 84.

45.  Ibid., pp. 48–49.

46.  Lao Tzu. *Tao Te Ching: A New English Version,* translated by Stephen Mitchell. New York: Harper and Row, 1988, Chapter 13.

46.  Adapted from *The Complete Works of Chuang Tzu,* p. 187.

47.  Waley, Arthur. *Three Ways of Thought in Ancient China.* Garden City, NY: Doubleday Anchor, 1939, p. 14.

47.  Lao Tzu. *Tao Te Ching,* translated by Gia-Fu Feng and Jane English. New York: Vintage Books, 1989, p. 21.

47.  Ibid., p. 31.

47.  Lao Tzu. *Tao Te Ching: A New English Version,* Chapter 41.

47.  Chuang Tzu. *The Way of Chuang Tzu,* p. 101.

page 48.  Ibid., p. 155.

49.  Chuang Tzu. *The Complete Works of Chuang Tzu*, p. 97.

49.  Zen Master Paichang. As quoted in *Oriental Humor*, by R. H. Blyth. Tokyo: Hokuseido Press, 1959, p. 90.

49.  Zen Master Lin-chi. Zen Master Ummon. As quoted in *Essays in Zen Buddhism: First Series*, by D. T. Suzuki. New York: Grove Press, 1949, pp. 294–295.

49.  Tokusan. As quoted in *Zen Buddhism and Psychoanalysis*, by Erich Fromm, D. T. Suzuki, and Richard DeMartino. New York: Harper Colophon Books, 1960, p. 48.

50.  Hui-Ch'ing. As quoted in *Zen Buddhism: Selected Writings of D. T. Suzuki*, edited by William Barrett. Garden City, NY: Doubleday Anchor, 1956, p. 22.

50.  Kerouac, Jack. *Last Words and Other Writings*. Zeta Press, 1985, p. 32.

50.  Watts, Alan W. *The Spirit of Zen*. New York: Grove Press, 1958, p. 50.

50.  Suzuki, D. T. *Zen Buddhism*, p. 10.

50.  Blyth, R. H. *Zen in English Literature*. New York: E. P. Dutton and Co., 1960, p. 2.

51.  Kerouac, Jack. *Last Words and Other Writings*, p. 32.

51.  Tao-wu. As quoted in *Zen Buddhism*, p. 132.

51.  Suzuki, D. T. *Essays in Zen Buddhism*.

51.  Blyth, R. H. *Zen in English Literature*.

51.  Bodhidharma. As quoted in *Essays in Zen Buddhism*.

51.  Watts, Alan W. *The Spirit of Zen*, p. 91.

52.  Hanh, Thich Nhat. *The Heart of Understanding: Commentaries on the Prajnaparamita Heart Sutra*, p. 1.

52.  Zen Master Feng. As quoted in *Zen and the Comic Spirit*, by M. Conrad Heyers. London: Rider and Company, 1974, pp. 105–106.

52.  Blyth, R. H. *Haiku: Volume One, Eastern Culture*. Tokyo: The Hokuseido Press, 1981, p. 202.

52.  Heyers, M. Conrad. *Zen and the Comic Spirit*, p. 85.

53.  Rinzai. As quoted in *Zen: Tradition and Transition*, edited by Kenneth Kraft. New York: Grove Press, 1988, p. 85.

53.  Blue Cliff Record, Case 51. As quoted in *Zen: Tradition and Transition*, p. 85.

54.  Heyers, M. Conrad. *Zen and the Comic Spirit*, p. 47.

54.  Ryōkan. *One Robe, One Bowl*. Translated by John Stevens. Tokyo: John Weatherhill, Inc., 1977, p. 23.

55.  Ibid., p. 26.

55.  Ibid., p. 26.

55.  Ibid., p. 16.

56.  Cold Mountain. *Riprap and Cold Mountain Poems*, translated by Gary Snyder. San Francisco: Grey Fox, 1958.

57.  Cold Mountain. *The Selected Songs of Cold Mountain*, translated by Red Pine. Port Townsend, WA: Copper Canyon Press, 1983, stanza 30.

page 57. Stonehouse. *The Mountain Poems of Stonehouse*. Port Townsend, WA: Empty Bowl Press, 1986.

58. Issa. From *Haiku: Volume 2, Spring*, by R. H. Blyth. Tokyo: The Hokuseido Press, p. 608.

58. Issa. From *The Penguin Book of Zen Poetry*, by Lucien Stryk and Takashi Ikemoto. New York: Penguin Books, 1977, p. 103.

58. Buson. From *Haiku: Volume 4, Autumn-Winter*, by R. H. Blyth. Tokyo: The Hokuseido Press, 1982, p. 1004.

58. Issa. From *The Oxford Book of Aphorisms*, chosen by John Gross. New York: Oxford University Press, 1987, p. 8.

59. Bashō. From *An Introduction to Haiku*, by Harold G. Henderson. Garden City, NY: Doubleday Anchor, 1958, p. 35.

59. Issa. From *Haiku: Volume One, Eastern Culture*, by R. H. Blyth. Tokyo: The Hokuseido Press, 1981, p. 306.

59. Issa. As related by Gary Gach.

59. Issa. *Haiku: Volume 3*, p. 794.

59. Issa. *Haiku: Volume 3*, p. 833.

59. Shiki. *Haiku: Volume 2, Spring*, p. 452.

59. Buson. *Haiku: Volume 3*, p. 691.

59. Bashō. *Haiku: Volume 3*, p. 896.

59. Issa. *Haiku: Volume 4*, p. 1242.

59. Buson. *Haiku: Volume 4*, p. 1254.

59. Milarepa. *The Hundred Thousand Songs of Milarepa: Volume One*, translated by Garma C. C. Chang. Boulder: Shambala, 1977, p. 65.

60. Milarepa. *Tibet's Great Yogi Milarepa*, edited by W. Y. Evans-Wentz. New York: Oxford University Press paperback, 1969, p. 8.

60. Kunley, Drukpa. *The Divine Madman: The Sublime Life and Songs of Drukpa Kunley*, translated by Keith Dowman. Clearlake, CA: Dawnhorse Press, 1980, p. 105.

61. Ibid., p. 112.

62. Ecclesiastes 1:18. *The New Oxford Annotated Bible*.

62. Aristotle. As quoted in *Irrational Man*, p. 89.

63. Lao Tzu. *Tao Te Ching: A New English Version*, Chapter 20.

63. Plato. Quoted in *The Great Thoughts*. Compiled by George Seldes. New York: Ballantine Books, 1985, p. 337.

63. Chuang Tzu. *The Complete Works of Chuang Tzu*, p. 293.

63. Barrett, William. *Irrational Man*, pp. 80–81.

63. Lao Tzu. *Tao Te Ching*. Translated Gia-Fu Feng and Jane English, p. 50.

64. Merton, Thomas. *The Wisdom of the Desert*. New York: New Directions, 1970, p. 73.

64. Psalm 150. *Selections from the Old and New Testaments*. New York: Reinhart and Co. Inc., 1953.

64. The Book of Mark. *Selections from the Old and New Testaments*, p. 302.

page 65.   Merton. *The Wisdom of the Desert*, p. 74.

65.   Ibid., p. 74.

66.   Baal Shem Tov. Buber, Martin. *Tales of the Hasidim: Early Masters*. New York: Schocken Books Inc., 1947, p. 74.

66.   Ibid., p. 72.

66.   Ibid., p. 35.

67.   Ibid., p. 82.

67.   Rumi. As quoted in *The Sufi Path of Love: The Spiritual Teachings of Rumi*, by William C. Chittick. Albany, NY: State University of New York Press, 1983.

68.   Rumi. *Open Secret: Versions of Rumi*. Translated by John Moyne and Coleman Barks. Putney, VT: Threshold Books, 1984, quatrain #82.

68.   Rumi. *Rumi and Sufism*, p. 43.

68.   Rumi. *Open Secret*, quatrain #158.

69.   Rumi. From "The Sheikh Who Played with Children," in *This Longing*, pp. 4–5.

69.   Rumi. From "The Long String," in *This Longing*, p. 15.

71.   Tyler, Hamilton A. *Pueblo Gods and Myths*. Norman, OK: University of Oklahoma Press, 1964, p. 195.

71.   Adapted from "Booger Event" in *Technicians of the Sacred*, edited by Jerome Rothenberg. Berkeley: University of California Press, 1968, p. 129.

74.   Lawrence, D. H. "A Propos of Lady Chatterley's Lover" in *A Selection from Phoenix*. Harmondsworth, Middlesex, England: Penguin Books, 1971, p. 356.

75.   Plato. From "The Apology," as quoted in Bertrand Russell's *A History of Western Philosophy*. New York: Simon and Schuster, 1945, p. 84.

76.   Ibid., p. 86.

76.   Ibid., p. 89.

77.   Ibid., p. 128.

77.   Ibid., p. 137.

78.   Barrett, William. *Irrational Man*, p. 83.

79.   Wittgenstein, Ludwig. *Tractatus Logico-Philosophicus*, translated by D. F. Peers and B. F. McGuinnes. London: Rutledge and Kegan Paul, 1961.

79.   Descartes, René. "Meditations on First Philosophy," as quoted in *The European Philosophers: Descartes to Nietzsche*. New York: The Modern Library, 1960, p. 46.

79.   Ibid., p. 48.

80.   Leibnitz, Gottfried Wilhelm Von. "First Truths" in *The European Philosophers*, pp. 248–254.

80.   Spinoza, Baruch. "Ethics: Part V" in *The European Philosophers*, p. 222.

80.   Lao Tzu. *Tao Te Ching: A New English Version*, Chapter 1.

81.   Wittgenstein, Ludwig. *Philosophical Investigations*, translated by G. E. M. Anscombe. Oxford: Basil Blackwell, 1967.

page 82. Camus, Albert. *The Myth of Sisyphus and Other Essays*. New York: Vintage Books, 1955, p. 20.

82. Kierkegaard, Søren. As quoted in *Irrational Man*, p. 149.

82. Camus, Albert. "Helen's Exile" in *The Myth of Sisyphus and Other Essays*, p. 135.

83. Nietzsche, Friedrich. "The Antichrist" in *The Portable Nietzsche*, translated and edited by Walter Kaufmann. New York: The Viking Press, 1954, p. 611.

83. Camus, Albert. "An Absurd Reasoning" in *The Myth of Sisyphus and Other Essays*, p. 15.

84. Heidegger. As quoted in *The Myth of Sisyphus*, "An Absurd Reasoning," p. 18.

84. Camus, Albert. "Helen's Exile" in *The Myth of Sisyphus and Other Essays*, p. 136.

84. Camus, Albert. "Absurd Creation" in *The Myth of Sisyphus and Other Essays*, p. 70.

85. Camus, Albert. "An Absurd Reasoning" in *The Myth of Sisyphus and Other Essays*, p. 38.

85. Nietzsche, Friedrich. *The Gay Science*, translated, with commentary, by Walter Kaufmann. New York: Vintage Books, 1974, p. 31.

86. Nietzsche, Friedrich. "Twilight of the Idols" in *The Portable Nietzsche*, p. 494.

86. Nietzsche, Friedrich. "Beyond Good and Evil" in *The Portable Nietzsche*, p. 444.

87. Nietzsche, Friedrich. "Twilight of the Idols" in *The Portable Nietzsche*, p. 501.

87. Ibid., p. 485.

87. Ibid., pp. 485–486.

87. Ibid., p. 467.

88. Nietzsche, Friedrich. *The Gay Science*, p. 75.

88. Nietzsche, Friedrich. "Thus Spake Zarathustra" in *The Portable Nietzsche*, p. 311.

88. Ibid.

88. Sartre, Jean-Paul. *Essays in Existentialism*. Seacacus, NJ: Citadel Press, 1965.

89. Apollinaire, Guillaume. As quoted in *Theories of Modern Art: A Source Book by Artists and Critics*, by Herschel B. Chipp. Berkeley: University of California Press, 1968, p. 231.

90. Camus, Albert. "An Absurd Creation" in *The Myth of Sisyphus and Other Essays*.

90. Foucault, Michel. *The Order of Things*. New York: Vintage Books, 1973.

90. Duncan, Isadora. *Isadora Speaks*. San Francisco, CA: City Lights Books, 1981.

90. Barnett Newman. As quoted in *The Painted Word*, by Tom Wolfe. New York: Bantam Books, 1975.

90. Blyth, R. H. *Zen in English Literature and Oriental Classics*. New York: E. P. Dutton and Co., 1960.

91. Camus, Albert. "Absurd Creation" in *The Myth of Sisyphus and Other Essays*, p. 72.

page 91.  Ibid., p. 72.

91.  Cage, John. *Silence.* Middletown, CT: Wesleyan University Press, 1973, p. 174.

91.  Nietzsche, Friedrich. As quoted in *The Myth of Sisyphus and Other Essays,* by Albert Camus, p. 69.

91.  Martinetti, F. T. "The Foundation and Manifesto of Futurism," as quoted in *Theories of Modern Art: A Source Book by Artists and Critics,* p. 286.

92.  Breton, André. *Manifestoes of Surrealism.* Ann Arbor: University of Michigan Press, 1972, p. 46.

93.  Tzara, Tristan. *Seven Dada Manifestos and Lampisteries.* New York: Riverrun Press, 1981, p. 41.

93.  Ibid., p. 43.

93.  Lao Tzu. *Tao Te Ching: A New English Version,* Chapter 37.

93.  Tzara, Tristan. *Seven Dada Manifestos and Lampisteries,* p. 24.

93.  Lao Tzu. *Tao Te Ching: A New English Version,* Chapter 56.

94.  Tzara, Tristan. *Seven Dada Manifestos and Lampisteries,* p. 45.

94.  Ibid., p. 111.

94.  Lao Tzu. *Tao Te Ching: A New English Version,* Chapter 14.

95.  Tzara, Tristan. *Seven Dada Manifestos and Lampisteries,* pp. 107–108.

95.  Cage, John. *Silence.* Middletown, CT: Wesleyan University Press, 1973, p. 174.

95.  Ibid., p. xii.

96.  Cage, John, in conversation.

97.  Cage, John. *John Cage: Documentary Monographs in Modern Art.* New York: Praeger, 1970, p. 12.

97.  Cage, John. *Silence,* p. 8.

97.  Lawrence, D. H. From "Introduction to 'Chariot of the Sun' " in *A Selection from Phoenix,* p. 430.

98.  *Bhagavad-Gita.* Translated by Swami Prabhavananda and Christopher Isherwood. New York: Mentor Books, 1944, p. 59.

98.  Blake, William. *The Essential Blake.* Edited by Stanley Kunitz. New York: The Ecco Press, 1987, p. 91.

98.  Ibid., p. 87.

98.  Ibid., p. 68.

99.  Ibid., p. 86.

99.  Ginsberg, Allen. *Kaddish and Other Poems: 1958–1960.* San Francisco: City Lights Books, 1961, p. 61.

99.  Kerouac, Jack. *Mexico City Blues.* New York: Grove Press, 1959, p. 176.

100.  Snyder, Gary. *Regarding Wave.* New York: New Directions, 1970, p. 39.

101.  Jeffers, Robinson. *Rock and Hawk: A Selection of Shorter Poems.* Edited by Robert Hass. New York: Random House, 1987, p. 25.

## Part II

page 105. Kabir. As quoted in *Deep Ecology*, by Bill Devall and George Sessions. Salt Lake City: Peregrine Smith Books, 1985, p. 191.

105. Wagner, Jane. *The Search for Signs of Intelligent Life in the Universe*. New York: Harper and Row, 1986, p. 19.

107. Bellow, Saul. *Herzog*. New York: Penguin Books, 1965.

107. Blake, William. *Blake: The Laurel Poetry Series*. New York: Dell, 1960, p. 156.

108. Lankavatara Sutra. From *A Buddhist Bible*, translated by D. T. Suzuki and Dwight Goddard. Thetford, VT: Dwight Goddard, 1938.

108. Wilson, Colin. *The Laurel and Hardy Theory of Consciousness*. Mill Valley: Robert Briggs Associates, 1986.

108. Roethke, Theodore. *Words for the Wind: The Collected Verse of Theodore Roethke*. Bloomington: Indiana University Press, 1961, p. 211.

108. James Joyce. As quoted in lecture given by Jack Kornfield.

108. Ornstein, Robert. *The Psychology of Consciousness: Second Revised Edition*. New York: Penguin Books, 1986, p. 185.

109. Ibid., p. 200.

109. Rilke, Rainer Maria. From *The Selected Poetry of Rainer Maria Rilke*, edited and translated by Stephen Mitchell. New York: Vintage Books, 1984, p. 247.

110. Jung, C. G. From his commentary on *The Secret of the Golden Flower*, translated by Richard Wilhelm. New York: Harcourt Brace and World, Inc., 1962, p. 93.

111. Kerouac, Jack. *Visions of Gerard*. New York: Farrar, Straus & Giroux, 1963.

112. Jeffers, Robinson. *Rock and Hawk*, p. 24.

112. Chief Seattle. As quoted in *Thinking Like a Mountain: Toward a Council of All Beings*, by John Seed, et al. Philadelphia: New Society Publishers, 1988, p. 68.

112. Issa. *Haiku: Volume I, Eastern Culture*, p. 207.

112. Camus, Albert. *The Myth of Sisyphus and Other Essays*, p. 135.

113. Watts, Alan. *Nature, Man and Woman*. New York: Vintage Books, 1970, pp. 122–123.

114. Wittgenstein, Ludwig. From *Zen To Go*, compiled and edited by Jon Winokur. New York: New American Library, p. 119.

114. Einstein, Albert. From "The World as I See It," in *Ideas and Opinions*. New York: Crown Pubs. 1982, p.11.

114. Wagner, Jane. *The Search for Signs of Intelligent Life in the Universe*, p. 206.

114. P'ang Chu-Shih. *The Spirit of Zen*, p. 52

115. Chuang Tzu. *The Collected Works of Chuang Tzu*, p. 85.

115. Zee, Anthony. *Fearful Symmetry: The Search for Beauty in Modern Physics*. New York: Collier Books, 1986, p. 249.

115–116. *The Flower Ornament Scripture*, translated by Thomas Cleary. Boston: Shambala Publications, 1986, pp. 201–203.

117. Sixth Chinese Zen Patriarch. As quoted in *Chan and Zen Teachings: First Series*, by Charles Luk. Berkeley: Shambala Publishing, 1970, p. 19.

page 117.  Luk, Charles. *Chan and Zen Teachings: First Series*, p. 159.

118.  Chinese Zen Saying. *Chan and Zen Teachings: First Series*, p. 19.

118.  Rumi. *These Branching Moments*, translated by John Moyne and Coleman Barks. Providence, RI: Copper Beech Press, 1988, p. 7.

118.  Shunryu Suzuki. *Zen Mind, Beginner's Mind*, p. 111.

118.  Ram Dass. From address delivered to the International Transpersonal Psychology Conference, Santa Rosa, California, February, 1989.

119.  Ornstein, Robert. *The Psychology of Consciousness*, p. 199.

119.  Koan of Master Tosotsu Etsu. As quoted in *Zen: Tradition and Transition*, p. 76.

119.  Zen koan. From *Chan and Zen Teaching: First Series*, p. 37.

120.  Snyder, Gary. *Earth House Hold*. New York: New Directions, 1969, p. 92.

120.  Sina'i. From *Rumi and Sufism*, p. 24.

121.  Wilde, Oscar. *The Wit and Wisdom of Oscar Wilde*, p. 65.

121.  Artaud, Antonin. From "No More Masterpieces," reprinted in *Evergreen Review Reader*. New York: Grove Press, 1979, p. 183.

121.  Rumi. *These Branching Moments*, p. 2.

123.  Mencken, H. L. As quoted in *Zen To Go*, p. 119.

124.  Serbian proverb. As quoted in lecture by Joseph Campbell, Esalen Institute, Big Sur, CA, 1979.

124.  Snyder, Gary. From an interview for the Buddhist journal, *The Inquiring Mind*, March 1987.

125.  Twain, Mark. From *The Oxford Book of Aphorisms*, p. 22.

125.  Mencken, H. L. *A Mencken Chrestomathy*. New York: Vintage Books, 1982, p. 5.

126.  Twain, Mark. *Letters from the Earth*, p. 181.

126.  Ibid., p. 181.

126.  Oates, Joyce Carol. From "Against Nature," in *The Pushcart Prize, XII*. New York: Penguin Books, 1987, p. 245.

126.  Gould, Stephen Jay. From an interview conducted by Terry Gross on the program "Fresh Air," broadcast on KQED radio in San Francisco, December 1989.

128.  Calder, Nigel. *Timescale: An Atlas of the Fourth Dimension*. New York: Viking Press, 1983, p. 78.

128.  Gould, Stephen Jay. From "Fresh Air."

129.  Ardrey, Robert. As quoted in conversation with physicist Robert Fraser.

130.  Fineberg, Gerald. As quoted in *The Cosmic Code*, by Heinz R. Pagels. New York: Bantam Books, 1982, p. 187.

130.  Zee, Anthony. *Fearful Symmetry*, p. 249.

131.  Ginsberg, Allen. "I Beg You Come Back and Be Cheerful," from *Collected Poems: 1947–1980*. New York: Harper and Row, 1984, p. 235.

131.  Calder, Nigel. *Timescale*, p. 43.

page 132. Williams, Heathcote. *Autogeddon*. Read in manuscript form and excerpted for *The Inquiring Mind*. Later published in *City Lights Review: Number 2*. San Francisco: City Lights Books, 1988, p. 171.

133. Rumi. *Open Secret*, quatrain 1359.

133. Freud, Sigmund. As quoted in *The Great Thoughts*, compiled by George Seldes. New York: Ballantine Books, 1985, p. 146.

134, 135. Franklin, Jon. *Molecules of the Mind*, p. 260.

135. Wagner, Jane. *The Search for Signs of Intelligent Life in the Universe*, p. 75.

135. Vonnegut, Kurt. *Galapagos*. New York: Dell Publishing Company, 1985, p. 166.

136. Bly, Robert. From *The Seventies: Spring 1972*, a journal edited by Robert Bly, published by the Seventies Press, Madison, MN.

136. Brown, Norman O. *Love's Body*. New York: Vintage Books, 1968, p. 98.

136. Rumi. *Unseen Rain: Quatrains of Rumi*. Translated by John Moyne and Coleman Barks. Putney, VT: Threshold Books, 1986, p. 63.

137. Chuang Tzu. *The Complete Works of Chuang Tzu*, p. 94.

137. Wilde, Oscar. *The Wit and Wisdom of Oscar Wilde*, p. 64.

137. Kafka, Franz. As quoted in *The Portable Curmudgeon*, compiled by Jon Winokur. New York: New American Library, p. 172.

138. Beckett, Samuel. *Waiting For Godot*. New York: Grove Press, 1965, p. 52.

138. Greek Proverb. As related in conversation with Steven Kaplan.

138. Campbell, Joseph. *The Power of Myth*, p. 229.

139. Stein, Gertrude. As quoted in *Zen To Go*, p. 11.

139. Yiddish saying. As related in lecture by Professor Abraham Joshua Heschel, Brandies Camp, 1965.

140. Thoreau, Henry David. As quoted in *The Great Thoughts*, p. 416.

141. Usher, James. As quoted in *The Experts Speak*, by Christopher Cerf and Victor Navasky. New York: Pantheon Books, 1984, p. 3.

141. Lightfoot, Dr. John. Ibid., p. 3.

144. Krassner, Paul. As related in conversation, Hollyhock Farm, British Columbia, 1984.

144. Eliade, Mircea. From *Man and Time: Papers from the Eranos Yearbooks*, edited by Joseph Campbell. Princeton: Princeton University Press, 1983, p. 181.

145. Einstein, Albert. As quoted in *The Cosmic Code*, p. 45.

146. Chuang Tzu. *The Complete Works of Chuang Tzu*, p. 177.

147. Dalton, John. *The Experts Speak*, p. 214.

147. Lord Kelvin. *The Experts Speak*, p. 236.

147. Hartmann, Johann. *The Experts Speak*, p. 29.

147. Hardin, Robert. As related in conversation.

148. Buddhist saying. As quoted in lecture by Joseph Goldstein.

148. Genesis III. *The Bible: Selections from the Old and New Testaments*. New York: Rinehart and Company, 1953, p. 7.

page 148.  Chuang Tzu. *The Complete Works of Chuang Tzu*, p. 113.

149.  Nietzsche, Friedrich. From "Twilight of the Idols," in *The Portable Nietzsche*.

149.  Bohr, Neils. As related in conversation with physicist Jack Sarfatti, Cafe Trieste, San Francisco, May 1989.

149.  Whitehead, Alfred North. As quoted in *1,911 Best Things Anybody Ever Said*, p. 128.

150.  Jung, Carl Gustav. As quoted in *The Great Thoughts*, p. 217.

150.  Chogyam Trungpa. As related in lecture, July 1975, Boulder, Colorado.

151.  Wordsworth, William. From "The Tables Turned," as quoted in *Zen in English Literature and Oriental Classics*, by R. H. Blyth. New York: E. P. Dutton and Co., Inc., 1960, p. 168.

151.  Vonnegut, Kurt. *Galapagos*, pp. 270, 8.

151.  Swift, Jonathan. *Gulliver's Travels and Other Writings*, pp. 127–128.

152.  Rumi. *These Branching Moments*, p. 9.

152.  Wittgenstein, Ludwig. *Philosophical Investigations*, translated by G. E. M. Anscombe. Oxford: Basil Blackwell, 1967.

152.  Genesis 11:7. *The New Oxford Annotated Bible*.

152.  Wittgenstein, Ludwig. *Wittgenstein: Language and Philosophy*, by Warren Shibles. Dubuque, IA: Wm. C. Brown Book Company, 1969, p. 95.

153.  Wittgenstein, Ludwig. Ibid., p. 93.

153.  Rumi. "The Name," from *Open Secret*, p. 73.

153.  Shakespeare, William. *Romeo and Juliet*. New York: Penguin Books, 1960. Act 2, Scene 2, p. 63.

153.  Burroughs, William. As quoted in conversation with Steven Kaplan.

154.  Rumi. *These Branching Moments*, p. 14.

154.  Neruda, Pablo. "Flies Enter a Closed Mouth," from *Five Decades: Poems 1925–1970*. New York: Grove Press Inc., 1974, pp. 201–203.

## *Part III*

159.  Diderot, Denis. *The Oxford Book of Aphorisms*, p. 31.

159.  Allen, Woody. *Side Effects*. New York: Ballantine Books, 1981, p. 81.

160.  Glashow, Sheldon. As quoted in *Beyond Einstein: The Cosmic Quest for the Theory of the Universe*, by Michio Kaku and Jennifer Trainer. New York: Bantam Books, 1987, p. 148.

164.  Snyder, Gary. *The Real Work*. New York: New Directions, 1980.

164.  McKibben, Bill. *The End of Nature*. Excerpted in *The New Yorker*, September 11, 1989.

166.  Durant, Will and Ariel. From *The Great Thoughts*, p. 117.

166.  Spengler, Oswald. *The Decline of the West*, p. 28.

167.  Nixon, Richard. From a campaign speech, September 1972.

167.  Tao Te Ching. *The Way and Its Power: A Study of the Tao Te Ching*, by Arthur Waley. New York: Grove Press, 1958, p. 199.

page 168. Chief Sealth (Seattle). Taken from a broadside displayed in the window of Cody's Books, Berkeley, September 1989.

168. Spengler, Oswald. *The Decline of the West*, p. 34.

170. Bohr, Niels. As quoted in *God and the New Physics*, by Paul Davies. New York: Simon and Schuster, Inc., 1983, p. 100.

171. Wagner, Jane. *The Search for Signs of Intelligent Life in the Universe*, p. 18.

171. Niels Bohr to Wolfgang Pauli. *Beyond Einstein*, p. 12.

171. DeWitt, Bryce. As quoted in *Quantum Reality: Beyond the New Physics*, by Nick Herbert. Garden City, NY: Anchor Press, 1985, p. 19.

173. Niels Bohr to Albert Einstein. As related in conversation with physicist Robert Fraser.

173. Feyerabend, Paul. *Against Method*. London: Verso, 1988, p. 256.

174. Heisenberg, Werner. As quoted in *Apocalypse Culture*. New York: Amok Press, 1987, p. 196.

174. Davies, Paul. *God and the New Physics*. New York: Simon and Schuster, Inc., 1983.

174. Casti, John L. *Paradigms Lost*. New York: William Morrow and Company, 1989.

174. Nietzsche, Friedrich. *The Portable Nietzsche*.

175. Zee, Anthony. *Fearful Symmetry*, p. 241.

175. Camus, Albert. *The Myth of Sisyphus*, p. 15.

176. Bohr, Niels. *Sympathetic Vibrations*, p. 155.

176. Democritus. *Selections from Early Greek Philosophers*. New York: Meredith Publishing Company, 1964, p. 197.

177. Ruckeyser, Muriel. Related in conversation with Djuna Odegard.

177. Lawrence, D. H. *A Selection From Phoenix*, p. 548.

178. Gautama the Buddha. *The Dhammapada*. Kandy, Sri Lanka: Buddhist Publication Society, 1985, verse I.

180. Artaud, Antonin. From *Evergreen Review Reader*, p. 181.

180. Dadaist Slogan. *Theories of Modern Art*, p. 376.

181. Kundera, Milan. *The Art of the Novel*. New York: Harper and Row, 1986, p. 19.

181. Ginsberg, Allen. From "Howl," in *Howl and Other Poems*. San Francisco: City Lights Books, 1956.

181. Breton, André. *Manifestoes of Surrealism*. Ann Arbor: University of Michigan Press, 1974.

181. Beckett, Samuel. From "Exorcising Beckett," by Lawrence Shainberg. *The Pushcart Prize, XIII*. New York: Penguin Books, 1988, p. 105.

181. Spengler, Oswald. *The Decline of the West*, p. 31.

182. Wilde, Oscar. As quoted in "Notes on Camp," from *A Susan Sontag Reader*. New York: Farrar, Straus and Giroux, 1982.

182. Motto of Constructivism. *Theories of Modern Art*.

182. Sontag, Susan. *A Susan Sontag Reader*.

182. Kandinsky, Wassily. *Theories of Modern Art*.

page 182. Beckett, Samuel. From "Exorcising Beckett," in *The Pushcart Prize, XIII*, p. 109.

183. Rauschenberg, Robert. As quoted in *The Bride and the Bachelors*, by Calvin Tomkins. New York: Viking Press, 1968, p. 194.

183. Sontag, Susan. From "Notes on Camp," in *A Susan Sontag Reader*.

184. Ferlinghetti, Lawrence. From "Adieu à Charlot" (Second Populist Manifesto). *Wild Dreams of a New Beginning*. New York: New Directions, 1988.

185. Shaw, George Bernard. From *The Great Thoughts*, p. 280.

185. Krassner, Paul. In conversation, Esalen Institute, May 1987.

185. Campbell, Joseph. *Transformations of Myth Through Time*. New York: Harper and Row, 1990, p. 16.

186. Santayana, George. *The Life of Reason*. New York: Charles Scribner and Sons, 1945, p. 28.

186. Hasidic saying. From *The Joys of Yiddish*, by Leo Rosten. New York: Pocket Books, 1970, p. 4.

186. Xenophanes. From *The Will of Zeus: A History of Greece*, by Stringfellow Barr. New York: J. P. Lippincott Company, 1961, p. 54.

186. Campbell, Joseph. *The Power of Myth*, p. 220.

187. Williams, William Carlos. *Paterson*. New York: New Directions, 1958, p. 6.

187. Jarry, Alfred. From *Evergreen Review Reader*, p. 314.

188. Krassner, Paul. In conversation, September 1976.

188. Zen Master Lin-Chi. From *Zen and the Comic Spirit*, p. 105.

188. Bruce, Lenny. *The Essential Lenny Bruce*. New York: Bell Publishing Company, 1970.

188. Twain, Mark. *Letters from the Earth*, p. 46.

190. Mencken, H. L. *A Mencken Chrestomathy*, pp. 95–96.

191. Van Gogh, Vincent. *A Self Portrait*. Letters selected by W. H. Auden. New York: Paragon House, 1989.

191. Kerouac, Jack. From "Lucien Midnight," in *Scattered Poems*. San Francisco: City Lights, 1971, p. 14.

192. Tao Te Ching. *Tao Te Ching*. Translated by Gia-Fu Feng and Jane English, p. 7.

192. Krassner, Paul. In conversation.

192. Einstein, Albert. From *1,911 Best Things Anybody Ever Said*, p. 352.

194. Japanese proverb. From *Zen in English Literature*, by R. H. Blyth.

194. Schell, Jonathan. *The Fate of the Earth*. New York: Avon Books, 1982.

195. McKibben, Bill. *The End of Nature*.

195. Seed, John. Excerpted from an interview in *Yoga Journal*, November/December 1989, p. 106.

196. Seed, John. From "Anthropocentrism." Appendix E in *Deep Ecology*, by Bill Devall and George Sessions. Salt Lake City: Peregrine Smith Books, 1985, p. 243.

## Part IV

page 201. Gautama the Buddha. "The Parinirvana Sutra" as excerpted in *The Sacred Art of Dying*, by Kenneth Kramer. New York: Paulist Press, 1988, p. 43.

201. Parker, Dorothy. Attributed.

201. Chuang Tzu. *The Complete Works of Chuang Tzu*, p. 47.

202. Allen, Woody. From *1,911 Best Things Anybody Ever Said*, p. 12.

202. Borges, Jorge Luis. As related in conversation by writer Steven Kaplan.

202. Al-Ghazali. *The Sacred Art of Dying*, p. 157.

202. Rumi. *These Branching Moments*, p. 7.

203. Castaneda, Carlos. *Journey to Ixtlan*. New York: Pocket Books, 1972, p. 34.

203. Chuang Tzu. *The Way of Chuang Tzu*, p. 100.

204. Gautama the Buddha. As presented in a lecture by meditation teacher Joseph Goldstein.

204. The Japanese death poems are all taken from *Japanese Death Poems*, compiled and introduced by Yoel Hoffmann. Rutland, VT: Charles E. Tuttle Company, 1986.

204. Franklin, Benjamin. *Death: An Anthology of Ancient Texts, Songs, Prayers, and Stories*, edited by David Melzter. San Francisco: North Point Press, 1984, p. 188.

205. Yeats, William Butler. *Selected Poems and Two Plays of William Butler Yeats*, p. 193.

205. Zen Master Bunan. From *The Sacred Art of Dying*, p. 62.

206. Pound, Ezra. *The Cantos of Ezra Pound*. New York: New Directions, 1970. From Canto CXVI, p. 810.

206. Chuang Tzu. *The Collected Works of Chuang Tzu*, p. 42.

206. Mencken, H. L. From *Zen To Go*, p. 106.

207. Barnett, Lincoln. *The Universe and Dr. Einstein*. Mattituck, NY: Amereon, Limited, 1948.

207. Twain, Mark. *Letters from the Earth*, p. 170.

208. Chuang Tzu. *The Collected Works of Chuang Tzu*, p. 139.

208. Yeats, William Butler. Quotation submitted to *The Inquiring Mind*, by author Dr. Myron R. Sharaf.

208. Allen, Woody. *Getting Even*, p. 42.

209. Hasidic saying. *The Joys of Yiddish*, p. 307.

209. Neruda, Pablo. *Estravagario*. New York: Farrar, Straus and Giroux, 1974.